Elizabeth and Hazel

Elizabeth
and Hazel

Two Women of Little Rock

David Margolick

Yale UNIVERSITY PRESS
New Haven and London

Yale University Press books may be purchased in quantity for educational, business, or promotional use. For information, please e-mail sales.press@yale.edu (U.S. office) or sales@yaleup.co.uk (U.K. office).

Set in Minion type by Keystone Typesetting, Inc.
Printed in the United States of America.

The Library of Congress has cataloged the hardcover edition as follows:
Margolick, David.
Elizabeth and Hazel : two women of Little Rock / David Margolick.
p. cm.
Includes bibliographical references and index.
ISBN 978-0-300-14193-1 (hardback)
1. Eckford, Elizabeth, 1941–. 2. Massery, Hazel Bryan, 1942–. 3. School integration—Arkansas—Little Rock—History—20th century. 4. Central High School (Little Rock, Ark.)—History—20th century. 5. Interracial friendship—Arkansas—Little Rock. 6. Little Rock (Ark.)—Race relations—History—20th century. 7. Little Rock (Ark.)—Biography. I. Title.
F419.L7M37 2011
379.2'63—dc22
2011014101

ISBN 978-0-300-18792-2 (pbk.)

A catalogue record for this book is available from the British Library.

10 9 8 7 6 5 4 3 2

To my mother, Gertrude Margolick, with love and gratitude

My interest in any man is objectively in his manhood
and subjectively in my own manhood.

Frederick Douglass

Contents

Elizabeth and Hazel

Prologue: Two Dresses

Early in the morning of September 4, 1957, two girls in Little Rock, Arkansas, each fifteen years old, dressed for school.

On a block of black families nestled in the west side of town, in the small brick house she shared with her parents and five brothers and sisters, Elizabeth Eckford put on a skirt that her older sister, Anna, and she had made just for this day. The immaculate white cotton piqué felt cool and soft to the touch; when Elizabeth and Anna, who had labored over it for several weeks, had run out of fabric, they'd trimmed the deep hem with navy blue and white gingham. The new skirt's double rows of gathers made it seem to have tiny pleats, and it appeared especially crisp because Elizabeth had ironed it one last time the night before. Buoyed by the petticoat she wore underneath, it encircled her tiny waist like a bell—one that rang out the tidings of new beginnings. Fashionable and yet modest, descending well below her knees, the pretty skirt was complemented by the rest of what she had chosen to wear that morning: the plain white blouse (which she'd also made), the loafers, the bobby sox. She could just as easily have been going to church, and in a way she was, because for Elizabeth, learning was much more meaningful, and useful, than prayer.

1

A few miles away, in a house much like Elizabeth's but in a neighborhood that was all white, Hazel Bryan selected something very different. It was a sleek dress of cool mint-green, with a triangular white sash at the top pointing suggestively to her bosom, and a ribbon tied provocatively around her midriff. She'd bought it a few months earlier at one of the "classy" department stores downtown, maybe Blass or Pfeiffer's, with around ten of the scarce dollars her mother earned making lightbulbs at Westinghouse. Hazel wasn't signaling the start of an earnest new undertaking so much as making a fashion statement: taking her cues from Marilyn Monroe, Jayne Mansfield, Elizabeth Taylor, and the other movie stars she followed, Hazel hoped to show off her petite figure, to look older and more sophisticated and maybe more promiscuous than she really was. She wanted to impress her girlfriends, but with any luck the boys forever hovering around her would notice, too. (That the dress was a mite too tight would help.) She'd worn the dress before, probably earlier in the summer. Then again, for Hazel this day wasn't quite as special as it was for Elizabeth. Like all of the white kids, she'd begun school the day before, unperturbed by the soldiers who encircled it, and she had been at this particular school for a year already.

Two girls, one black, one white, born less than four months apart, each about to begin eleventh grade. Within a few minutes of each other, they set out for the same destination: Little Rock Central High School. They did not know, nor—in the world of the South in the 1950s—would they have ever encountered, each other before, except perhaps when they rode the same buses or passed on a downtown street or sat—on different *levels—in a local movie theater. But within an hour or so they would, and from that moment on, their lives would be inextricably intertwined. For long after that—as long, in fact, as the tortured saga of relations between the races, in the United States and everywhere else, still mattered, or as long, when it came right down to it, as people can see—they would be linked.*

When Hazel got home that afternoon, she took off the dress and changed into something more comfortable—boy's jeans, perhaps; they didn't yet make them for girls—and hung it up for the next time. Doubtless, there would be many next times— dances, dates, more school days—to put it on. But when Elizabeth removed her skirt that night, then folded it up and handed it to her mother, she already knew she would never wear it, or even want to see it, again. As everyone else was coming to recognize it—for a time, that simple cotton skirt was just about the most famous piece of clothing in the world—Elizabeth set out to forget about it. It promptly went into the attic, and no one— Elizabeth included—ever laid eyes on it again.

ONE

———————————

Elizabeth Eckford's house sat on a short stretch of West 18th Street, just off Peyton. Everything about the building and the land it rested on was compact, as if someone had sat down and figured out the smallest and most inexpensive way to fulfill a dream—a place of one's own. The home was squat and square, with two bedrooms on a single floor, along with a crawl space below and a small attic, accessible only via a ladder. The place was rudimentary, unfinished: the pine floors, for instance, had never been varnished. The front yard was tidy, and tiny. There was room for a small garden, or a lawn, but not really enough for both, and certainly not enough for a tree. No one had ever bothered with the backyard, where a big rock stuck out of the dirt. A local black doctor, who'd grown rich performing abortions and speculating in real estate, had built it in the late 1940s, and the Eckfords—Elizabeth's parents, Oscar Jr. and Birdie; her older sister, Anna; and her younger brothers, Oscar 3rd and Bolden—were the first folks ever to live there, moving in on Elizabeth's eighth birthday in October 1949. That was a time, shortly after World War II, when if you scrambled enough, even the relatively poor could own their own homes. The house had grown with the family: as two more children, Melbert Don and

Katherine, had come along, the Eckfords had added a couple of rooms to the back.

Little Rock in the Eisenhower era was a racial checkerboard, with blocks of whites and blocks of blacks interspersed throughout large parts of the city. To delineate the racial boundaries, one needed only to look up (there were no streetlights in the black neighborhoods) or down: the white blocks were paved, while the black ones were clay, though they were always covered with oil—it tamped down the dust—whenever elections loomed. Elizabeth's mother had always hated the neighborhood. She'd grown up in the sticks, in the hamlet of Pettus, Arkansas, thirty-five miles or so east of Little Rock. Her education there was spotty, scheduled around the crop year; like promising and ambitious blacks throughout the state, she'd come to Little Rock by herself as a teenager to attend the prestigious all-black Dunbar High School, earning her keep by cleaning the home of the black schoolteacher with whom she lived. (The schoolteacher had evidently taken on the country girl as her personal project, refurbishing her language and cleaning up her grammar; Birdie became a stickler herself, correcting her children whenever they split infinitives.) She never liked the home on West 18th Street; with many lots either still wooded or empty (a cow grazed on one), the area reminded her of the countryside she had fled. (Once a year, Elizabeth would visit her blind grandfather in Pettus; his farm had a mule, and the water tasted different there.) Near the city limits, Elizabeth's new neighborhood also housed various illicit businesses. Sundays, the kids watched gleefully as ladies in their church finery tiptoed toward the nearby gin mills to gamble or drink.

Within Little Rock's black community, the Eckfords were known

Elizabeth's house (Photo by Brian Chilson)

for their intelligence and seriousness. They'd always thought of themselves as something special, or, as Birdie Eckford once put it, "something on a stick." *"Aren't you Eckford's?"* someone once asked Elizabeth's brother Bolden when he stumbled into a bootlegging joint. "Don't tell your parents you were down here!" The patriarch of the family was Elizabeth's grandfather, Oscar Eckford, Sr., a large and imperious man—his second wife (Elizabeth's step-grandmother), and even some white people, called him "Mr. Eckford"—who ran a small grocery store and café called Eckford's Confectionary on West 15th Street. He had served in France in World War I (when the state VFW wouldn't admit him and other blacks, he had helped set up a VFW post of their own) and started his store during the Depression, selling the ribs his wife cooked up in the front room of their house. Though the shelves were never very full, there were big jars of barbecue sauce—made from vinegar, root beer, brown sugar, and mustard—along with enormous bags of cornmeal and flour and lots of penny candies. The place smelled of Dubble Bubble gum. From behind the counter, sitting with his fat legs crossed, Oscar Eckford presided over his domain, barking out orders to his wife and everyone else.

Her grandfather was the only black man Elizabeth knew who spoke to white people without fear—in part, she figured, because he paid his bills on time and never owed anybody anything. He was very principled, with little patience for people who, like the white man who delivered bread to his store, refused to take a stand on the issues of the day. (Such a fellow wasn't "worth the gunpowder it would take to blow him up," he liked to say, and that was typical, for he often spoke in aphorisms.) He had blue eyes and traced the family name back to a chaplain in the Confederate Army. He was acutely aware of lineage; "Who are your people?" he regularly asked. Of all his grandchildren, Elizabeth was, if not necessarily his favorite, the one for whom he held the highest hopes. "EEE-lizabeth," he would always ask, looking her squarely in the eye, "what did you learn in school today?" From "Pop-Paw," as his grandchildren called him, she always understood she would go to college, though she never knew quite how.

Elizabeth's father was neither as ambitious nor as accomplished, though he surely put in his time. He worked nine days a week, he told people. Seven were for the Missouri Pacific Railroad, where, after a few unhappy years waiting tables in dining cars, he'd taken a lower-paying job—stocking trains, renting pillows—that let him stay in town. Weekends, he was an "extra man," hauling junk in his pickup, performing odd jobs for three white families. Birdie Eckford also worked, teaching laundering at the Arkansas School for the Negro Blind and Deaf, five blocks from the Eckford home. That let her look after Oscar 3rd, who was badly handicapped. He appeared autistic (the term used then was "retarded"; Elizabeth's father once described him as an "idiot"). Late in her life, Birdie disclosed that he'd been dropped during delivery, when she'd given birth by herself. "Baby Brother" could have lived at the school, but Birdie brought him home every night; he was a familiar sight in the neighborhood, running up and down the street or rocking back and forth on the porch.

Birdie watched her other children just as vigilantly. She let them do very little, like dance or ride a bike or roller skate. Birthday parties were generally forbidden, unless she knew the parents. "The Queen of No," Elizabeth called her. When her girls met with their Brownie troop a few blocks from home, Birdie knew exactly how long the sessions lasted and how many steps away they were. When they attended shows at the segregated Gem Theater (where there were films with black casts, and the audience talked back to the screen), a teenage girl to whom the family was close always went along. When any of them strayed even slightly from her orbit, Birdie Eckford suffered; whenever one was in trouble or pain, she somehow always knew. The Eckfords had no phone—it was too costly—but they did have a television, the better for her to keep her children in her sights. When Elizabeth returned from some event, her mother always asked whether there had been any men there. Perhaps, Elizabeth later theorized, she had been sexually molested when she was young.

Elizabeth's mother was pious: you could tell her mood by whether she sang hymns or the blues. Once she took voice lessons, which she paid for by letting her teacher use the converted player piano the Eckfords owned to teach other children. She was also superstitious, and mixed in with her Methodism was some sort of hoodoo. She thought certain people—she called them "readers"—were endowed with supernatural powers, and paid them for their prophecies. (One of them lived in a dilapidated house. If she had such magical powers, Elizabeth used to wonder, why had she remained so poor?) But her superstition was ecumenical. She spent time in the Baptist bookstore and often clutched a rosary. To some, she seemed a little off—"an elevator that didn't go up all the way," as one of Elizabeth's childhood friends put it. Elizabeth's parents had a troubled marriage; her father was abusive and strayed regularly, though it was something Elizabeth knew only from her mother's complaints. Perhaps that was why the Eckfords ignored certain family rituals; for instance, never did they sit for a family portrait. Only in some years could Elizabeth afford to buy her school picture.

Early on, Elizabeth became a reader. When, at age seven, she finished her first book, Dr. Seuss's *The 500 Hats of Bartholomew Cubbins,* she felt like shouting with joy: a whole world had just opened up to her. In sixth grade, she overheard a teacher saying she read at an eleventh-grade level. Sensing this, Elizabeth's parents let her sit in her Daddy's chair and read even while her siblings had to clean the house. When you saw her, nine times out of ten she had her head buried in a book. The kids in her neighborhood thought of her as the "professor girl"; whenever they had a question about something, they turned to her. But Elizabeth was modest. She got good grades not because she was smart, she thought, but because it was expected of her, and because she worked hard. And, at least in ninth-grade civics, because she had a crush on her teacher.

TWO

There was one other thing everyone noticed about Elizabeth, or at least she thought they did: her smile was crooked. The Crumpton twins had welcomed her into her new neighborhood by throwing rocks at her and calling her "Buck Teeth." White children, she knew from the sitcoms on television, could fix their teeth with braces, but that wasn't an option for her. She didn't like looking at herself in the mirror and sometimes covered her mouth when she spoke. It made her even shyer than she naturally was.

Though her mother let her join the pep team in ninth grade, Elizabeth was essentially a loner. Classmates knew they'd never see her at dances or "socials." *Their* parents were strict, too, but they, unlike Elizabeth, had learned how to get around the rules. To them, Elizabeth was eccentric—a homebody, a square. Her first date Anna had to arrange for her, picking the boy and helping make her dress. When she was comfortable with someone, like Minnijean Brown, who was in her class and lived for a time next door, she could be clever and wickedly funny. More often, people couldn't coax full sentences from her, and even when they could, they sometimes couldn't hear the end. Elizabeth would raise her hand in class and then, once all eyes were on her, wonder why on earth she had. Though she'd occasionally blow her bus money on doughnuts, she was slight. No one had yet diagnosed her as depressed, but it ran in her family.

The Eckfords regularly attended the Allen Temple African Methodist Episcopal Church, nine blocks from their home. Elizabeth welcomed the diversion; it was one of her only avenues out of the house and, when the children went by themselves, a chance to get away from her mother. But religion provided her little comfort: it all seemed very illogical to her. You'll get over that, her mother had cockily predicted, but she never really had. For hours at a time she'd daydream on the big rock in her backyard, pretending she was sitting by a campfire somewhere far away, realizing that wherever she found herself, she didn't quite belong.

And yet, much to the amazement of those who knew her, in the fall of 1957 Elizabeth was among the nine black students who had enlisted, then been selected, to enter Little Rock Central High School. Central was the first high school in a major southern city set to be desegregated since the United States Supreme Court had ruled three years earlier in *Brown vs. Board of Education* that separate and ostensibly equal education was unconstitutional. Inspired both by Thurgood Marshall, who had argued *Brown,* and Clarence Darrow (she'd watched the Spencer Tracy version of him in *Inherit the Wind*), Elizabeth wanted to become a lawyer, and she thought Central would help her realize that dream. She knew that in the Jim Crow South, the best of everything went to the white schools, and Central was far and away the best high school in Arkansas. Even more miraculously still, her overprotective mother had gone along with her decision.

For months, in a campaign of growing vituperation, white

groups had mobilized to keep the black students out of Central. Three nights earlier the governor of Arkansas, Orval Faubus, had announced that to maintain peace and order when the school opened, he was surrounding it with members of the state's National Guard. To Elizabeth, that was reassuring; soldiers would be there to protect her. Besides, there would be some familiar faces on hand: not just a few of the other black students, like Minnijean, but some white children for whose parents her mother had worked, or who lived nearby. Elizabeth had had scant exposure to white people, and knew too little about them even to be scared. Most worrisome to her was having to find her way around the place; Central was enormous, far larger than any of the black schools she'd attended.

But on that first morning of school, her primary concern was looking nice. Her mother had done her hair the night before—an elaborate two-hour ritual, with a hot iron and a hotter stove, of straightening and curling. Then there were her clothes. People in black Little Rock knew that the Eckford girls were expert seamstresses; practically everything they wore they made themselves, and not from the basic patterns of *McCall's* but from the more complicated ones in *Vogue*. It was a practice borne of tradition, pride, and necessity: homemade was cheaper, and it spared black children the humiliation of having to ask to try things on in the segregated department stores downtown. Huddled over the pedal-operated Singer in their living room—the largest open space in their crowded home—the Eckford girls made themselves outfits for Christmas, Easter, and always, the beginning of school.

Calm as Elizabeth was that morning, her mother was her usual apprehensive self. The night before, she'd urged Elizabeth to turn to her Bible, and Elizabeth had picked the 4th Psalm: "Answer when I call, my saving God. In my troubles, you cleared a way." On the television as Elizabeth ate her breakfast, a newsman described large crowds gathering around Central. It was all Birdie needed to hear. "Turn that thing off!" she shouted from the kitchen. Should anyone say something nasty at her, she counseled Elizabeth, pretend not to hear them. Or better yet, be nice, and put them to shame. Elizabeth's father, who worked nights and would normally have been asleep, was up and agitated too, even though the police chief had personally assured him there'd be no trouble. He paced the room, holding his pipe, chomping on an unlit cigar.

After making sure everyone looked right and that they all had their pencils and notebooks and lunch money, Birdie Eckford gathered her children around her in the living room. Then, together, they recited the 27th Psalm.

> *The Lord is my light and my salvation; whom shall I fear? The Lord*
> *is the strength of my life; of whom shall I be afraid?*
> *When the wicked, even mine enemies and my foes, came upon me to*
> *eat up my flesh, they stumbled and fell.*
> *Though an host should encamp against me, my heart shall not fear:*
> *Though war should rise against me, in this will I be confident.*

She instructed Elizabeth to say it to herself, over and over again, at the school. If she did just that, her mother said, she had nothing to fear.

Around 7:30, Elizabeth, carrying a green notebook, left the house with Anna, one year older than she, who had elected to stay at Horace Mann, the black high school to which Elizabeth had gone the previous year. The day was bright and sunny, still more summer than fall, and Elizabeth put on her sunglasses, dark orbs in a clear plastic frame that were a little too big for her face; her eyes were extremely sensitive to light. Together, she and Anna walked to 16th and Peyton, only two blocks away but already into a white neighborhood, with concrete streets, and boarded the War Memorial bus. For a few years now, Elizabeth had been able to sit wherever she wanted. (But the old folkways persisted: whether out of habit, or fear, older blacks still clustered toward the rear, while mischievous black children planted themselves alongside elderly white women who, much to their delight, would leap up as if nudged with red-hot pokers.) The ride to Central cost twenty-five cents and took only about fifteen minutes. Little Rock *was* little: very different worlds were very close together.

The bus went down to Lewis, then took a left to 13th, where it headed east, through a white working-class neighborhood. At South Pine was the all-white Robert E. Lee Elementary School, and across the street, the Lee Theatre, where Elizabeth sometimes watched movies, though only from the balcony. On the bridge over the Missouri Pacific tracks just beyond Woodrow, she felt her first fears. She was approaching Central: the football stadium was visible to her right. She got off at Dennison, then walked up to Park, where she turned. Up the hill, on Park and 14th, was a Mobil station; beyond that, on the other side of the street and stretching for two blocks, lay Central. Instantly, she sensed something amiss: there were more parked cars than usual, and she heard the muffled murmur of a crowd. Then the military Jeeps and half-tracks came into view, and then the soldiers.

To Benjamin Fine of the *New York Times*, who had been there since 4:30 that morning, the crowd had at first seemed cheerful, even festive. "If anyone had a popcorn concession, they could have had a picnic," he later recalled. Some of the white girls flirted with the National Guardsmen, many of them scarcely older than they, some Central graduates themselves. A few boys waved Confederate flags; a man played "Dixie" on his cornet. But not everything was so upbeat. "They don't want to be in your school, they want to be in your bedroom!" a minister shouted through a bullhorn. Standing shoulder to shoulder, the ragtag group of soldiers encircled the school. Across the street, bystanders gathered; a young newsman with NBC, John Chancellor, counted ninety-two of them by around the time Elizabeth left home. Suddenly, a commotion: "They're coming!" someone shouted. "The niggers are coming!" The "they" was really just a "she": Elizabeth, a black face in a cloudlike splotch of white in the bronzed, late summer streetscape, was approaching. Shortly, the world would learn all about the "Little Rock Nine."[1] At this moment she was the Little Rock One.

THREE

I n 1927 Little Rock witnessed two seemingly contradictory
events, occurring only a few miles apart. Together, they help
illustrate how, even thirty years later, the city could be a
place of both lofty aspirations and deep-seated intolerance.
The paradox was, in fact, nothing new: Little Rock was also where,
in 1889, Frederick Douglass was welcomed by the state legislature,
but turned away by a local restaurant.

In May 1927 a thirty-five-year-old black man named John Carter, the married father of five, fled into the woods after supposedly
assaulting a white woman and her daughter on the road to Hot
Springs. A search party tracked him down, and before long a
lynch mob had gathered around him. The men tied together a
rope and chain, placing one end atop a telephone pole and the
other around Carter's neck before forcing him to climb onto the
hood of a Ford roadster. "Start praying, nigger, because you are
getting ready to go!" someone shouted. Strictly as a matter of
visual dramatics, this lynching was a bust; when the car pulled
away, Carter dangled only five feet off the ground. But it sufficed.
He hung there for two minutes—just long enough to die. Then
fifty men riddled him with some two hundred bullets.

The corpse was tied to a rear bumper, and a procession of thirty or forty cars, filled with howling men and boys, made its way into Little Rock, passing undisturbed by the police station and court-house en route. After driving around for an hour, the mob placed the body on the trolley tracks at West 9th Street and Broadway, in the heart of the black part of town, then doused it with gasoline. Four or five thousand people, including women with babies, con-verged on the scene, and for the next three hours or so, they celebrated around the blaze. Whenever the fire died down, more gasoline, along with boxes, doors, windows, and furniture, some of it lifted from nearby black homes and a black church, brought it back to life. The police stood by; the mayor showed up only after Carter was but a charred crust. His bones became prized souvenirs.

Little Rock's blacks, who had huddled in terror as the events unfolded, slowly emerged from their homes and businesses as the furor died down. (Those who had stuck around, that is: Eliza-beth's grandfather had hidden his children under a bed, then spirited them via the Rock Island Line to Forrest City, ninety-five miles to the east.) Afterward, from the relative safety of the North, the black press recapitulated what had happened. To the crowd, the *Chicago Defender* related, Carter's culpability hadn't really mattered: "All they wanted was to see human blood—hear human cries for mercy—smell human flesh as it burned itself out. They wanted their children to grow up with the memory of a human being hanging from a tree, his head almost shot away, blood streaming from a hundred holes in his body!" When it was all over, the *Defender* reporter wrote, "the crowd, tired from its exer-tions, hungry but happy, dispersed. Some went back to their busi-nesses, some returned to their pulpits, some to finish their house-work, and the children to their classrooms. It was a perfectly gorgeous affair, and everyone was happy. That is a picture of Arkansas."[1]

Over the next few weeks, the Missouri Pacific sold record numbers of tickets to blacks fleeing Little Rock. The lynching, the city's first in thirty-six years, horrified respectable whites—"a Saturnalia of savagery," the *Arkansas Gazette* called it—but only to a point: no one involved was ever prosecuted, nor was any official ever removed from office (though both the *Defender* and another leading black weekly, the *Pittsburgh Courier,* were soon banned from Little Rock because, in the words of the local censorship board, "they agitated the state of mind of the colored populace of the city"). In the next thirty years nothing remotely similar had happened. But how many eyewitnesses, including all those children who'd either looked on or cowered in corners, remained part of Little Rock, circa 1957? How quickly or completely could such hatred, and fear, ever dissipate? How much, in fact, would it only have been stoked as blacks, however tentatively, began pressing for their rights, including the right to have their children attend the same schools as whites?

The glow from the funeral pyre that night surely illuminated the glorious new home for Little Rock High School—the "Central" part came much later—that was rising only a few miles away, on Park between 14th and 16th Streets. A Gothic structure of buff-colored brick enveloping two full city blocks, it was monumental, stately, self-confident—emanating what the *Arkansas Democrat* called "an almost ancient cathedral permanence." Clearly, it was too big and grandiose for its present purposes, but the city fathers were thinking epic thoughts: one day and soon, it all but shouted, progressive, forward-thinking Little Rock would grow into it. In a

Central High School

region so wedded to, and crippled by, its past, here was a building that looked resolutely forward. "Helping to Make Little Rock Famous," the Little Rock Gas and Fuel Company said of the school in an advertisement that ran when the building formally opened that November. And this turned out to be prophetic. It would prove an ideal backdrop to epochal events.

Five thousand people—presumably a very different five thousand from those who'd gathered around the trolley tracks at Ninth and Broadway a few months earlier—attended the dedication. The day's speeches abounded with those superlatives Americans so love: the biggest this, the most expensive that. One even graced the new letterhead: "The most beautiful high school in America." Another could have said: "the most archetypal." Could there ever have been a high school that looked, well, so much like a high school? Most striking were the four stone sentinels above its monumental entryway, each symbolizing one of the values to be imparted inside: "Ambition," "Personality," "Opportunity," and "Preparation." Another of Central's tenets went unrepresented, though it, too, could have been depicted in stone, perhaps by a figure with its hands held up, palms out: "Exclusion." Little Rock's new high school was, naturally, for whites only. Built like a fortress, for the next three decades it proved impregnable to Little Rock's black children. For them, its manicured grounds might just as well have been a moat.

When Central was built, blacks in Little Rock had their own primitive, ramshackle school; another few years would pass before Dunbar High School—largely funded, as were thousands of schools for blacks throughout the South, by the Jewish philanthropist Julius Rosenwald—would open. It was designed by the same local architects who'd done Central, and, standing only a few blocks away, was modeled consciously, almost poignantly, after it. Not surprisingly, it was far smaller and less sumptuous, with fewer classes to take, fewer frogs to dissect, fewer fields to play on. Its textbooks were hand-me-downs from Central, bequeathed after many years' use, sometimes arriving—the white students knew where they were destined—with racial epithets on their pages. But Dunbar, too, was considered the best of its kind, "the most modern and complete public high school building in the United States erected specifically for Negroes," as a Works Progress Administration guide put it. "The dream of the colored people of Little Rock has come true . . . far beyond in beauty, modernity and size what the boldest had ever hoped for," the local black paper declared when it opened.

Of all the states in the Old Confederacy, Arkansas was probably, on racial matters, the most enlightened. In the ferment following World War II, several graduate departments of the University of Arkansas admitted black students; when Silas Hunt entered its law school in 1948, he was said to have been the first black student at any state university in the Old Confederacy since Reconstruction. A handful of smaller towns peacefully integrated their schools following the *Brown* decision; Fayetteville so decided within a week of the ruling. (It was part the relative open-mindedness of a college town, part economic necessity: without a black high school of its own, the cash-strapped city had spent five thousand dollars the previous year to put up the nine black students it shipped off to segregated schools in Fort Smith and Hot Springs, fifty and two hundred miles away.) Faubus had been elected governor in 1954 as a racial moderate, someone who idolized Lincoln and, he liked to boast, would have backed the Union during the Civil War.[2] Little Rock, population 100,000 at the time, was one of the most progressive cities in the region. Things had settled down since the lynching, in part because blacks had resumed their traditional places. "Accustomed since birth to characteristically Southern environmental factors, the Negroes of Little Rock and North Little Rock accept them with little outward evidence of resentment," stated a WPA report from 1941.[3]

By the mid-1950s, though, blacks could use some parks and, on certain days, the zoo; some of the "whites only" and "colored" signs had been removed from drinking fountains. Thanks to court cases and protests, black schoolteachers earned as much as whites; black policemen patrolled 9th Street.[4] In 1954, the year before Martin Luther King, Jr., led his famous boycott in Montgomery,

Alabama, Little Rock quietly desegregated its buses. So when Elizabeth's mother set off to clean the houses of wealthy white families in Pulaski Heights, she could sit wherever she pleased. The handful of white professors at the local black college, Philander Smith, could eat at the "strictly colored" Charmaine Hotel without being prosecuted, as they would have been in Mississippi. Little Rock boosters noted with pride that white salesmen now waited on black women when they bought shoes. Even the conservative *Arkansas Democrat* had come to use "Miss" and "Mrs." when writing about black women.[5] With his "Land of Lincoln" Illinois license plates, the NBC newsman Sandor Vanocur was terrified to enter places like Jackson, Mississippi, or Birmingham, Alabama, but in Little Rock he felt just fine.

But beneath this comparatively tolerant façade, Jim Crow was alive and well in Little Rock. Newspaper policy notwithstanding, whites invariably called blacks by their first names. The train and bus stations still had separate waiting rooms, though more now by custom or habit than by stricture, integrated whenever some oblivious outsider stumbled into the forbidden realm. "Sometimes a white person drinks from the 'wrong' fountain, discovers his mistake and ambles away with a sheepish grin," one reporter noted. Blacks could not patronize local soda fountains and coffee shops, or the restaurants in the downtown department stores; the first lady of the black press, Ethel Payne of the *Chicago Defender*, couldn't find a place to eat, at least in the white part of town, while seated; like other blacks, she had to order her victuals through the back door. (To Payne, who'd traveled all over the segregated South, Little Rock was "the crummiest corner on the map.") Harold Isaacs of MIT, who came to study race relations in Little Rock in November 1957, learned that there wasn't a single establishment where he could have a cup of coffee with a black man. Were a white man to sit with a black woman in one of the colored establishments on 9th Street, he was told, there would inevitably be trouble, requiring police intervention.[6] No hotel would accommodate Carl Rowan, then a young reporter for the *Minneapolis Tribune.* Daisy Bates, who besides running the Arkansas NAACP copublished (with her husband, L. C. Bates) the weekly black newspaper the *State Press,* effectively turned her home into a rooming house for visiting black reporters. (Their paper barely scraped by, threatened by both black penury [and timidity] and fickle white patronage. "Can you vision [*sic*] what it takes to build up a newspaper in the deep south, contrary to the white man's wishes and way of thinking among a bunch of 'Uncle Toms' who do not even know that the Emancipation Proclamation has been signed?" L. C. Bates once wrote to an impatient black creditor.) For all the rules, written and unwritten, guiding relations between the races, there were dangerous areas of gray. As one local black lawyer, Robert Booker, told Isaacs, sometimes one was lured into them by an ostensibly friendly gesture.[7]

Even in her insular and constricted world, Elizabeth had had brushes with southern racial reality. To get ice cream—and eat it before it melted—she and her family had to go to the colored waiting room of the Little Rock train station. Though the main library was officially integrated, blacks had to *read* the books somewhere else. She could watch movies only in the (segregated) Gem Theater or, as in the Lee, from the balconies of a few white theaters. The one time Elizabeth prepared to sit down and eat with the family for whom she did occasional housework, the mother—

a Girl Scout troop leader—had quickly found something else for her to do. For a white neighbor, Elizabeth waxed the floors the woman's own daughters refused to do. As payment, she was given two old hand-me-down skirts.

Because the Eckfords traveled little, Elizabeth had been spared the segregated (or nonexistent) restrooms, restaurants, and hotels she would have encountered on the road. But she came instinctively to recognize the invisible borders of Jim Crow culture. She noticed that white and black children played together easily until around age ten, when the word "nigger" crept into the white kids' vocabularies. She learned that white people were to be feared: they could hurt you and your parents, without cause or cost. She saw that white children were more spontaneous and uninhibited than black children, perhaps because they didn't fear the white man's wrath. She noticed, too, that black children from the North felt freer than children like her. That became painfully apparent with the notorious case of Emmett Till, the young black boy from Chicago who'd been murdered in Mississippi in 1955 after supposedly whistling at a white woman; Till had been two months older than Elizabeth. She remembered seeing the famous picture of him in his casket, his body beaten and bloated, that appeared in *Jet*. But that was Mississippi, and Mississippi, she believed, was a different world from Arkansas.

FOUR

F ive days after the *Brown* decision, and more than a year before the High Court offered its ambiguous order for southern schools to desegregate "with all deliberate speed," the Little Rock School Board pledged to comply with the decision. It was in some ways a forward-looking commitment, befitting what the local superintendent of schools, Virgil Blossom, called "a friendly, open-handed town where the easy comradeship of the West and the hustling spirit of the Middle West blended with the traditions of the Old South," one garnering considerable attention, and applause: "a likely model for other cities," *U.S. News and World Report* declared in 1956. But Blossom, a pragmatist with political ambitions, feared getting too far ahead of public opinion. It took him three years to decide to enroll only a token number of blacks in only three grades at only one school: Central High School. In May 1957 school administrators set out to find the black trailblazers: children who were simultaneously old enough to attend Central, close enough to get there easily, smart enough to cut it academically, strong enough to survive the ordeal, mild enough to make no waves, and stoic enough not to fight back. And, collectively, scarce enough to minimize white objections.

Black students at Dunbar and Horace Mann were asked that

spring whether they wanted to participate in the great experiment. Of the roughly two hundred who were eligible, only eighty or so volunteered. Elizabeth was not among them; she couldn't decide anything so momentous so quickly. That was fine with her folks. Though the Eckfords felt black pride— *"There's a Negro on television! There's a Negro on television!"* someone would shout when Nat King Cole or Harry Belafonte or Ella Fitzgerald appeared on the screen—Elizabeth's parents were hardly activists. What most concerned Oscar Eckford, Jr., was making a living, and getting by. When a white woman approached, he instinctively crossed to the other side of the street. If anything, Elizabeth's mother was even more deferential. Her entire career in political activism consisted of collecting signatures once to have streetlights installed in the neighborhood. "I have never had trouble with white people," she told one reporter. "I always gave in, if necessary." They'd have been perfectly content had Elizabeth stayed put, continuing her studies at Horace Mann.

At Blossom's request, the principals of Horace Mann and Dunbar (which had become a junior high school) winnowed down the candidates to a couple dozen. The superintendent interviewed them all, filtering out those whom he felt might cause problems— one girl, for instance, was too pretty—and scaring away others by telling them everything they *could not* do. Even were they to be greeted warmly, Central's pioneering black students would not enjoy a traditional high school experience. To mollify white fears of "race mixing," they were to be barred from all extracurricular activities: they could not act in school plays, sing in the school choir, go to the prom. "You know, this whole problem [of school desegregation] could be solved if they'd give us a Negro student who could run the 100 in 9.8 and also throw a decent forward pass," a white student told the *New York Post*. But under Blossom's plan, that could not happen: blacks couldn't play on Central's teams (including the famous football Tigers) either.

For weeks, Elizabeth weighed whether to add her name to the list. Were she to stay at Horace Mann, her path would be clear, and circumscribed: she would surely wind up at Philander Smith, then go on to teach history to black students in some Podunk town. Central offered more courses, like speech, that could help her become a lawyer. It also had a far better library. While it had always been off-limits to her, it was also oddly familiar: she passed it all the time en route to her grandfather's store; summers, she played on its tennis courts, which were integrated long before its classrooms were. As for the ban on extracurricular activities, that posed no problem for her: she was shy by nature and "The Queen of No" was actually *happier* with her home. On the other hand, she knew her parents might suffer retaliation—both could lose their jobs—were she to enroll.

Sometime that summer, Elizabeth made up her mind: she wanted to go. Birdie Eckford demurred, hoping her daughter would forget about it. Several weeks passed, and Elizabeth, showing a persistence with her mother that was unusual for her, brought it up again. Wasn't it time, she asked, for her mother to speak to the principal of Horace Mann, LeRoy Christophe? Anna lobbied for her. So did her grandfather. "Maybe Papa felt that he and I didn't do nothing, so maybe Elizabeth would," her father later said. Christophe told Elizabeth's mother that the list was already complete, and that they'd have to go see Blossom himself. When they did, he kept them waiting until all the whites had left the office. An owlish, jowly man, Blossom satisfied himself that Elizabeth had no ties to the local NAACP, which had sued the school board the year before to speed up desegregation, proposing its own slate of students; Blossom wanted none of them. He cautioned Elizabeth that she would have to emulate the black baseball pioneer Jackie Robinson, ignoring all provocations. Elizabeth found Blossom intimidating and patronizing. But a week later, he got back to them: sensitive, brooding, fragile Elizabeth had, improbably, made the cut. Even more improbably, her worrywart mother went along, not even wavering as the mood in Little Rock darkened.

Throughout the summer, a group of segregationists, including several prominent local churchmen, campaigned to halt the Blossom plan. Cheering them on were racial hard-liners throughout the South, who feared that if desegregation, even in so diluted a form, proceeded in Little Rock, their own communities would inevitably follow suit. Advertisements and fliers conjured up black boys and white girls dancing together and kissing in school plays, and warned of venereal disease contracted from communal toilets. A newly formed Mothers League of Central High School sued the Little Rock School Board. Convinced that political survival lay in supporting the hard-liners, Faubus spoke out on their behalf, citing dubious reports that both whites and blacks were stockpiling weapons. Exacerbating race prejudice was class resentment. Little Rock's elite would not fully participate in the plan; just as blacks were entering Central, the brand new Hall High School—nicknamed Cadillac High—was opening in wealthy Pulaski Heights, and, like the neighborhood, it would be lily-white. Thus the whites bearing the brunt of the change were, by and large, poorer and less educated: mixed in for them with traditional race prejudice was a more undifferentiated kind of rage. The hate descending upon Little Rock in the summer of 1957 reminded Blossom of what he'd read about Germany in 1933.

Quite understandably, some of the black students who'd signed up for Central got cold feet. Soon, only nine of them remained, to enter a student body of approximately two thousand. No man is an island, perhaps, but nine black boys and girls were about to become an archipelago in an ocean of whites. "There's strength in numbers, especially when you're having trouble," Thurgood Marshall told a reporter. "One student is horrible and nine or ten is bad."

Little Rock's black community was small and interconnected, and in addition to Minnijean Brown, Elizabeth had ties to several of the pioneering black students. She'd had a crush on the self-assured, highly intelligent Terrence Roberts in junior high, and had seen Carlotta Walls, who was energetic and athletic and had long, thick braids, around the neighborhood. Her mother had once lived with people close to Ernest Green, and Elizabeth knew Ernest, the only senior in the group, as a highly social sort who liked jazz. Thelma Mothershed she'd met through her family. Only Melba Patillo, Jefferson Thomas, and Gloria Ray were complete strangers to her. Collectively, they were what Blossom had wanted: well-mannered children from good families, the offspring of schoolteachers and postal workers and others in the small black middle class, or those with middle-class aspirations. Most were genuine Jackie Robinson types, sufficiently tough and talented to withstand the inevitable abuse. But anyone in the know could see how hasty and haphazard the process had been.

Why pick Thelma, a tiny, fragile girl with a heart defect? Or the proud and pugnacious Minnijean? Or, for that matter, Elizabeth? With her sensitivity and intelligence, she would surely feel whatever punishment was to be meted out more keenly and convey her pain more compellingly should she ever find her voice.

Underfunded as they were, Little Rock's black schools had a proud tradition, teaching black pride before the term existed and black history before there were any texts. They represented community and continuity: some of Elizabeth's teachers had also taught her parents. It was a point of pride that many of them had better credentials—that is, more graduate degrees—than their counterparts in the white schools. The schools provided a refuge from the racism outside. Whatever benefits Central conferred, then, would come at a cost. The very institutions—schools, churches, stores—that insulated Elizabeth from whites left her largely ignorant about them. When she got to Central, she actually had trouble understanding some of the children: their accents were too foreign. White people were stick figures to her, exotics whom she scrutinized only to stay safe. Her ignorance extended to the virulence and depth of white antipathy. Part of what would prove so terrifying to her was that it was so unfamiliar, so unexpected.

Blossom had directed the black parents to send their children to the first day of school at Central without them. Having adults around, the authorities reasoned, would only inflame things more. Would the soldiers dare block the black students? To the black parents, that seemed hard to believe. In fact, unbeknownst to them, their orders that day were, as one of the Guardsmen present later recalled, quite explicit: "No niggers in the building." That soldier, a Central graduate himself, knew the school had many black employees—janitors, boiler operators, cafeteria workers, the folks who really kept the place going—and asked his superior officer whether exceptions would be made for them. "No niggers in the building," the officer reiterated.[1]

The local NAACP decided that the black students should not come to school that first day, pending a decision in the segregationists' latest court challenge. But on September 3, Federal Judge Ronald Davies, on loan from North Dakota, ordered that the process proceed. Late that night, the principals of Dunbar and Horace Mann informed the nine black students that they would be going to Central the next day. Daisy Bates, who had taken charge of the group, also called the families. The students should not come individually to Central, as Blossom had requested; it would be too dangerous. Instead, they were to assemble at her home. From there they would proceed to a spot near the school, where they'd meet with a small group of local ministers, including the few white pastors she'd been able to enlist. The clergymen would then escort the black students to the school. But the Eckfords did not have a phone. As Bates later wrote, she knew that Elizabeth's father worked nights at the train station; she'd have driven down there to tell him the plan had she not been so dog tired. It could wait till morning. But when morning came, she forgot.[2]

FIVE

Will Counts was the son of a sharecropper. He'd grown up in Plum Bayou, a community south of Little Rock built by the Farm Security Administration. After World War II his family moved to Little Rock, and he'd graduated from Central in 1949. While there he'd gotten his first camera: a Kodak Brownie Hawkeye. Now twenty-six years old, he was back at the school—or at least outside it—documenting everything for the *Arkansas Democrat*. It was his first big story for the afternoon paper, which he'd joined only a few months earlier. Sensing that there'd be trouble, wanting to make sure he wouldn't be mistaken for a carpetbagging Yankee, he had put on a countrified plaid shirt that morning, something he'd been given the previous Christmas but had never worn. (Sure enough, the three *Life* photographers attacked that day sported jackets and ties.)

Slight and youthful, Counts could easily have been mistaken for the student he had only recently been. His hero was Henri Cartier-Bresson, the French photographer who strived to capture the "decisive moment"—that instant defining the essence of a situation. Counts's task was made easier by his Nikon S2 rangefinder, with its wide-angle lens; he could shoot away while his competitors

Will Counts on the job, 1957 (Robert Troutt, *Arkansas Democrat.*
Courtesy *Arkansas Democrat-Gazette*)

fumbled with their clunky old Speed Graphics. Alone among the photographers, most of whom had gathered at the other end of the block, Counts had positioned himself toward the north end of the school, not far from where Elizabeth had gotten off the bus. Only he had spotted her as she approached. Then he went to work.

Lots of white people lined Park Street as Elizabeth headed toward the school. As she passed the Mobil station and came nearer, she could see the white students filtering unimpeded past the soldiers. To her, it was a sign that everything was all right. But as she herself approached, three Guardsmen, two with rifles, held out their arms, directing her to her left, to the far side of Park, toward all the onlookers. She asked the soldiers for the time. "Six minutes to eight," one replied. She stepped into the street, then resumed her walk. A few steps farther along, she crossed back and approached a different knot of soldiers. This time they closed ranks, then crossed rifles. "Don't let her in!" someone shouted. Perhaps, she thought, she hadn't found the right door; hadn't Blossom said something about using the main entrance, the one with all the statues on top?

By now a crowd had started to form behind Elizabeth, and her knees began to shake. She continued down Park. For an instant, she faced the school: it just looked so big! The white students, books in hand, continued to walk nonchalantly past the Guardsmen. She steadied herself, then walked up to another soldier. He didn't move. When she tried to squeeze past him, he raised his carbine. Other soldiers moved over to assist him. When she tried to get in around them, they moved to block her way. They glared at her. She walked back toward the street, where the protestors were concentrated. After she did, John Chancellor approached the soldiers. "You couldn't let her in?" he asked. "We couldn't let her in," one of them replied.

Now, as Elizabeth continued walking south down Park, more and more of the people lining the street fell in behind her. Some were Central students, others adults. They started shouting at her. The primitive television cameras, for all their bulkiness, had no sound equipment. But the reporters on the scene scribbled down what they heard: *"Lynch her! Lynch her!"* "No nigger bitch is going to get in our school!" "Get out of here!" "Go back where you came from!" "Go home, nigger!" "Throw her out!" "Nigger, go back to where you belong!" "Send her back to the NAACP and Eleanor Roosevelt!" "You've got a better school of your own!" Looking for a friendly face, Elizabeth turned to an old white woman. It was what she had been trained to do, and besides, there was little choice. One in four local residents was black, but the crowd that day included no black faces. The woman spat on her. It was the last time that Elizabeth turned her head in any direction. From that moment on, she gazed resolutely ahead. For all the turmoil she felt inside, outwardly she remained calm. Her sunglasses made her look all the more impassive. One could not look into her eyes, which would have betrayed her fear.

Walking backward, the cameramen and photographers recorded Elizabeth's advance. Meantime, reporters pulled up beside her, peppering her with questions: *What's your name? Did you come here to register?* Elizabeth ignored them, and kept on walking forward. With the mob at her heels, she felt she could not turn back. A block ahead, she remembered, was another bus stop; if she could only get there, she would be safe. She wanted to run, but feared she might fall down if she tried. So, looking straight ahead, she kept on walking. "Lynch her!" someone shouted. "Go home, you burr head!" "Send the nigger back to the jungle!" Meantime, Counts took his pictures. He felt sorry for Elizabeth, but he had a job to do. He had picked the right film—Kodak Plus-X, good for sunny mornings—but hoped he had read the light correctly, for it was spotty, weaving its way through the still-leafy trees. He also hoped he had enough film. There were only thirty-six exposures on the roll, and by the time he'd recorded the various Guardsmen turning Elizabeth away, he had already used up nine. He couldn't just shoot indiscriminately; with things moving so quickly, there would be little time to rewind one spool and load another.

Three young girls, barely into their teens, fell in directly behind Elizabeth. They were clearly together, and clearly students; two of them, like Elizabeth, carried books. They wanted to be at the very center of things. And they wanted to get really close to Elizabeth—close enough to let her know that they didn't want her in their school. It was easy: everyone—the television reporters, the grown-ups in the vacant lot across the street, the other kids—was either egging them on, or, like the soldiers and policemen, paying them no mind. No one was telling them *not* to do anything. *"Two, four, six, eight! We don't want to integrate!"* they chanted. Walking closest to Central, carrying a small metallic purse, was Mary Ann Burleson. She had a mild, almost bemused quality on her face, or maybe it was a nervous smile; later, she recalled that as she shouted, she felt nausea, even a knot in her stomach, as if she knew that what she was doing was wrong. The pretty girl next to her, Sammie Dean Parker, wearing a dark dress with a sailor's ribbon on top, also shouted, though without any great passion. But the girl to her right, Hazel Bryan, looked livid, her face poisoned with hate. As Benjamin Fine of the *New York Times* later described her, she was "screaming, just hysterical, just like one of these Elvis Presley hysterical deals, where these kids are fainting with hysteria." Her eyes narrowed, her brow furrowed, her teeth clenched as if about to bite, Hazel shouted, then shouted some more: "Go home, nigger! Go back to A—"

Click.

"—frica!"

Will Counts had his picture.

SIX

U nlike many of the rabble-rousers that morning, who had come in from the sticks, Hazel Bryan, age fifteen and a half, actually lived in Little Rock. But her roots, too, were rural. She had been born—on January 31, 1942—and raised in the hamlet of Redfield, population a hundred or so, roughly thirty miles to the south. Her parents had married in 1940; her father, Sanford, had been thirty years old, her mother, Pauline, only fourteen. The town's economy revolved around a sawmill; people on both sides of her family worked there. Hazel grew up in a small house, with a privy in the back and two sycamores her father had planted in the front. Their street ran parallel to the train tracks and Highway 365, which they took periodically to Pine Bluff.

In January 1944, five days short of Hazel's second birthday, Sanford Bryan had gone off to World War II, leaving Hazel and her younger sister, then only a few months old, behind with their mother, who had taken a job making bombs in the Pine Bluff Arsenal. Fighting in France that November, he had taken shrapnel in his hip, shoulder, and stomach, and after a prolonged hospitalization overseas and stateside, had come back to Arkansas with a gimpy, shriveled-up left leg, one that always required him to attach a metal brace to his shoe. Hazel never knew him any other way; one of her earliest memories was of walking alongside her limping father shortly after his return, and of his stopping to take off his Bronze Star and Purple Heart and pin them on her chest.

Sanford Bryan had been physically active before going overseas —as a young man, he had run away with Ringling Brothers—and his injury left him frustrated and embittered, rough and profane. One night, after mixing alcohol and pills, he'd stumbled into the open sewer in front of the local beer joint and had to be rescued. (As Hazel later saw it, it was a botched suicide.) So embarrassed was he by his disability, and by the unsightly equipment it required, that as much as he'd always liked to swim, only once did Hazel actually see him go in the water. He couldn't really work, so Hazel's mother did. He favored more sedentary pursuits, like playing the fiddle and harmonica and working wood, which he'd do while waiting to shoot squirrels for his family's table. To Hazel, he was more nurturing, more mothering than her mother, forever loading up her and her baby sister and cousin on the back of his truck and taking them swimming or dancing or roller skating. Hazel was his favorite; whenever her mother or sister wanted something from him, they would always go through her.

Sometimes he'd bring Hazel to his favorite bar, stand her up on the counter, and have her sing, with his buddies chipping in afterward to buy her a Coke. Maybe this was when she first realized how much she loved to perform. She had shown some promise in school—her first-grade teacher once let her spend the night at her home because she was the best reader in the class—but Hazel never cared much about her studies. What she loved was being on a

Hazel in Redfield, June 1944. Her father carried the picture with him
throughout Europe during World War II. (Courtesy Hazel Bryan Massery)

stage, real or make-believe. Of course, there was little place for
such things in the fundamentalist Christian faith to which the
Bryans had been converted by an itinerant college student who
had come through Redfield once selling silverware. (From him,
and from the purple book he left behind, Hazel first learned how
to set a table, something the Bryans had never previously done.)

Redfield was too tiny to be segregated. Living close at hand were
elderly black ladies like "Old Nigger Eller" and "Boot Fanny," who
trod the town's unpaved streets in giant rubber galoshes. None-

theless, there were racial lines: when Hazel's grandmother invited one of the black women onto her porch, her Uncle Charlie had reproached her. (One of the old ladies had a dog that followed her everywhere, a fact that amazed him. Imagine that! A dog could love niggers, too!) Sometimes Hazel played with black children; once, they pretended to be in church—a black church, of course: they were much more fun—with an upended washboard serving as their pulpit. After one such experience, her daddy had jokingly told her to check her hands: maybe some of their blackness had rubbed off on her. All this stopped when the black children got a bit older; because there was no place for them to go to school locally, they were around only in the summer.

Lore had it that there was some black blood in Hazel's family— that after his wife died, her paternal great-grandfather, who'd had a plantation in Natchez, had taken up with one of his slaves and may have had a child by her. So livid was Hazel's grandfather over this turn of events, the story went, that he renounced his family, and family fortune, signing away his rights one night by the head-lights of a big city lawyer's Model T Ford. And an aunt on her mother's side had suspiciously kinky hair and big lips.

When Hazel was ten they had moved to the city so that Pauline Bryan could be closer to the Westinghouse plant where she worked. The family bought a small house in the industrialized southeast part of town known as Biddle Shop. The house was the same size, and shape, and vintage as the Eckfords'. (But for the Bryans it was more of a step up, with such unaccustomed luxuries as indoor plumbing, hot water, and a washing machine.) Politically, too, the two families were congruent: both were Democrats; both had voted for Faubus. The only thing separating them was race.

After Redfield, Little Rock seemed positively cosmopolitan. Only there, for instance, did Hazel hear her first symphony orchestra. But the segregation was more pronounced. Her new neighborhood was all white. In fact, she lived right off Confederate Boulevard, and passed Little Rock's Confederate cemetery— 640 rebel soldiers are buried there—every day en route to Central. As long as they lasted, Hazel rode on segregated buses, drank out of segregated bubblers, and, though they didn't eat out much, sat at the segregated lunch counters of the five-and-ten-cent stores, without ever thinking much about it. Segregation and integration were, in fact, terms that Hazel barely recognized. When black performers like Bo Diddley came to Robinson Auditorium, there would be separate performances for blacks and whites. To her, blacks were the folks who picked up the garbage, or worked (and ate) in the backs of restaurants. The only black person ever to enter her home was the woman who came occasionally to iron. Hazel liked her—she found her motherly—and used to play sick sometimes just to stay home and be with her.

Matters of faith were just as segregated. The East Side Church of Christ had no black members. The preacher put it bluntly: "The birds don't mix; why should the races?" (As Hazel remembered it, he'd had this smug, all-knowing smile on his face as he'd said it.) Sundays, everyone would sing, "Jesus loves the little children of the world / Red and yellow, black and white / We are all precious in his sight," but the lyrics were about as far as it went. Theirs was an abstemious faith: no drinking, swearing, dancing. "A praying knee and a dancing foot don't grow on the same leg," the preacher liked to say. It was a hard regimen for an exuberant young girl to follow.

Hazel didn't read the papers much and knew nothing about the

Brown decision except that the grown-ups had grumbled about it, and about Martin Luther King, too: a "troublemaker," they called him. As Central's day of reckoning approached, she was almost entirely oblivious. To the extent she had any, her racial attitudes mirrored her parents': for instance, her father would not let black clerks wait on him, and when stores began hiring black cashiers, he stood in other lines. (Of course, he'd also complain that blacks were lazy.) The one exception for Hazel was music. She actually preferred Johnny Mathis (and Little Richard and Chuck Berry and Fats Domino) to Elvis, though she didn't exactly broadcast it.

Hazel had entered Central her sophomore year, when she was fourteen. Though it was all white, it was also stratified: poor whites like Hazel from Little Rock's East and West Sides next to children from the more affluent Heights, from which the student leaders and academic stars generally came. Her extracurricular activities weren't the sort that made yearbooks. To be more precise, what mattered most were boys, and she was the envy of her girlfriends. All the things teenagers do—dating, dancing, dressing up—she did well. Boys forever buzzed around her; during the seven nights of the Arkansas State Fair one year, she had nine dates. (A couple of also-rans had to settle for afternoon slots.) One suitor, named Billy, actually fired his gun unhappily into the air before she crawled out the window of her house to get him to leave before he woke up her father. Hazel acted, and dressed, older than she was. She experimented with makeup, and when she wasn't starching crinoline slips for the full-circle skirts that were all the rage, she wore snug sweaters like Marilyn Monroe. Her girlfriends, like Sammie Dean Parker, thought her desperate to get married, which was really just another way of getting out of the house.

Hazel met her first real boyfriend, who worked in a parking lot downtown, in the fall of her sophomore year. Billy owned a Ford convertible, and she loved going on drives with him. At Christmas, he gave her a music box that played "Let Me Call You Sweetheart." Her parents disapproved of the relationship, and Hazel, feigning illness, played hooky to see him. She failed some courses as a result, and the school summoned her father. Central's vice principal for girls, Elizabeth Huckaby, remembered him as "a small, wiry, highly nervous man." "Mr. Bryan was sure that Hazel had not been ill," she wrote after the meeting. "He hoped, he said, that he would not have to whip her, for he sometimes lost his temper when he did that and whipped her harder than he intended." (Hazel later insisted such things never happened.) Feeling the heat, poor Billy broke things off. Ever one for histrionics, Hazel promptly swallowed some aspirin and rubbing alcohol and landed in the hospital, having her stomach pumped. It had been a bit of a performance—she could get down only a little of the stuff, certainly not enough to be life-threatening—but the story made the papers, and Mrs. Huckaby sent the school nurse to check up on her. Hazel bounced back quickly. There was Gary, with the motorcycle. And James, who went on to become a doctor. But the most serious was Mickey, a lonesome young airman whom she met shopping at Walgreen's in the spring of 1957, when he was stationed at the nearby military base. Before long he'd given her his class ring and then they were engaged, or at least he'd bought her a diamond, purchased on layaway before he'd shipped out to England. They agreed that she could date other boys in the meantime; for the hapless airman, that was not a wise move.

Hazel's other diversion was *Steve's Show*, the daily dance party program on a local television station. Every afternoon after school, Hazel hopped on the bus and headed for the studio. It wasn't something a good Fundamentalist Christian girl should do, but Hazel loved dancing to rock-and-roll records, and having folks watch her on their brand-new television sets. A forerunner of *American Bandstand* (which made its debut six months later), the program brought together students from all classes of Little Rock; on the dance floor, everyone was equal, as long as they were white.[1] Often joining her was Sammie Dean Parker, whom Hazel had met shortly after her thwarted suicide attempt. Sammie Dean thought of herself as a caregiver, and Hazel was someone who clearly needed care (and, could, incidentally, teach her a thing or two about boys). When they weren't dancing together, the two shopped for clothes at Blass or one of the other fancy Jewish department stores downtown. Sometimes they bought themselves matching outfits. In the summer of 1957, as school administrators, police officials, lawyers, and parents braced themselves for desegregation, Hazel and Sammie Dean daydreamed around jukeboxes at Lake Nixon, Windy Beach, or Willow Springs.

In the year and a day she'd been going to Central, Hazel had generally taken the bus. But anticipating trouble, her father had driven her on the morning of September 4, 1957. Unlike Mary Ann and Sammie Dean, whom she met up with once she arrived, she carried no schoolbooks—only her purse and, improbably, a newspaper, rolled up in her right hand. Hazel's mother was at the school as well: alarmed by the reports over the radio, Westinghouse had let parents with children at Central go down to the school to take them home, if necessary. But Mrs. Bryan hadn't seen Hazel around the grounds and assumed her daughter had gone inside with the others. Hazel, who never knew her mother was around, would have, too—she hadn't planned on protesting—but she was having too much fun: all those people, and reporters, and young men in uniforms! Rebuffed by the soldiers, Elizabeth was now making her way toward the bus stop, and Hazel, walking directly behind her, was hamming it up. To the extent she was even thinking about Elizabeth (barely), Elizabeth was less a person than the disembodied stand-in for something she'd been told was foreign and repugnant: the federal government, shoving something down Little Rock's throat. So she started yelling awful things, awful enough for people to notice, even before it was frozen on film. As for Hazel herself, as soon as her words had dissolved in the torpid September air, she had forgotten all about them.

SEVEN

The men of the Arkansas National Guard continued to ring the school, watching idly as Elizabeth walked by. Since she was no longer physically trying to enter Central, she was of little consequence to them. But others continued to watch her. "Here she is this little girl, this tender little thing, walking with this whole mob baying at her like a pack of wolves seeking to destroy a little lamb," Benjamin Fine of the *New York Times* later recalled. Buddy Lonesome of the *St. Louis Argus*, a black weekly, was also looking on. "The mob of twisted whites, galvanized into vengeful action by the inaction of the heroic state militia, was not willing that the young school girl should get off so easily," he wrote. "Elizabeth Eckford had walked into the wolf's lair, and now that they felt she was fair game, the drooling wolves took off after their prey. The hate mongers, who look exactly like other, normal white men and women, took off down the street after the girl."

Elizabeth's goal remained the bus stop on 16th and Park. She was scared, especially after someone shouted "Push her!" But if she let herself go, she feared she'd begin to cry, something she didn't want to do in front of so many people. She worried that if she said or did anything unusual, the crowd might turn even uglier. There were more shouts: "Go home, nigger! You will never get into this school! We don't want you here!" "Go back where you came from!" But she looked placid, unflappable, as if she wasn't hearing anything. At one point a major in the Guard wearing command pilot wings held up his hands and forced the mob to back off a bit. Another soldier, holding his billy club at both ends, stared vacantly into space. John Chancellor was among the many reporters looking on. "He wanted a story, a good story," David Halberstam later wrote, "but this was something beyond a good story, a potential tragedy so terrible that he had hoped it really wasn't happening. He was terribly frightened for her, frightened for himself and frightened about what this told him about his country." Chancellor's cameraman got it all on film.

By the time she reached the bus stop, Elizabeth felt as if she couldn't walk another step. She sat down at the edge of the empty bench and, for the first time, began to cry. The catcalls continued, largely from grown-ups; the school bell had rung, and most of the students had gone inside. "Drag her over to this tree!" someone shouted. Some reporters drifted back to the school, where by now the seven other black students had been rebuffed en masse, with little of the pain or menace Elizabeth encountered.[1] (The other black girls, one reporter noted, didn't appear nervous; one even smiled.)

Some thirty or forty people milled around the bench. No one made any move to harm Elizabeth, but there was lots of laughing and jeering. The country might just as well be handed over to the Communists, one man shouted repeatedly. Someone, perhaps a plainclothes policeman, moved the crowd away. A few newsmen— Jerry Dhonau and Ray Moseley of the *Arkansas Gazette,* Paul

Elizabeth at the bus stop, September 4, 1957
(Lloyd Dinkins/ *Commercial Appeal*)

Welch of *Life*—created an informal cordon around Elizabeth, though she thought they were only trying to overhear whatever she might be saying.[2] A reporter for *Time* tried to interview her. "No comment," she told him. "I'm minding my own business." Then a black man—one of the very few in the crowd—offered to escort her away. It was L. C. Bates, Daisy's husband, whom Elizabeth recognized from his pictures in the *State Press*. Given the explosiveness of the situation, and the conspicuousness of any black face in that immaculately segregated crowd, it was remarkable that Bates had even shown up; the day before, when he had also made an appearance, he admitted that he'd been "scared as hell."[3] Even more remarkable, as he furtively showed Elizabeth, he was carrying a gun, tucked into his pants pocket. It frightened her; she wanted it—and him—nowhere near her. He offered to escort her out of there, but Elizabeth knew that her mother would never approve of her going off with a strange man, however honorable his intentions.

Benjamin Fine sat down alongside her, introduced himself, and asked for her name. "I'm not here to hurt you," he added. "Nothing's going to happen. You'll be alright, honey." Then Fine, the father of three young daughters himself, put his arm around Elizabeth. "Don't let them see you cry," he urged. That gesture—the act of a white man touching a black girl—appeared to ignite the crowd, already smoldering over the presence of the Yankee press. "Then the scream went up: 'There he is! The nigger lover! He's from the *Times*! Throw him out! Let's lynch him! Let's cut his nuts out! We'll fix him!'" Fine recalled afterward. Years later, a woman interviewing Fine asked him whether, by seeking to comfort Elizabeth that day, he had crossed some ethical line. "A reporter has to be a human being, my dear," he replied.

Robert Schakne of CBS also approached Elizabeth. Television news was in its infancy, a strange hybrid of newsreels and radio; its ground rules had yet to develop. Schakne could see that Elizabeth was petrified, but he pressed ahead. "Can you tell us who you are?" he asked, as gently as a gruff-looking and -sounding man wielding a microphone could. Elizabeth said nothing. Schakne looked back uncertainly toward his crew—"Rolling," his cameraman piped in—and tried again. "Can you tell me your name, please? Are you going to go to school here at Central High?" Again, Elizabeth remained silent. "You don't care to say anything, is that right?" It was.[4]

Terrence Roberts also appeared and urged Elizabeth to leave with him. Terrence, the young man Elizabeth had fancied at Dunbar, was dignified and polite. (One of his ancestors had clearly been a tribal chieftain or something like that in Africa, Mrs. Huckaby theorized.) But he lived closer to Central than Elizabeth did and, she figured, would accompany her only partway home, turning off on Howard Street. Better to stay put, she thought: this way, if something were to happen to her, at least someone would see it.

One of those who'd accompanied Elizabeth on her walk that morning had been the Rev. Colbert Cartwright of the Pulaski Heights Christian Church, one of Little Rock's wealthiest white congregations. He had wanted to express his solidarity with the black students, but didn't know quite how: he'd considered joining the black pastors accompanying the children, but feared that might seem paternalistic. So as Elizabeth had made her way down Park, he had resolved to be a witness, following slightly behind her, taking notes. When the screams flew at Elizabeth—"epithets I had never heard before or since," he later recalled—he too had been impressed by the "calm dignity with which she made her lonesome pilgrimage."

When he reached the bench, Cartwright saw a lone white woman sit down alongside Elizabeth. "What struck me with force was the fact that neither segregationist nor integrationist preachers had bothered to help," he wrote. "Her only help came from this single woman who was generally regarded as an intellectual Communist. Who was neighbor unto that girl?" Actually, the woman's name was Grace Lorch, and no one who had ever encountered (and either admired or reviled) her and her husband in prior years and locales would have been surprised to see her on that bench, alongside that black girl, in Little Rock.

EIGHT

—————

For Grace Lonergan Lorch and her husband, Lee, civic engagement had long been second nature. Grace had been first to the barricades, fighting for herself and other women teaching in the Boston public schools during and after World War II for the right to keep their jobs after marriage. (A plaque honoring her still hangs outside a school there.) In 1949 Lee, a mathematician, lost his position at City College in New York for leading the fight to integrate Stuyvesant Town, the massive housing complex on Manhattan's East Side then owned by the Metropolitan Life Insurance Company. Lee Lorch was subsequently fired by Penn State, where he'd found another teaching job, for attempting to sublet his vacant Stuyvesant Town apartment to a black couple. For five years after that, the Lorches lived in Nashville, where Lee taught at Fisk University, a historically black institution. While there, they petitioned to enroll their daughter in an all-black public school; it was, they argued, the school closest to their home. They were turned down.

Lee Lorch had once been a Communist; whether or not he stayed in the Party, he remained a sympathizer. This made him a prime target for various Red-baiting investigations. When he refused to answer questions from the House Un-American Activities Committee, Fisk, too, let him go. Only one school in the country would then have him: Philander Smith, the historically black college in Little Rock, to which the family moved in September 1955. "Because he believed in the principles of decency and justice, and the equality of all men under God, Lee Lorch and his family have been hounded through four states from the North to the South like refugees in displaced camps," Ethel Payne of the *Chicago Defender* wrote in May 1956. "And in the process of punishing Lee Lorch for his views, three proud institutions of learning have been made to grovel in the dust and bow the knee to bigotry." The Lorches again moved into a black neighborhood, and—this time, with the *Brown* decision behind them—again tried to send their daughter to an all-black school, again without success; when the young girl was barred from using the public roller skating rink with her black friends, her father protested to the Little Rock Parks Commission. He also became an official with the state NAACP, just as he had been in Tennessee.

On the morning of September 4, Lee Lorch was at one end of Central, observing how the great drama was unfolding. Meantime, his wife, who had just left their daughter at her junior high school, approached Central from the other direction and happened upon Elizabeth, sitting on the bench. To the catcalls of the milling crowd, she, too, tried speaking to the girl, without success. Then she turned toward her detractors. Couldn't they see that this was just a kid? Six months from now, she told them, they'd all hang their heads in shame. Her scolding only made things worse; Elizabeth was sorry she'd come, and hoped she'd quickly leave. Cries of "nigger lover!" and "Yankee!" filled the air. Lorch then took Elizabeth by the arm and, pushing aside anyone in her path,

Grace Lorch, right, with protestors, September 4, 1957
(Courtesy *Arkansas Democrat-Gazette*)

headed toward Ponder's, the ice cream and sandwich shop across the street, to call a cab. The store owner saw her coming and promptly locked the door in her face. "Won't somebody please call a taxi?" Lorch pleaded. She was told to go back to New York, or at least to act like a white person.

Elizabeth now got a bit of protection from an unlikely source: the National Guard. After seeing her rebuffed outside the drugstore, Maj. Lilburn Harris ordered a subordinate, Sgt. William Corker, to keep an eye on Elizabeth until the city bus arrived, then to help her to board it. When Elizabeth and Grace Lorch resumed their places on the bench, Corker positioned himself unobtrusively nearby—so unobtrusively, in fact, that Elizabeth never knew he was there. Though he had a carbine and thirty rounds of am-

munition, Corker was nearly as frightened as she: there was menace in the air. While he wanted to console her—he could see the
tears running down her cheeks—he felt it wiser to say nothing.

Afterward, Elizabeth couldn't guess just how long she'd sat on
that bench. *Time* put it at thirty-five minutes. The bus finally
pulled up. Again taking Elizabeth's arm, Lorch shoved her way
toward the open door. Two boys tried to block their way. "I'm just
waiting for one of you to touch me!" Lorch shouted. "I'm just *ach-
ing* to punch somebody in the nose." Some hooligans tried to board
the bus, but the driver threw them off. As it pulled away and the
crowd began to disperse, the "Call to Colors" sounded outside
Central. What struck Bobby Jones of the *Pine Bluff Commercial* was
that everyone—students, protestors, soldiers—stood at attention:
all considered themselves good patriotic Americans. Then, once the
last note sounded, they all resumed whatever they'd been doing.

Afterward, Elizabeth was to tell the press how relieved she had
been when Lorch showed up that day, but she was just being
polite. She, too, saw Lorch as a provocateur, come to stir up trouble. She assured the older woman that she could now fend for
herself, and as the bus approached Woodrow, Lorch got off. Elizabeth never saw her again.[1]

For what she did that day, which was widely reported, Grace
Lorch came in for both praise and abuse. The "warm and coura-
geous heart of a gentle white-haired woman in Little Rock" embodied mankind at its best, wrote *Time*. But the Lorches also had a
cross burned on their lawn and dynamite shoved under their
garage door. Classmates shunned and abused their daughter. And
they were implicated in a grand international conspiracy. There
was but a handful of Communists in Little Rock, and here was at

least a fellow traveler at center stage—confirming, at least for some, that desegregation was yet another Red plot. One state official charged that Lorch's "Communist masters" had directed her; Little Rock's newly elected segregationist congressman, Dale Alford, later charged on the floor of the House of Representatives that Lorch's "yeoman service to the Communist apparatus was so great that she was sent to Arkansas, via Nashville, Tennessee, and other points, to help create racial incidents in my state." (As for her "exhibition of alleged friendship" with Elizabeth, she had performed that "stunt" only after making sure the cameras were rolling.) Grace Lorch was hauled before the Senate Internal Security subcommittee, where Senator William Jenner of Indiana labeled her a "troublemaker." "You want to attract attention by protecting that little colored girl in Little Rock," he charged. (That she'd been subpoenaed, one observer said, raised the question "of whether it is subversive for a Southern white woman to treat a Negro child with kindness.") Fearful of being Red-baited, the NAACP quickly distanced itself from her and her husband. "Thurgood Marshall has been busy poisoning as many people as he can against us," Lee Lorch complained in October 1957. The following month the group's field secretary, Clarence Laws, made the ostracism official. "The best contribution you could make to the cause of full citizenship for Negroes in Arkansas at this time would be to terminate, in writing, your affiliation with the Little Rock Branch, NAACP," he told Lee Lorch.

While there was plenty of hate mail, letters of praise were few, or so the Lorches initially thought. One night, a black man visited their home. Like the Lorches themselves, he presumed that the house was being watched, and he insisted that the porch light be turned out before stating why he'd come. He then explained that he worked at the local post office, and handed them a package. In it were letters to Grace Lorch from all over the world, about to be returned to their senders: despite her sudden notoriety, "Grace Lorch, Little Rock, Arkansas" was technically an insufficient address. After the man left, the Lorches read portions of the letters to each other. "We have spoken with much deference of you in our lessons of ethics," some Catholic high school girls wrote from Brussels. The man, whose name the Lorches never learned, later returned with a second package. But such gestures were rare and, taking it from all sides, the Lorches' days in Little Rock were numbered.[2]

In film footage of Elizabeth at the bus stop, one can spot a very serious-looking young woman brushing by. It's Hazel, purposefully proceeding to play hooky. Rather than report to classes, she had decided to make a holiday out of the occasion. Off to Sammie Dean's house she went; she may even have danced on *Steve's Show* that afternoon. Not for an instant did she think she'd done anything wrong. Or momentous. Or that would mark her for life.

NINE

T here are times," Elizabeth later observed, "when you just *know* you need your Mama." When she had boarded the bus with Grace Lorch, Elizabeth knew where she had to go: to the School for the Blind and Deaf Negro. When she got there, walking along the unpaved street from the bus stop to the main entrance, she headed straight down the stairs to the laundry room. Reports from Central, some highly inaccurate, had gone out over the radio, though Birdie Eckford hadn't needed them; she already knew something terrible had happened. When Elizabeth entered the room, she found her mother turned away, looking out the window; simply from her posture, she could see that Birdie had been praying. Elizabeth walked up quietly, but her mother sensed that she was there. When Birdie swung around, Elizabeth could see that she'd also been crying.

Elizabeth tried to say that she was all right, but she couldn't speak. "Don't let anybody see you crying, baby—brace up," her mother told her. "That's just what some people want to do—see you crying." Then she sent Elizabeth home. She quickly followed, making her a bacon-and-tomato sandwich, with Kool-Aid, for lunch. That afternoon Elizabeth, along with the other black students, went to the local FBI office to give a statement. When

Elizabeth's father had heard the reports, he had gone looking for her, bringing along a .38-caliber gun with the only three bullets he could find. (He had reconciled himself to being killed but took a roundabout route to Central; friends dissuaded him en route from doing anything rash.) Daisy Bates had also tuned in. " 'A Negro girl is being mobbed at Central High!' *'Oh, my God!'* I cried," she later wrote. " *'It must be Elizabeth! I forgot to notify her where to meet us!'* " In the black community, there was a pregnant pause as word spread that the Eckford girl had been mobbed; no one was quite sure what had happened to her.

For a time, Will Counts had been too busy taking more pictures to consider what he already had. After getting four shots of Elizabeth on the bench, he'd scurried back to the other end of Central, just in time to record Lt. Col. Marion Johnson, nightstick in his hands, turning away the other black students. At that point the action—at least at Central, at least that day—was over. If Counts lingered, he might not get into that afternoon's paper. So he rewound the film (eleven frames remained on the roll) and rushed back to the *Democrat.* Only in the darkroom, when he unspooled the newly developed film—and zeroed in on negative number 15— did he realize he'd gotten something special. That small rectangular frame had captured everything: the dignity and determination of the black girl and the vituperation of the whites, all crystallized in one particular, readily understandable face. The white girl's name he never got. As for the black girl's, because he'd written it down either wrong or illegibly, "Echford" was how it would get to, or emerge from, the typesetter.

At least two other photographers—Johnny Jenkins of the United Press and Lloyd Dinkins of the *Memphis Commercial Appeal*—had

Elizabeth and Hazel, September 4, 1957, by Will Counts
(Will Counts Collection, Indiana University Archives)

captured almost the exact same moment (though, judging from the positions of various bystanders, Counts actually took his shot last, following Dinkins and then Jenkins). Working for the afternoon *Democrat,* though, Counts's would be the first in print. Jenkins's picture appeared on the front page of the next morning's *Gazette.*[1] As for Dinkins's, it didn't appear at all; perhaps it was too incendiary, or incriminating, for the more conservative Memphis paper. Instead, the *Commercial Appeal* ran a far less heartrending picture of Elizabeth at the bus stop, and understated what it showed. She "sat composedly," the caption stated, "surrounded by newsmen, photographers, and curious onlookers. She ignored

Elizabeth and Hazel, September 4, 1957, by Johnny Jenkins (Bettmann/Corbis)

Elizabeth and Hazel, September 4, 1957, by Lloyd Dinkins
(Lloyd Dinkins/*Commercial Appeal*)

the crowd, a few of whom mildly heckled her." The Memphis paper was not alone; even ostensibly progressive southern papers didn't run the picture.

Within hours of the episode at Central, Elizabeth—and Will Counts—were all over the front page of the *Democrat*. There was Elizabeth approaching the school, then Elizabeth talking to the Guardsmen, then Elizabeth taking directions from them. Finally, nestled in the bottom right-hand corner, was Elizabeth with Hazel. "CAT CALLS," the caption declared. "Elizabeth Echford [*sic*], 15, the first Negro student to attempt entry to Little Rock Central High today, walks down Park followed by a crowd of some 250 shouting whites." Hazel was not identified, nor would she be in the next morning's *Gazette*. Gene Foreman, then a young reporter on the *Gazette*, explained why: to the editors, she was merely a generic segregationist white kid, whose name didn't really matter. And why would so sensational a picture not have been displayed more prominently—bigger and, as the newsroom types say, "above the fold"? Little Rock was a tinderbox, Foreman explained; it seemed foolhardy to inflame things even further.

Cloaked in anonymity, cropped to look a bit less central than she was, Hazel had gotten a bit of a pass—but only in those two small respects. Everything else about Counts's picture—the light, the positioning, the choreography, the medium itself—conspired to make her more conspicuous, and odious. In the first several shots Counts took that day, Hazel was directly behind Elizabeth, either partially or completely obscured. Only when Elizabeth—in part to avoid walking directly into the photographers—turned slightly to her left, was Hazel revealed, and at that point, she merely glowered. But then Elizabeth walked forward—toward the edge of the frame.

She is slightly out of focus, her expression almost impossible to discern, though if you study it carefully, you notice that her left eyebrow is slightly arched, and her left eye, barely visible behind the sunglasses, betrays a profound sadness—the faint outline of a broken heart. Meantime, Hazel came fully into view, squarely in the ground-glass center of Counts's range finder. And at that very instant, she screamed. As Hazel stepped into prominence, her confederates all but vanished. At the moment the shutter clicked, Sammie Dean Parker had turned around, apparently because someone—was it her father?—had called her name.[2] Though Sammie Dean was to become the most flamboyant of the segregationist students at Central, for now the world saw only the back of her head. The two older, frumpy women to Elizabeth's left, who leered at her in Jenkins's picture, were momentarily becalmed in Counts's. And Mary Ann Burleson, who had been hollering with the others, looked mild, detached, even distracted when Counts captured her.

When it comes down to it, Counts's famous photograph of Elizabeth Eckford is really more of Hazel Bryan: it is on Hazel that the eyes land, and linger. Despite the tricky lighting, her face is perfectly exposed: the early morning September sun shines on her like a spotlight. It hits her from the side, painting her face in a stark chiaroscuro that makes it look more demonic still. She's caught mid-vowel, with her mouth gapingly, ferociously open. At that instant, and in perpetuity, Hazel Bryan, always the performer, has the stage completely to herself. Others played their own small parts in the picture, but "the mouth," she later said, "was mine." And dressing that morning as she had, trying to look all grown up and sexed up, she had masked how young she really was. She was only fifteen, but she would always be seen, and judged, as an adult.

And then there was the solemnity and permanence of film itself, and of the era in which it had been exposed. Hazel's act hadn't been an expression of some grand, well-developed worldview; it had been tossed off, flippant, fleeting. But in a photograph—a stark, black-and-white photograph—it would appear premeditated, even ordained.

Were others in the picture conspicuously misbehaving as well, Hazel might have found some small solace. But everyone else is just milling about; no one is moving menacingly, and no one else is *saying* much of anything. Only one face—the smiling young man behind Hazel, wearing a V-neck shirt trimmed in black, looking to his left—could conceivably share some of Hazel's culpability. He appears to be another of those blithe, sadistic bystanders who pop up in photographs of horrific events—the smiling spectators at lynchings, the German soldiers cheerily looking on as the beards of Orthodox Polish Jews are shorn. In fact, far from relishing Elizabeth's predicament, that young man, Joe Holland, was thinking other thoughts. To Holland, a sophomore at Central new to Little Rock, going to school with blacks was no big deal: he'd done it elsewhere. He admired Elizabeth's bravery that morning. What had so struck, and amused, him—enough for him to turn smilingly to his friend to talk about it—was Hazel. Listen to the mouth on her! he'd said. Why, he'd never heard a girl cuss like that before! No apologies would ever be demanded, or expected, from anyone else in Will Counts's photograph. In the universe he had created, if nowhere else, Hazel was every bit as alone as Elizabeth.

By afternoon, the picture had already sparked controversy. At a press conference, Faubus was asked whether the police had been ordered *not* to help Elizabeth. "Definitely not," he replied. In the meantime, paperboys were delivering the evening *Democrat* all over Little Rock. One subscriber was Elizabeth Huckaby, who, as Central's vice principal for girls, was officially responsible for both Elizabeth and Hazel. "Read the awful story," Mrs. Huckaby, who'd been teaching at Central since 1930, wrote in her diary that night. "Saw the awful pictures—the dignity of the rejected Negro girl, the obscenity of the faces of her tormentors. Graded papers to occupy mind." The picture was presumably the topic of many a dinner conversation in Little Rock that night, conversations that did not always fall along predictable racial lines. The segregationist father of a Central student named Anne Childress expressed his outrage over it. "I don't want those niggers going to school with my kids," he declared, "but those people didn't treat that little girl right."

Even segregationist leaders weren't about to defend Hazel: she'd given bigotry a bad name. The head of the segregationist Mothers League, Margaret Jackson, had specifically told her daughters to avoid getting into such situations—or, as she liked to put it, becoming "stirrers." The editor of the pro-segregation *Arkansas Recorder*, John Wells, also found the spectacle disgusting. White anger, he wrote, should be directed at meddlesome courts, a weak-kneed governor, and the NAACP, and not at Elizabeth and her compatriots. "It is one thing to assert that the Negro children should remain at Dunbar; another to threaten and intimidate them," he wrote. "They are the last who should be condemned."

Given the paper's segregationist leanings, many of Little Rock's blacks didn't take the *Democrat*. But that evening, footage of Elizabeth's walk made the national news. Among those watching, in Chicago, was Gerald Bullock, an official with the Illinois NAACP, who filed a mock report to Lee Blackwell of the *Chicago Defender*.

Dear Lee,

Today—Sept. 4, 1957—I witnessed an amazing display of military daring. I flicked on my television set to a news program and suddenly I was in Little Rock, Ark.

There before my startled eyes were ranged a magnificent group of soldiers, armed to the teeth, bayonets fixed, surrounding a large stone and brick structure. The commentator said there were 2,000 troops and they were Arkansas' finest National Guardsmen.

Splendid in their battle dress, they were there on orders from Gov. Orval Faubus to give their lives if necessary to protect the state's vital institutions from an implacable invader.

At the moment I saw no invading military force, but lining the streets were throngs of admiring citizens, obviously awed by this panorama of armed might. Then—suddenly—the camera picked up the invading force: striding resolutely forward through a jeering crowd of men, women and children.

It seemed to be a young girl, of perhaps some 15 years, and she must have weighed all of 98 pounds, Lee.

Quite pretty, too, but of course I was not deceived—no doubt this urbane appearance was camouflage, a sinister military disguise. Peering closely at her slender form, I saw she carried under her left arm what appeared to be a book but [was], no doubt, a terrible secret weapon.

At least the soldiers and crowd seemed to think so for suddenly the military might of Old Arkansas stiffened and the citizenry went scampering in all directions.

For a moment I thought the stout line might waver and break— but no—the long years of stern training now evidenced their value.

The line held and, rifles at the ready, these brave men faced the invader. She made no threatening motion, hurled no grenades, but she didn't falter either.

Clinging firmly to her secret weapon she marched straight up to the nearest soldier. His face was pale, his lips grim. Now I thought, I am about to see carnage unimaginable. I wondered if the courage of Arkansas' finest would be equal to the task. It was.

The girl seemed to be saying something to the soldier. I wondered what manner of monster from outer space this could be that she showed no fear. No question but it was confidence in her secret weapon which gave her such audacity.

But perhaps this was not meant to be a frontal attack, but only a reconnoitering maneuver, because she suddenly turned and left the scene. The danger at least momentarily averted, the military might relaxed.

Now, Lee, my wife tells me I misinterpreted the whole thing. She says that little girl was no invader from outer space, but only Elizabeth Eckford, the daughter of a taxpaying Arkansas citizen.

She was, it seems, only trying to enter a public school to enroll.[3]

Also watching in Chicago that night was Hazel's aunt, Katy Morris, who called to say she'd seen her on television. Hazel's parents were neither terribly surprised nor dismayed by what she had done—they knew Hazel wasn't shy, and they shared her sentiments—but they were displeased with her visibility. "It was just her up there: her and her big mouth," her mother said afterward.[4] Besides, she should have been in school. Perhaps because they were so close—they were about the same age, and both their fathers and their mothers were siblings—Hazel's cousin Linda had no qualms telling her that the picture would end up, as she put it, biting her in the butt. Hazel laughed that off.

Mrs. Huckaby's brother was alarmed enough to telephone. "Bill called again from N.Y. horrified by the picture of pupil insulting to Negro girl," Mrs. Huckaby wrote in her journal. Just about the only person paying no attention to the picture was Elizabeth. Perhaps she was still numb. Or perhaps living through it had been enough.

TEN

Reporters badgered Daisy Bates, either to let them interview Elizabeth or to chastise her for sending someone so fragile into the line of fire. It was just what the segregationists were saying: Elizabeth had been ill-used to induce sympathy. The syndicated columnist Bob Considine claimed that Bates had prepared Elizabeth as meticulously as the general manager of the Brooklyn Dodgers, Branch Rickey, had coached Jackie Robinson. "The Eckford girl underwent careful schooling and priming," he wrote. "By the time Mrs. Bates finished briefing her, the child would have walked across a mined field—which is just about what she had to do." In fact, until her father brought her to the Bates home on the afternoon of her walk, Elizabeth had never met Daisy Bates. And when she did, she let her have it. Why had Bates forgotten her? she asked, with what Bates later called "cold hatred in her eyes." From that moment on, Bates tried to win Elizabeth over, with little success. Elizabeth never stopped believing that to Bates and the rest of the NAACP, the nine black students were foot soldiers in a cause for which they'd been woefully unprepared.

The chaplain at Ole Miss, the Rev. Will Campbell, who'd been observing events in Little Rock for the National Council of

Churches, stopped by the Eckford home that night; after the way the white community had behaved, he felt he had to. Elizabeth's protectors, he noted, had been a Communist (Grace Lorch) and a Jew (Benjamin Fine); where had all of Little Rock's Christians been? Actually, the Rev. Colbert Cartwright, who'd walked alongside Elizabeth outside Central that first day, also came by the house, on the Saturday following the disturbances. He told her how much he admired her, and of the shame he felt as a white person. "Elizabeth clasped my hands with the same firmness she had shown in everything she had done," he later wrote. " 'No, Reverend Cartwright, it's just some of the white people who have stirred things up,' " was how he quoted her in his sermon the next day. She expressed no bitterness, but also said there was no way she would ever resume a segregated education. Cartwright told his congregation that Elizabeth had more guts than any of them; Central's whites were all the poorer for not yet knowing her. As he wrote in his unpublished memoirs, Cartwright devoted that sermon to Elizabeth because "I wanted to put a human face on the colored race." ("Portrait in Ebony," he called it.) Untouched by the gesture, some thirty members of his Sunday Bible class promptly demanded his dismissal, and the Arkansas State Police began compiling a file on him.

The day after the disturbances, the black children stayed home (though the *Memphis Commercial Appeal* reported that Elizabeth had again shown up at Central, and again been turned away). Returning to school made no sense until the politicians, and the courts, sorted things out. But for the trio of white girls in the picture, the attention proved addictive. They reappeared outside

Central, spouting the segregationist line for the newsmen. *They* were desegregation's real victims, they insisted: blacks now had their choice of schools, while whites were saddled with just one. Invariably Sammie Dean Parker and Mary Ann Burleson spoke first, with Hazel, her brow perpetually furrowed, chiming in a beat later. The minute the black students walked in, she declared, *they'd* walk out. "Whites should have rights, too!" she barked. "Nigras aren't the only ones that have a right!" Hazel's sudden visibility surprised the folks at *Steve's Show;* they had thought her passions ran only to dancing, and boys. Severe restrictions were promptly placed on reporters seeking statements from Central students, an edict that pretty much ended Hazel's brief career in commentary.[1]

That morning, September 5, Elizabeth and Hazel landed on millions of doorsteps. Elizabeth became, as Ted Poston of the *New York Post* put it, "probably the most widely known high school student in the whole United States," with the unidentified white girl to her rear running a close second. "Some day the people of Arkansas, North Carolina, Kentucky, Texas, Georgia and other states north and south of the line will recognize the quality of heroism in such persons as Elizabeth Eckford and Dorothy Counts," declared the *New York Times,* linking Elizabeth to another fifteen-year-old black girl who'd undergone a similar ordeal in Charlotte, North Carolina.[2] "Elizabeth was taunted, insulted and rejected, but she knows in her heart that she acted honorably, patiently and bravely," the *Chicago Daily News* observed. "In contrast, the snarling, hooting, menacing mob cannot face themselves in a mirror without recognizing brutishness, meanness and cowardice."

Murray Kempton of the *New York Post* compared Elizabeth to

the two United States senators from Arkansas, William Fulbright and John McClellan, neither of whom would fault Faubus. "We can only, with wonder and gratitude, reflect how much better a private child is than two public men," he wrote. Bob Considine called Elizabeth "aristocratic" and predicted that her walk through the "gantlet of vilification" would be a milestone in the annals of integration. Meanwhile, the *Fresno Bee* described "a white girl, a possible classmate, [who] bellows imprecations, her mouth open in hate like a dog's."

ELEVEN

Two days after Johnny Jenkins's picture of Elizabeth and Hazel ran in the *Gazette*, it appeared again, though in a very different guise. This time, it wasn't featured on the front page but on the lower right-hand corner of page 4A. It was set off from the news columns by a couple of thin lines, and labeled ADVERTISEMENT. "If you live in Arkansas—" it read above the photograph. Only after the eyes had taken in the two schoolgirls came the rest of the sentence, delivered in bigger, bolder type: **"Study This Picture and Know Shame."** "When hate is unleashed and bigotry finds a voice, God help us all," the text continued. Below that, almost as an afterthought, came a bit of information: "Adv. paid for by Davis Fitzhugh, Route 1, Augusta, Ark."

Who was Davis Fitzhugh? And why had he taken it upon himself, at his own expense, to convey such a message, one that could subject him to harm or harassment and which, at the very least, few people would have wanted to hear? Readers of the *Gazette* weren't told very much about him in a news article nearby—only that he owned a fifteen hundred–acre cotton and rice farm three miles north of Augusta, had been mayor of the town, and was the brother of the man who had helped bring public electricity to Arkansas. Only out-of-towners were curious enough to ask more.

Arkansas Gazette, September 7, 1957 (Courtesy *Arkansas Democrat-Gazette*)

"I'm not a carpetbagger, a Yankee or a Communist, but I'm in favor of a humane attitude toward other human beings," Fitzhugh told the *Daily Worker*, presumably by telephone. No one actually bothered tracking Fitzhugh down until Harold Isaacs of MIT— seeking to learn how the Cold War was affecting American race relations, as well as to understand why some people rose to historical challenges while others failed—came to town.

It's unclear how Isaacs, who was probably in Boston when it appeared, even knew of the advertisement. But arriving in Little Rock two months later, he promptly contacted Fitzhugh, who invited him to Augusta, a small town (oddly enough, where Hazel's mother had been born) seventy-five miles to the northeast. Fitzhugh—"a stocky man of mid-forties, with eyes large behind thick glasses, thin gray hair, dressed as for a Sunday of leisure"—met Isaacs on the outskirts of town, then led him to his home, a place, Isaacs noted, "with books that looked used." Isaacs, who had written for *Newsweek* before going into academia, got down to business quickly. "I said I had come out to discover what had made him put that ad in the paper," Isaacs later wrote.

The picture demanded reflection, Fitzhugh explained, because it captured a catastrophe. "I thought 50 years of progress had been destroyed in one afternoon," he said. What progress? "Progress in allowing a Negro person a sense of dignity, progress in a lack of bitterness—a kind of negative progress—against using the word 'nigger.' And economic progress, progress in the schools. Not much, but some. I thought things like this could happen in Georgia, perhaps, but not here! It amazed me." As the events in Little Rock unfolded, he said, he assumed some white people—at least those white people who appeased their consciences through

Davis Fitzhugh (Courtesy Bay Fitzhugh)

ELIZABETH AND HAZEL

paternalism, by informally looking out for one or two black families—would speak up. But no one had come forward, so he had. The picture appeared on a Friday morning; by that afternoon he was on the phone, buying an ad for the Sunday paper. Fitzhugh's family was prominent locally—the small town of Fitzhugh, named after his relatives, was only a few miles from Augusta—and, thanks to his late brother, known even in Little Rock; that, plus its relatively progressive politics, may have explained why the *Gazette* even accepted such an ad.

Fitzhugh, it turned out, was not your typical southerner. His mother had studied at the Sorbonne and campaigned for women's suffrage and birth control; he'd gone to high school in Chicago, met his wife in Chile, and studied short-story writing at Columbia, where he'd had several black classmates. During World War II—he had enlisted while mayor—he had first commanded a company of black soldiers in Texas, then helped reestablish local governments in newly liberated German towns. It was that experience that helped prompt his ad. "I tried to find out from people how they could stand by and see Jews persecuted and murdered," he explained. "They'd say they felt guilty, but didn't know what they could do; that it was dangerous to do anything. This is something like the feeling I feel here now, something of the same evil spirit, the same inability to act. It almost seems ridiculous to think that this could be, here, yet it is. And I ask myself: what do you do? What do you do next? What do we all do next?"

Local reaction to Fitzhugh's gesture fell into what for Isaacs had become a recurrent pattern throughout the Little Rock story: "politely not noticing the unpleasant." It was, Isaacs wrote, as if Fitzhugh "had committed some act of indecent exposure outside the church on a Sunday at noon." Ninety percent of his friends simply ignored the ad, said Fitzhugh, whose farm had both white and black tenants, living in houses with running water, electricity, even television sets. They chalked it up to his eccentricity. "They see me as a turncoat, I think, but they'd never say so to me," he said. "Some pool hall elements in town cussed me out on the street, but wouldn't stop and talk when I tried to do so." The few who complimented him looked around first, or took him behind something, before doing so. Only the preacher's wife had praised him openly—actually, to Fitzhugh's wife, interrupting her bridge game. The three other women at the table kept playing, saying nothing. Fitzhugh said he had received about 150 letters, only 3 or 4 of them hostile. Many congratulated him for his religious spirit, though the ad, he confessed, made him sound more religious than he really was. "I'm not much for the church," he explained.

The *Democrat*'s letters page carried no reactions to Counts's picture, either because its readers didn't care or because the editors spiked them. But the *Gazette* had plenty of comments about Jenkins's version of it. "If Governor Faubus, as he claims, called on the National Guard to protect the peace in this state," went one, "why did the National Guard not protect this innocent girl from these savages?" The picture "signifies one of the most disgraceful and uncivilized acts that has ever occurred in Arkansas," stated another. "It reminds me of the howling mob that crucified Christ. With a little egging I think they might have crucified that girl," went a third, signed "Patient, State Sanitarium." Readers elsewhere also reacted. "The picture in the newspapers of that poor girl holding her head high and brave while being followed and

spat upon and called ugly names by supposed Americans reminded me of Nathan Hale. And I cried," Louis Gerzog wrote to
the *New York Post*, which gave readers a post office box to which
they could send Elizabeth words of encouragement.

Checks flooded into the NAACP. One, from a Cincinnati
woman, included a copy of something she had written to Elizabeth. "It was after a harrowing day that I walked to the TV. . . . And
then, Elizabeth, I saw you, a 15-year-old girl, walk past a shouting,
jeering mob to enter a school you had every right to enter. . . .
How many of that ugly-faced mob would have the same courage?
By that supreme act of courage you have done something that no
double-talking politician can do. You have made the people of
America take sides."

In the black press—still influential, though far less luminous
than it had once been now that the journalistic mainstream had
finally begun picking off some of its talent—the image also rever-
berated. To Moses Newson of the *Baltimore Afro-American*, the
photograph had the same galvanizing impact on black Americans
as the photograph of Emmett Till two years earlier. "A Girl Without a Country," the Bateses called Elizabeth in the *State Press*. Such
an experience, they predicted, would mark her in a way that "only
death will erase." "ARKANSAS HATE! 15 Year Old Girl is Heroine of
Dixie Strife," declared the *St. Louis Argus*. "Don't you protect
colored children, too?" an Elizabeth-like figure standing alongside
a giant pair of army boots labeled "Gov. Faubus' Guard" asked in a
cartoon in the *Afro-American*. *Jet* predicted that Elizabeth would
be inscribed in the same book of heroes as Martin Luther King, Jr.

St. Louis Argus, September 13, 1957

"If the scales of history are in correct adjustment at all, a century from now in 2057, it will take a thousand Eisenhowers and a million [Secretary of State John Foster] Dulles to weigh as much in historical value as the one lone little Negro girl" in Little Rock, Langston Hughes predicted in the *Chicago Defender.* The picture "ought to be framed and hung up in every Negro home as a reminder to all to stand up more vigorously for their rights," urged J. A. Rogers in the *Pittsburgh Courier.* "Surely her example ought to touch the hearts of even some hostile whites and make in the years to come some of those who spat at her and shouted contemptuous names be ashamed of themselves."

Attention, and commentary, came from abroad as well. "One Girl Runs Gantlet of Hate," shouted a headline in the *Daily Express* in London. The *Arkansas Gazette* marveled at how the events had united in their outrage the newspapers of the Vatican, the Kremlin, and a country whose leader had snubbed Jesse Owens only twenty years earlier. The story and picture led off the Little Rock coverage in *Paris Match.* "The bowed head of Elizabeth Eckford" had become "perfectly familiar to the French by name, identity and meaning," the *New Yorker*'s Janet Flanner wrote in her *Paris Journal.* (Of course, what was interesting about that head was that it was, in fact, *unbowed.*)

Not surprisingly, Soviet Russia relished the black eye the photograph gave its Cold War rival. For the USSR, Little Rock epitomized America's racial shame, and Elizabeth Eckford epitomized Little Rock. Apparently the truth wasn't awful enough; depicting Elizabeth walking to school for a broadcast to Soviet schoolrooms, Radio Moscow embellished things a bit. "She stopped in fright, dropped her satchel with her books and felt her hair standing on end," the broadcast went. "A corpse hanging from a lamppost swung to and fro in the wind. On its chest was a board with the inscription: 'This will happen to all who dare to sit on a school bench next to a white person.'" The *Afro-American*'s correspondent in

Ethiopia reported that Russians in Addis Ababa "rub their hands in great glee and . . . drink big gulps of vodka over their apparently new-found allies in Arkansas." A Baptist clergyman in Little Rock showed Harold Isaacs the many clippings—with "their embarrassing photographs"—he'd received from missionaries in the Philippines, Ghana, Nigeria, and Argentina.

TWELVE

Officially, the NAACP discouraged what its executive secretary, Roy Wilkins, called "sideshows and exhibitions" involving Elizabeth or the other black students. Their education—that is, once it resumed —was to come first. But Elizabeth was produced to selected reporters, who made their way to the Eckford home, which they tended to describe as some variant of "_____ but _____." (Ted Poston's "spic-and-span but much used" was typical.) She knew that going to Central wouldn't be easy, Elizabeth told Walter Lister of the *New York Herald Tribune,* but her pastor had urged her once to take advantage of every opportunity. "I believe in being independent," she said. "I don't like to wait for somebody else." A picture of her, book in hand and pencil at the ready, appeared alongside the story on the front page. "It helps to know we have such support," Elizabeth—"her lips in a trembling smile"—told Virginia Gardner of the *Daily Worker.* Elizabeth was slighter than Gardner had anticipated, and her hands felt tiny. "She was terribly upset for a while, but she is pulling out of it," her step-grandmother told Gardner.[1]

Al Nall of the *New York Amsterdam News* asked the "cute little lass" what people had shouted at her. "I wouldn't want to repeat

Elizabeth studying at home, September 1957 (Bettmann/Corbis)

those words," Elizabeth replied. "Some of them I never heard before, but I don't like them."² So in awe of Elizabeth was Moses Newson of the *Afro-American* that sometimes he stopped taking notes while interviewing her, the better to contemplate her courage. (Her voice quiet and muffled, Elizabeth often had to repeat what she'd just said; to spare herself that, she cultivated a precise, articulate speaking style she was never to lose.) "Elizabeth Ann Eckford, 15, is the most sensitive of the children," a *New York Post* reporter wrote. "She's pensive, the kind of person who loves deeply and can be hurt deeply."

Elizabeth quickly wearied of all these reporters, however sympathetic they might be. "I wish they could get together and have one press conference and get it over with," she complained. The others in the Nine teased her that she should charge for interviews. Seeking to protect her, Daisy Bates told the press that she had sent Elizabeth out of town for the weekend, and rumors flew that the girl had gone to San Francisco for a speaking engagement. The *St. Louis Argus* reported "particular spirited bidding" for such appearances. But of course, that was quite impossible; even now, Birdie Eckford would have never let her leave home.

Virginia Gardner asked Birdie how she had prepared Elizabeth for desegregation, only to realize "that that is what Negro mothers in the South have been doing for generations." To the Associated Press, Elizabeth's mother was calm, and sanguine. Did she believe school integration would lead to socially awkward situations? "See that vacant lot across the street?" she replied. "Negro and white children play ball there and they get along fine." Long-distance telephone calls for Elizabeth came into her grandfather's store from Chicago, Detroit, New York, even Oklahoma. Though all of the Nine got letters, usually sent via Daisy Bates, Elizabeth got far and away the most, as many as fifty a day. Things got so lopsided that Bates—who'd publicly called Elizabeth the "star of the show"—privately urged NAACP branch presidents to send messages to the other eight. When the *Today* show devoted a program to the events in Little Rock, it felt compelled to ask for anyone *but* Elizabeth.

One letter, from a sixteen-year-old in Japan, was addressed simply to "Miss Elizabeth Eckford, Littol Rocke, USA." Another, from New Zealand, arrived with just her name and the picture. So much mail came from Germany that a schoolmate of German descent was recruited to translate it for her. (Elizabeth, characteristically, hoped for letters from France, so that she could work on her French.) An Englishman living in Zurich sent her a hundred dollars. She saved everything she received, putting it all in a cardboard box. Only from Arkansas was there was no mail: detractors would have been too ashamed, and supporters perhaps too fearful. But a few sympathetic whites left cash for her at her grandfather's store. And on her sixteenth birthday in early October, a white man whose name Elizabeth never learned stopped by her home with a Girard-Perregaux watch belonging to his dying wife. (Elizabeth used it for many years.) Not every gesture was so positive: someone threw a brick through the window of Eckford's Confectionary, and the filling station where her father bought gas for his truck cut off his credit.

Faubus, too, received an enormous amount of mail. Many of his correspondents praised him, but several who didn't enclosed the picture of Elizabeth for emphasis. "It is with real shock that I see the face of an otherwise beautiful girl distorted by arrogant hatred as in the inclosed [sic] picture. The serene dignity displayed by the negro girl whom the white girl is jeering is mute evidence of where real Christian virtue and superiority reside," stated Josephine Gomon of Detroit. "What ugly white women you have in Little Rock," Adelaide Forbush wrote from Los Angeles. "The Negro girl shows much more dignity and courage." Penny

Rover of Chicago proposed a monument in Elizabeth's honor. Several cited Scripture. "I also saw the picture of the colored girl leaving the school—by order of the Guard—walking alone," went one. "Reminded me of the picture of Christ—HE, too, walked alone on his trip to Gethsemane." "IT IS A SAD COM-MENTARY FOR THE LEADERSHIP OF ARKANSAS WHEN A 14 YEAR OLD NEGRO CHILD HAS MORE DIGNITY AND COURAGE THAN THE GOVERNOR OF ARKANSAS," wired a man named Raymond Burks.

Because she'd rarely been identified by name, Hazel got little mail. A few letters—all from the North, all critical—were sent to her care of Central. One simply had the picture pasted to the envelope. "To this girl," it was addressed. Hazel read them, found their critical tone surprising, then gave them little mind.

Some criticism went directly to the newspapers:

Miss Hazel Bryan:

I have often been told by my friends that I am the world's worst correspondent, but to you I will take the time to write this letter. I have just read the paper in which your name was mentioned, as having acted as a leader in persecuting a colored girl (not nigger) in connection with this mess you have down there.

I can only say that you are a disgrace to the female sex, a terrible American and, I am sure, a sore disappointment to God.

Maybe when you grow up, if you ever do, you will be ashamed of yourself. I hope so for your sake. I could say much more, but I won't bother.

> *A Disgusted Reader*
> *of the Milwaukee Journal*

P.S. I am white.

Anyone favoring what Hazel had done was probably disinclined to say so. But in one letter to the governor, Hazel came in for a bit of sympathy. "One feels compassion for the white children who have been handicapped with hatred by alleged adults," wrote Lucille Toll of Long Beach, California.

Around Hazel's church there was embarrassment over the photograph but little surprise: Hazel, they knew, didn't do anything halfway. But at Central, there were repercussions. Mrs. Huckaby didn't recognize the screaming girl in the picture at first, nor did any other school officials. "Small wonder," she later wrote. "We weren't used to seeing our pupils like that." But she soon realized it was Hazel Bryan, that girl who had tried to poison herself a few months earlier. She promptly hauled Hazel into her office. Hazel hadn't a clue why; she thought that maybe it was to hand over some more letters.

"I told her that I was distressed at the picture because hatred was a feeling that destroyed the people that hated," Mrs. Huckaby later wrote. "She shrugged. Well, that was the way she felt, she said. I hoped, anyway, that I would never see her pretty face so distorted again. I certainly hadn't recognized that that ugly face was hers. More breath wasted." Sure enough, the following Monday Hazel was at it again, telling the *Democrat*—in a line cribbed from her preacher—that had God meant for whites and blacks to mix, he'd have made them the same color. "The boys and girls pictured in the newspapers are hardly typical and certainly not our leading students," Mrs. Huckaby wrote her brother in New York. "The girl (with mouth open) behind the Negro girl is a badly disorganized child, with violence accepted in the home, and

Mrs. Elizabeth Huckaby (Central High School *Pix*, 1958)

with a poor emotional history." She returned to Hazel in a post-script. "Don't think I haven't reprimanded this child!" she added.

Hazel's parents found her sudden notoriety sufficiently alarming to pull her out of Central: whatever educational advantages it offered paled next to concerns for her safety. Only recently having been so intent upon keeping Elizabeth out of Central, Hazel soon ceased to be a part of Central herself. For a few days she attended a small high school near Redfield. But staying there meant living with her grandparents, who were poor and had neither a car nor indoor plumbing. For Hazel, accustomed to a doting father and the creature comforts of home, that wouldn't do. So she quickly transferred to Fuller High School in rural Sweet Home, on Little Rock's outskirts, which was actually closer to her house than Central had been. As linked as she became to the Little Rock Nine, then, Hazel Bryan did not in fact spend a single day inside Central with any of them.

The decision to move Hazel *did* protect her from a great menace: herself. Had she remained at Central, she would surely have joined in the despicable deeds to come. Instead, she returned to pursuits that mattered far more to her than race relations. While registering at Fuller, she spotted a handsome, dark-haired boy named Antoine Massery. "That one's mine," she told her sister, who had transferred with her. And before long, he was. Hazel traded in the airman's ring for a stereo.

America had seen its last of Hazel for the next forty years— except, that is, for the Hazel of the picture, which appeared with ever-increasing frequency as the Little Rock story evolved from current events to old news to history. In 1960 the picture graced the cover of its first textbook, a collection of materials on the schools crisis. With each iteration, her image increasingly became the official face of intolerance.

THIRTEEN

The 1957 college football season was about to begin for Sidney Williams. Williams, who'd grown up five blocks from the Eckfords, was a junior at the University of Wisconsin and was about to become the first black in the history of the Big Ten to begin a season as starting quarterback. He expected trouble, but Elizabeth's example helped embolden him whatever came his way.

John Lewis was a seventeen-year-old theology student in Nashville when he saw the picture. He couldn't discuss it with his parents back in Troy, Alabama, who had spent their lives keeping their heads down. But he, too, felt inspired by it. "We all walked through that crowd with her," he recalled. Later, he hung the photograph on the wall of his office, in the United States House of Representatives.

Roger Wilkins, twenty-five at the time, belonged to one of the first families of black America: Roy Wilkins was his uncle. He'd been about to join a New York law firm when he saw the photograph. Here, he realized, was someone confronting the impregnable wall of southern segregation—something, he realized, he could, and should, do, too. He embarked upon a career of civil rights activism instead. Seventeen-year-old Julian Bond, who later led the NAACP, began asking himself a simple question: Could he pass "the Elizabeth Eckford test"? Others were similarly moved.[1]

Back in Little Rock, though, things were at an impasse for the two and a half weeks that followed Elizabeth's walk. As lawyers, judges, and politicians wrangled, the Little Rock Nine stayed home. Having received their textbooks (and even some of their homework assignments) from Central, they were tutored. With the time they now spent together, largely at the Bates home, Elizabeth got to know those black students she hadn't previously met. Melba Patillo was highly dramatic and outspoken; Jefferson Thomas talked slowly but had what Ernest Green called a "hangman's humor"; Gloria Ray seemed confident. Of them all, she felt fully comfortable only with Minnijean Brown, whom she'd known from her neighborhood, and Thelma Mothershed, whose people were also seamstresses and who, with her health problems, was even more vulnerable than she. With several of the others, particularly those whose parents were college graduates, she sensed a class divide: only Minnijean and Thelma, she felt, would not disparage or belittle her family. The others got to know Elizabeth as well, at least as much as she allowed.

With events at a standstill, enterprising reporters like the Associated Press's Stan Meisler looked for stories in unusual places, like Little Rock's black community. Among those Meisler polled was Oscar Eckford, Sr. His granddaughter "did the right thing" by enrolling in Central, Eckford said, while stressing the need for goodwill between the races. "Among Negroes, humbleness is a way of life," he said. Meanwhile, the mob gathered daily outside the school. Faubus actually *needed* bloodshed to save face,

Daisy Bates charged. "This place is plenty hot, and growing hotter every day," she told NAACP officials in New York, noting that the local White Citizens Council was importing "red necks" from rural eastern Arkansas to keep things boiling. Bob Considine described the rabble-rousers as "town loafers, slattern housewives, old pappy characters and soiled children too young for school . . . what we used to call po' white trash." (One man entertaining the crowd, he wrote, "gave off a broken Roquefort cheese smile.") More fancy whites in Little Rock may have found them and their shenanigans embarrassing, but, as the Rev. Billy Graham wrote, they had a cause in common.

Only Washington, it seemed, could break the impasse. Intervention was not something for which President Eisenhower was temperamentally or politically suited. He was reluctant to call in the army, which had not been sent south since Reconstruction, and part of him actually sympathized with the segregationists. (To the author of the *Brown* decision, Chief Justice Earl Warren, Eisenhower wrote of understanding those southerners concerned that "their sweet little girls are not required to sit in school alongside some big overgrown Negroes.") So Ike did nothing, let alone follow Senator Hubert Humphrey's plea to "take those colored children by the hand and lead them into school where they belong." "In Washington, no strong voice is raised to tell the world the conscience of America is not that of Arkansas," the *Fresno Bee* editorialized. "Elizabeth Eckford and her people, however, have the assurance that their government is studying the situation."

Many, at least outside the South, shared such frustrations. Theatergoers attending a production of *South Pacific* on Long Island booed so lustily when the navy nurse Nellie Forbush said she hailed from Little Rock that the show had to be interrupted. But the most surprising—and, for that very reason, one of the most powerful—protests came from a hotel room in a small town in North Dakota.

FOURTEEN

When I see on television and read about a crowd in Arkansas spitting on a little colored girl, I think I have a right to get sore."

The speaker was Louis Armstrong, who on the night of September 17, 1957, was preparing to play with his All Stars in Grand Forks, North Dakota. There was a Grand Forks Nine, too: the nine blacks living in a town (as of 1950) of 26,836. Grand Forks did not figure to be a key front in the civil rights struggle. But this was not all Armstrong had to say that night to a twenty-one-year-old journalism student and jazz buff at the University of North Dakota named Larry Lubenow, who was moonlighting for $1.75 an hour at the *Grand Forks Herald*.[1]

With Armstrong in town—performing, as it happened, at Grand Forks' own Central High School—Lubenow's editor, an old-timer named Russ Davies, sent him to the Dakota Hotel to see whether he could land an interview. Perhaps sensing trouble—Lubenow was, he now says, a "rabble-rouser and a liberal"—Davies laid out the ground rules: "No politics," he ordered. That hardly seemed necessary, for Davies was a very conservative editor at a very Republican paper, and, with his famously sunny, unthreatening disposition, Armstrong rarely ventured into such things anyway. "I don't get involved in politics," he once said. "I just blow my horn." (It wasn't so simple, of course; during his long career Armstrong had broken down innumerable barriers, the latest of which was the ban on black guests at the Dakota Hotel.) But Lubenow had been following the Little Rock story; oddly enough, Federal Judge Ronald Davies (no relation to the editor), who had ordered that the desegregation plan there proceed, was from Grand Forks. And, like everyone else, Lubenow had seen the picture of Elizabeth.

Armstrong's road manager told Lubenow that he couldn't see Satchmo until after the concert. But that wouldn't work: it was past his deadline. So with the connivance of the bartender and bell captain, both of them drinking buddies, Lubenow sneaked into Armstrong's suite masquerading as a bellhop, delivering the trumpeter's room-service lobster dinner. He told Armstrong he'd be fired if he didn't come back with a story. The musician, dressed in a Hawaiian shirt and shorts, couldn't let that happen. He agreed to talk. And talk he did.

Lubenow stuck initially to his editor's script, asking Armstrong to name his favorite musician. (Bing Crosby, Armstrong replied.) But soon Lubenow brought up Little Rock, and he could not believe Armstrong's angry response. "It's getting almost so bad a colored man hasn't got any country," he said. Armstrong had been contemplating a goodwill tour of the Soviet Union for the State Department—"they ain't so cold but what we couldn't bruise them with happy music," he'd explained—but now, he confessed to having second thoughts. "The way they are treating my people in the South, the government can go to hell," he went on, offering further choice words about Secretary of State John Foster Dulles.

"The people over there ask me what's wrong with my country. What am I supposed to say?" As he spoke, he got progressively worked up. Eisenhower, he charged, was "two faced," and had "no guts," while Faubus was a "no-good motherfucker." (Writing for a family newspaper, Lubenow somehow turned that into "uneducated plow boy.") Armstrong bitterly recounted his experiences touring the Jim Crow South, like the times when whites, including some of the very folks who had just cheered him, rocked his tour bus menacingly when he and his musicians prepared to leave town. He broke out into the opening bar of "The Star-Spangled Banner," inserting enough obscenities—"Oh, say can you motherfucking see / By the motherfucking dawn's early light"—to prompt the band's vocalist, Velma Middleton, to try to hush him up.

Lubenow, from the small farming community of Northwood, North Dakota, was shocked by what he heard, but he also knew he had a story; he skipped the concert and went back to the office, typing up what he had on yellow copy paper. "The Ambassador of Jazz trumpeted a new tune today," he wrote, before laying out that novel song's jarring notes. The *Herald* printed his story the following morning (taking care to remove the word "hell"), but, dubious that Armstrong would have said such things, the Associated Press editor in Minneapolis refused to put the story on the national news wire until Lubenow could prove he hadn't made it all up. So he returned to the Dakota, and, as Armstrong was shaving, the *Herald* photographer took their picture together. (The caption referred to "Louis (Satchmo) Armstrong, who got all lathered up about segregation here Wednesday"; Lubenow himself was cropped out.) Lubenow then showed Armstrong what he had written. "Don't take nothing out of that story," Armstrong de-

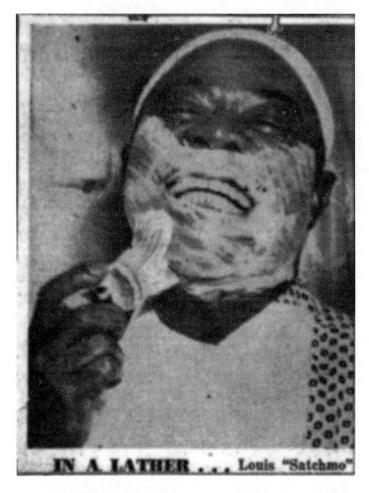

Louis Armstrong in Grand Forks, North Dakota, shaving and standing
by Larry Lubenow, September 18, 1957
(Courtesy Louis Armstrong House Museum)

clared. "That's just what I said, and still say." He then wrote "solid" on the bottom of the yellow copy paper, and signed his name.

The story flashed across the country. Douglas Edwards and John Cameron Swayze reported it that night on the network evening news programs. Armstrong's road manager quickly claimed that Satchmo had been tricked, and that he regretted his statements. But Armstrong would have none of that. "I said what somebody should have said a long time ago," he declared the following day in Montevideo, Minnesota, where he gave his next concert. He closed that show with "The Star Spangled Banner"— the traditional version, that is, minus the obscenities.

Armstrong took it from all directions: the writer Jim Bishop called for a boycott of his concerts; the Ford Motor Company threatened to pull its advertisements from a Bing Crosby special on which he was to appear; Van Cliburn's manager refused to let him perform a duet with Armstrong on Steve Allen's talk show; a radio station in Hattiesburg, Mississippi, threw out all his records. The Russians, an anonymous government spokesman lamented, would relish everything Armstrong had said. Meantime, Sammy Davis, Jr., criticized him for not speaking out ten years sooner. But Jackie Robinson, Lena Horne, Eartha Kitt, Marian Anderson, and Sugar Ray Robinson quickly lined up behind him.[2] In the black press there was surprise, and delight. Dulles might just as well have stood up at the United Nations and led a chorus of the Russian national anthem, declared *Jet*, which had once labeled Armstrong an "Uncle Tom." Armstrong had long tried to convince people throughout the world that "the Negro's lot in America is a happy one," it observed, but in one bold stroke, he had pulled nearly fifteen million American blacks to his bosom. Any white confused by Martin Luther King's polite talk need only listen to Armstrong, the *Amsterdam News* declared. Armstrong's words had the "explosive effect of an H-bomb," said the *Chicago Defender*. "He may not have been grammatical, but he was eloquent." "Louis made more friends with his statement than he has in a decade," Leslie Matthews wrote in the *New York Age*. But it was a letter in the *Afro-American* that put it best. "When Louis Armstrong gets riled up," it read, "the country is really going to hell."

Because of its "total unexpectedness," wrote Buddy Lonesome of the *St. Louis Argus,* Armstrong's statement "in all probability had more devastating effect on President Eisenhower's administration and national leaders than many mouthings of recognized Negro leaders." Whether, as Satchmo's devoted fans believe, what Ike was about to do in Little Rock can be attributed to Louis Armstrong is unclear. But there can be no doubt that what Louis Armstrong did in Grand Forks, North Dakota, could be attributed to Elizabeth Eckford.[3]

FIFTEEN

American diplomacy faced greater problems than the cancellation of Armstrong's tour. The U.S. Information Agency, then showing Edward Steichen's famous photographic exhibit "The Family of Man" around the world, now had to juxtapose its inspirational images of brotherhood against the pictures coming out of Arkansas. One USIA report complained that photographs from Little Rock "were particularly damaging to U.S. prestige"; the agency scoured its archives for pictures of blacks and whites in harmony to offset them.[1] The State Department created "Talking Points to Overcome Adverse Reaction to Little Rock Incident" for all field missions in sub-Saharan Africa but conceded that the damage done "by sensational newspaper accounts and photographs cannot be repaired overnight." Dulles lamented that Little Rock was harming America more than the suppression of the revolt in Hungary the previous year had hurt the Soviets. American tourists were not immune. "Everywhere Americans have gone in recent years they have gotten Little Rock thrown in their faces," W. E. B. Du Bois remarked in 1959.

Faubus insisted that he was both maintaining order and reflecting the wishes of his constituents. Forced integration, he said, was bad for both races. Mike Wallace, hosting an interview program for ABC News, caught up with the governor only a few days after Elizabeth's walk. "Probably every newspaper in the country has published a picture of the fifteen-year-old Negro girl walking to and from school with a crowd of white students behind her, sneering, snarling, and probably even cursing," Wallace said. How did the governor feel about that? He hated violence and enmity, Faubus replied; his childhood hero, after all, was Lincoln, who had counseled malice toward none. But Elizabeth, he suggested, was a tool of outside agitators.

It was a point Faubus repeated, and elaborated upon, over the years. Masters at garnering sympathetic publicity, he contended, the Communists had meticulously choreographed the whole thing: where Elizabeth had gotten off the bus; how far she had walked; how often (and where) she approached the Guardsmen; and the path she took afterward, where—of course—dozens of cameramen, photographers, reporters, and observers just happened to be. The planning, charged Faubus, began with the selection of Elizabeth herself. "They picked one of the sweetest, most appealing, innocent-appearing Negro girls to take the key role," he said. "All of this was very carefully worked out, and planned just like you'd work out a military maneuver. . . . As we say in the army, they'd G-2d the place"—that is, had done sophisticated intelligence work. "I have to marvel at the way they handled it."

"The Echford [sic] girl followed these directions to the letter, and the success in reaping publicity was phenomenal," Faubus later wrote. "The lone, shy, well-mannered Negro girl, notebook in hand, turned back by lines of armed Guardsmen and ringed, temporarily at least, by heckling whites—what more appealing picture could be portrayed to gain the desired sympathetic publicity? The planners of this publicity stunt chose the students well." (He never said whether Hazel, and her histrionics, were also part of the planning.) "She'd had all this prior instruction, to come to a certain point and then walk down this way, and all the cameras grinding," Faubus recalled at another point. And then, who should be awaiting Elizabeth at the finish line but one of her Communist puppet masters: Grace Lorch! Daisy Bates, too, had Communist ties, Faubus claimed, and may well have been in cahoots with the party apparat.[2]

The court challenge to the desegregation plan dragged on. On September 20 Elizabeth testified briefly before Judge Davies, talking so quietly that he'd had to urge her to speak up. Again, Davies ordered Faubus to stop interfering, and to admit the black children. Another date for implementing the plan was set: September 23. With the National Guard having been withdrawn, only the Little Rock police would be there to protect the black students. Once more, Daisy Bates notified the families to bring the children to her home. By now, the Eckfords had a telephone. (The novelty quickly wore off as the hate calls started coming.) But dreading a conversation with them—how could she ask Elizabeth's mother to send her daughter out *again?*—Bates put off contacting them. When she finally did call, Birdie Eckford demurred: she had to ask Elizabeth. When she returned to the phone, Elizabeth's mother had but one question: What time should Elizabeth show up? The next morning, Elizabeth was among the first to arrive. This time, though, she would not have to go to school alone.

The Nine reached Central, where more than one thousand protestors had already gathered. They came from all over Arkansas;

even some of Oscar Eckford's coworkers at the Missouri Pacific were on hand. The Little Rock police, thoroughly overmatched and ambivalent at best about their mission, managed to slip the black students, accompanied by Daisy Bates, Lee Lorch, and a couple of others, in ignobly through a side door, partly because the simultaneous arrival of three black newsmen in front of Central momentarily distracted the mob. The three were quickly set upon. Bearing the brunt was L. Alex Wilson, the editor of the *Memphis Tri-State Defender*. Despite pleas from his colleagues, Wilson refused to flee, even after being hit over the head by a brick. Only one policeman moved, ineffectually, to help him. From the front steps of the school Central's football coach, Wilson Matthews, looked on with amazement. "I never thought I'd see it," he remarked. "They're killing those niggers." This moment, too, Will Counts captured.[3] Little Rock, declared Alistair Cooke after the latest pictures appeared, had become "as universally infamous as Rome at the height of its decadence." A marine during World War II and later a correspondent in Korea, Wilson insisted on keeping on his hat throughout the assault; that's what a gentleman did. Besides, he didn't want his attackers to know how badly he'd been hurt. "I fought for my country in the war, and I'm not running from you," Wilson, the father of a five-month-old daughter, told them. Later, he offered another reason he'd stood his ground. Elizabeth Eckford hadn't run, he noted; how, then, could he? He soon developed Parkinson's disease, presumably because of his beating, and within three years he died, age fifty-one. Though the assailants were readily identifiable from Counts's photographs, no one was ever prosecuted, nor even, it appears, seriously investigated, for the assault.

Word quickly spread among the demonstrators that the black students had entered Central. There were calls to go inside and drag them out. Some of the white students in the building tried to flee; Hazel's pal Sammie Dean jumped out a second-story window, the first of her many flamboyant and highly publicized protests.[4] For the next three hours, a crowd of seething whites hovered outside the place, repeatedly trying to break through the fragile police lines. Meanwhile, the Nine went to their first classes. Someone photographed Elizabeth in one of them; the next day's *Democrat* ran the picture on its front page. But school and police officials quickly concluded the situation was too volatile to let the black children remain. It was scary enough with them in the building; what would happen at the end of the day, when they had to go home?[5] So after a couple of hours, officials decided to pull the students out. They were brought to the principal's office, then led to the basement, where they were ordered to lie down on the floors of two unmarked police cars and covered with blankets as the cruisers sped off.[6] Elizabeth always thought the officers saved their lives that day.

Once again, Little Rock's experiment with desegregation was suspended. That afternoon, Bates told reporters that the children wouldn't return to Central until the president of the United States supplied some protection. That night, policemen patrolled outside the homes of each of the Nine, as well as the Bates home. An anonymous caller told Daisy Bates that someone connected to the desegregation campaign had just been killed, that she was responsible, and that more deaths would follow that night. "My heart stood still," she later wrote. "I thought of Mr. Eckford, the father of Elizabeth, returning home from his night employment. I could

Elizabeth outside the home of Daisy and L. C. Bates, Little Rock, fall 1957.
From left, Elizabeth, Minnijean Brown, Daisy Bates, Melba Patillo,
Thelma Mothershed (Getty Images)

envision him being shot down, and his warm blood running in the street."

The next day, September 24, the black students stayed away from Central; had they shown up, Bates feared, some of them might have been killed. "Little Rock was a frightened city that evening," Louis Cassels later recalled in the *New York World-Telegram*. "It half expected a race riot to break out at any moment." Along West 9th Street, where memories of the 1927 lynching remained vivid, the cafés and pool halls were deserted; in black neighborhoods, the shades were drawn. The deteriorating situation finally prompted Eisenhower to act. Elizabeth and the others were at the Bates home when he announced on television that he was sending the 101st Airborne Division into Little Rock. She, too, saw what became another iconic photograph from that drama: the procession of

Jeeps and other military vehicles, their headlights piercing the Indian summer steaminess, crossing the river into Little Rock, a billboard—"WHO will build Arkansas *if her own people do not?*"—illuminated in the background. Unlike the kids in the National Guard, the "Screaming Eagles" of the 101st were the real deal.[7] ("Their khaki-clad rigidity was in marked contrast to the exquisite boredom displayed by the Guardsmen," according to the Central High School *Tiger*.) By nightfall, 319 members of the 101st encircled the school, and while Bates expected a day's delay, their commander insisted that the black children come to Central the next morning.

After more frantic phone calls, the Nine once again gathered at the Bates home. They said a prayer, then hopped into two army station wagons, this time sitting upright rather than lying hidden under blankets on the floor. Then, with soldiers sporting helmets, rifles, and combat gear riding shotgun at either end of the motorcade, they arrived at Central. Faced with this show of force, the mob suddenly lost its ardor. Escorted by twenty-two soldiers, first up the stately steps and then through the monumental wooden doors, Elizabeth and the others entered. Inside, each was assigned a personal escort, who took her to class, waited outside, then took her to the next. Never before had the black students been treated so respectfully, and by white people at that! The soldiers actually called the black girls "ma'am."

In various documentaries, it is at this point that the music usually swells, and the credits roll: the story is triumphantly over. "If you decide to walk into the schools with the little colored kids, take me along, Daddy," Louis Armstrong wired Eisenhower. A cartoon appearing in the German paper *Tagespiegel* showed Eisenhower in a tank, talking to an Elizabeth surrogate. "Come, little girl," he beckons. "I'll take you to school."

SIXTEEN

The initial reports from inside were encouraging. "They [the white students] were so wonderful," Melba Patillo told one reporter. "They treated us so good. Nothing I can say describes just how happy I am."[1] A picture taken during the morning of the first day of classes—in the midst of a "fire drill" that was actually a bomb scare—showed Elizabeth chatting, apparently casually and comfortably, with two white girls from her history class. (In fact, anticipating problems when the soldiers were not around, Elizabeth was asking one of them, Priscilla Thompson, to describe the layout of the lunch room and the gymnasium for her.) The photograph ran throughout the country the following day, counteracting a bit the pictures from three weeks earlier, and corroborating what the black students themselves said. "The teachers are very nice. Nothing went wrong, there were no catcalls. I especially enjoyed my history and English classes," Elizabeth reported after that first day. "Everything will be all right, for the majority of the white students themselves are all right." "This nervous town has simmered down to a slow beat," Bill Patten wrote a few days into the new era in the *New York Age*. "Nine Negro boys and girls have been attending classes at Central High School for a week and the walls haven't crumbled nor has the color rubbed off on any of the students they chanced to meet."

Soon, though, there were disquieting signs. On October 1, while walking down the hall, Elizabeth was struck from behind with a pencil. In gym class the next day, someone threw a rock at her. When a soldier asked who, the white students just laughed. All this bore watching, but suddenly, there was something else for the world to see. On October 4—the day Little Rock's papers described Central students hanging a black body in effigy—up went Sputnik. Something that humbled and terrified most Americans left Mrs. Huckaby, for one, feeling relieved. "We'll be glad to take second billing for a while," she wrote her brother. Not so fast, the Soviets seemed to reply. On October 9, while stating the times the first man-made satellite would be visible from the world's largest cities, Radio Moscow amended its list, announcing that it would pass over Little Rock, and Central High School, at 9:36 the following night. Standing on the very street where Elizabeth had just felt the grim present, one could now gaze skyward—and see the future.

By the time people stopped looking up and resumed looking across, things had changed dramatically at Central—for the worse. While hardly enthusiastic about integration, most students were willing to tolerate it. But lurking in the shadows was a hard core—estimates ranged from fifty to two hundred—of sadistic segregationists, either freelance, precocious bigots or pawns of grownup diehards, bent on wreaking as much havoc as they could. The question was whether anyone—administrators and teachers, the soldiers, the police, the community, their fellow students—would rein them in.

Under intense political pressure, Eisenhower withdrew the paratroopers as quickly as he could, sending them back in only whenever conditions worsened. For the most part, the protection of the black students fell to the same Arkansas National Guardsmen who had previously kept them out. It was a job for which they had little training or inclination; many hated desegregation as ardently as the protestors. (Some were kids, still in or barely out of high school themselves, who could occasionally be spotted walking arm-in-arm with Central girls.) Whenever trouble occurred, they seemed to be somewhere else or looking the other way. So, too, were most school officials. Some of them—notably, Central's principal, Jess Matthews—were lukewarm themselves about having the black students around, and resented enforcing what meddlesome outsiders had foisted on them. Matthews had done nothing to prepare students (or teachers) for what was happening, let alone inspire them to rise to the occasion.

In fact, he stood in the way. During the summer, some members of the incoming student council had arranged a formal welcome for the black pioneers, thereby signaling to one and all that whatever their reservations about integration might be, they would uphold the law. The date was set—Friday, August 30—and invitations were printed. But after all the turmoil in the days before—the segregationist Mothers League had been formed; the desegregation plan had been challenged in court; the superintendent's daughter had been threatened—Matthews nixed the idea at the last moment. Later attempts to revive the plan were also thwarted. Similarly, nothing had come of the principal's notion, one he'd broached during practice one day, of having the football players help maintain order around the school once desegregation started. The black students would be on their own; none of Central's student leaders would ever get to know any of them or feel much of a stake in their well-being.

Like everyone else, the president of the student body, Ralph Brodie, had seen the picture of Elizabeth and Hazel. It embarrassed him, of course, but he hadn't thought of it for more than a minute or two. A new school year was beginning; there were students to motivate, teams to launch, and, as it turned out, aggressive northern reporters with agendas to talk to. When Mike Wallace, then a young television reporter as well as a columnist for the *New York Post,* telephoned Central on September 3 in search of a big man on campus to interview, it was Brodie—a defensive back and backup quarterback in football, a letterman in basketball, and a three-time state track champion in high and low hurdles and relays, in addition to governor at Arkansas Boys State—who quite naturally was summoned. As Mrs. Huckaby hovered over him, Brodie, seventeen years old, sat behind the principal's desk, fielding the reporter's inquiries. Three questions or so in, he distinctly felt that Wallace was setting him up—trying to coax him into saying something stupid, and thereby confirming for his citified readers that all Arkansans were rednecks.

Was he alarmed by the situation? No. How long would it last? It's up to Governor Faubus. Did he think the Negro students could come to school tomorrow? Sir, it's the law. We are going to have to face it sometime. Would you mind sitting next to a Negro? No. Would there be much resistance to integration? I don't believe there'll be any at all. Do you have Negro friends? No, sir. Had he done any soul-searching about segregation? Not particularly. Would it make a difference to him to see a white girl dating a Negro boy? I believe it would. Why? I was just brought up that way. Do you think Negroes are equal to whites? That is a matter of opinion. What's yours? If they have had the same benefits and advantages, I think they're equally as smart. Should southerners live by the law of the land? I don't see why we shouldn't. We've been living under it all our lives.

It lasted just a few minutes, and after Wallace had hung up, Brodie turned to Mrs. Huckaby. "That man was trying to make us all look bad!" he cried out. To Brodie, Wallace was like many of the reporters who had descended on Central. At night he'd watch their reports on television, and what they described scarcely resembled what he'd seen at the school earlier in the day. After his interview with Wallace was reprinted in the *Gazette,* out-of-town reporters began badgering Brodie for quotes—all, he was convinced, to buttress their biased portrayals. It got so bad that he and his father had to ask the local prosecutor to keep the press away from him and, for as long as Brodie needed it, the prosecutor did. Brodie himself did the rest: twenty years passed before he granted another interview. Barely into the new school year, then, Brodie already believed Central's whites had not been allowed to show their good character, and that the northern press wouldn't have believed them even if they had. They were feelings that would last a lifetime.

SEVENTEEN

Elizabeth's homeroom teacher, Miss Poindexter, was a disciplinarian who kept things largely under control, making some boys take off their Confederate caps and stand for the Pledge of Allegiance. Nothing bad happened to Elizabeth there. At least at first, some white classmates befriended her and the other black students. But in the official vacuum the segregationists quickly came to set the tone, intimidating all the others—in the South, few labels were more toxic than "nigger lover"—into silence. Elizabeth was surprised by how quickly the tolerant kids gave up; within a few weeks, most of the goodwill had evaporated. She'd believed that as people got to know her—and she could show them that she was a "*good* Negro"—she'd be accepted, but that was not the case. As time passed, her every day inside Central came to resemble that first day outside it. It was worse, really, because now, no one was taking pictures.

Already scattered—only rarely were two of them in a class together—the black students became almost entirely isolated. Elizabeth sat by herself in her classes, always at the rear, often with no one nearby. Even the few white children she'd known previously now steered clear of her: *Please don't let them know you know me,* their eyes seemed to plead. Only during her last class of the day—

speech—were there any friendly faces. To be precise, there were two, belonging to Ken Reinhardt and Ann Williams, who felt free to be nice only because their teacher, Miss McGalin, was both sympathetic and strict. Decades later, Williams still recalled how isolated Elizabeth was that first day; *no one* deserved to be that lonely. (Miss McGalin remembered Elizabeth as "a very fragile little girl . . . looking like I could blow her away with one puff.") It became the only class in which she sat in the front row, rather than off by herself somewhere in the back. That small bit of friendliness, and security, helped Elizabeth to blossom a bit. It was in front of this class, for instance, that she first appeared on a stage, delivering Portia's courtroom speech from *The Merchant of Venice* in Central's massive auditorium. Williams, Reinhardt, and the handful of students like them suffered for their solicitude.[1] A few other students did speak to Elizabeth, but only to hear what "it" sounded like.

(Some tried to do the right thing: Ted Poston of the *New York Post* wrote of a visit paid by seven white schoolchildren, along with their pastor, to Daisy Bates. The occasion was marred for Poston when he answered the phone. "Is Mrs. Eckford back from New York?" the caller—it sounded like a teenage boy—asked. Elizabeth's mother had never left Little Rock, Poston replied. "Don't give me that shit, you black babooning son of a bitch," the boy went on. "You know you sent her back up there to visit her family, just like you brought her and that little Elizabeth ape down from there to stink up our schools." Calls like this led Elizabeth's mother to forbid her from answering the Eckfords' phone.)

Anyone doubting that the South could ever be redeemed, the columnist Max Lerner wrote, could "learn from the quiet confidence of Elizabeth Eckford, who will never waver in her purpose, no matter what hurts she must suffer and whatever psychic price she must pay." They were pretty words, but it wasn't really so. Less than a week into school, Elizabeth came into Mrs. Huckaby's office "red-eyed, her handkerchief in a damp ball in her hands." So bad was the harassment that she wanted to go home early. Appealing to Elizabeth's courage, Mrs. Huckaby persuaded her to stay. A week later, *Paris Match* ran another picture of Elizabeth with her white classmates during that "fire drill," only in this one, she seemed very much alone. "Elizabeth Ann Eckford is in school, but she is in quarantine," the caption declared.

Mrs. Huckaby asked some of Elizabeth's teachers to look out for her, though she estimated that a third of them considered desegregation "just terrible." One was Elizabeth's history teacher, Miss Emily Penton. Ever since the fourth grade, when her mother gave her a well-worn world history textbook, with tales of the Fertile Crescent and the Ottoman Empire, history had been Elizabeth's favorite subject. She savored the black history she'd learned at Dunbar, even though it was rudimentary, noncontroversial stuff: more Booker T. Washington than Frederick Douglass, more George Washington Carver and his peanuts than slave rebellions, abolitionists, and Buffalo Soldiers. Every year she relished Negro History Week, when *Ebony* highlighted something from the African-American past.

With Miss Penton, a schoolmarm with a pince-nez who had already been teaching Little Rock's high school students for four years when Central opened, the lessons were very different— something out of *Birth of a Nation*. In them, slavery had civilized blacks; the Ku Klux Klan defended white womanhood; Lincoln

Elizabeth with her history teacher, Miss Emily Penton, September 1957
(Courtesy *Arkansas Democrat-Gazette*)

freed the slaves strictly for tactical reasons; the black office holders during Reconstruction were all ignoramuses and buffoons. As shocking as this was to Elizabeth, more shocking was that no one ever objected, even though many of her classmates, the superintendent's daughter among them, came from prominent families. Miss Penton did call on Elizabeth occasionally. But when there was money to collect—say, for the *Weekly Reader*—she refused to touch her, insisting that Elizabeth put the coins down on her desk. When Elizabeth complained about her to the principal, she was informed that Miss Penton was a graduate of the University of Chicago and a pillar of the community.[2]

EIGHTEEN

When Jackie Robinson broke into major league baseball, a decade before blacks entered Central High School, he was spiked on the base paths, shunned by some of his own teammates, taunted mercilessly from the opposing dugout. Yet he had managed to maintain his composure so admirably that when the black students were told how to carry themselves inside Central, his example was invariably cited. But when the recently retired Robinson spoke to seven of the Nine by phone on October 18, he insisted that *he* was in awe of *them*. He had had the backing of the general manager of the Brooklyn Dodgers, the president of the National League, and the commissioner of baseball; the Nine, by contrast, had been largely on their own. "I think it makes my job look like nothing—what I had to go through," he told them.

Elizabeth missed the call, having been home with the flu.[1] But Mrs. Huckaby's disciplinary files give some sense of what she encountered that fall when she was in school, and it was a litany Jackie Robinson would have recognized. October 28: Elizabeth shoved in hall. November 20: Elizabeth jostled in gym. November 21: Elizabeth hit with paper clip. In fact, most incidents went unrecorded, especially once Elizabeth, convinced it did no good, stopped reporting them. The Guardsmen who had taken over for the paratroopers were instructed to intervene only in the most egregious cases. Once, after she was body-slammed, timid Elizabeth actually grabbed her assailant. "Tell me you didn't see that!" she shouted at the nearby soldier. He ordered her to let the girl go. The Guardsmen's ranks gradually thinned. But as meager as their protection was, the head of the segregationist Mothers League cautioned that there would be bloodshed were they taken away. (Self-serving scare tactics, perhaps, but the mildly pro-integration *Gazette* warned of the same thing.)

In late October, the parents of the Nine met with Blossom to complain about the situation. Meanwhile, some of the black students devised ways to cope with, or at least to cushion, the pain: laughing off their tormentors, as did Minnijean Brown and Jefferson Thomas; gritting their teeth, like Carlotta Walls; verbally sparring with harassers (or silently reciting poetry), like Terrence Roberts.[2] Ernest Green's maturity and stature seemed to help him endure. And with her heart problems, Thelma Mothershed appeared to be off limits; killing one of the Nine was surely bad strategically. Elizabeth had no such defenses. Indeed, maybe her fame made her more of a target. She seemed to take, and absorb, every blow.

Fearful of rallying those who wanted to scuttle the experiment, Bates and the NAACP played down the difficulties inside the school. On November 25 the black students gathered at the Bates home for an early Thanksgiving. More than the turkey was stuffed that day: the small dining room was crammed with reporters and photographers invited to look on as the Little Rock Nine feigned normality, and thanks. The evening's theme wasn't just gratitude but patriotism: each of the black students had to explain why, in spite of everything, he or she preferred life in America to the Soviet Union. "Elizabeth Eckford started a statement and then dropped the microphone, apparently distraught," reported the *Democrat*. " 'That's all,' she said, and left."

December 10: Elizabeth kicked in gym class. Tells Mrs. Huckaby such kicks "happened all the time." December 18: Elizabeth punched and hit by books. Beyond the individual indignities—having a dead fly tossed onto your cafeteria tray, say, or hearing someone mutter, "Remember the Till boy"—there were group insults, too, like seeing "Nigger, go home!" soaped onto the bathroom mirrors. Far from penalizing the worst offenders, Matthews tried appeasing, and even empathizing with, them. In an embittered unpublished memoir, Central's vice principal, J. O. Powell, himself a graduate of the school, described a typical Matthews "dressing-down." "You're not going to solve this thing by punching niggers," he would tell the latest miscreant. "This thing is bigger than you and me and Congress and the Governor and everybody else, and it's not going to be solved any time soon. We don't like it any more than you do. But it's here. . . . Now you just quit causing trouble and stay out of the vice principal's office or I'm going to have to do something about you. You start thinking about your education and quit worrying about integration and niggers." To the black students, Matthews was someone who did nothing, though always with a smile. "Grinning Chicken Jess," they called him.

Despite the brave public front, Daisy Bates was candid with her colleagues. "Conditions are yet pretty rough in the school," she wrote Roy Wilkins on December 17—rough enough, in fact, for her to ask that FBI agents be sent there. That, it turned out, was also the date of what soon became a celebrated episode in the school cafeteria. Not surprisingly, it involved Minnijean Brown; confident and combative, she, more than the eight other black students, acted as if she *belonged* at Central, which only roused the troublemakers more. After some boys attempted to trip her while she carried a tray of food to her table, she dumped a bowl of chili on one of them. The black women working the lunch line broke out in applause, but Minnijean was summarily suspended. Elizabeth happily yielded the distinction of being the most famous of the Nine; what mattered far more to her was that Minnijean was her closest friend at Central, someone who understood, and protected, her. And now she'd be gone a while.

NINETEEN

One Sunday morning in November, Harold Isaacs of MIT was picked up at his hotel in Little Rock by a World War II buddy of his named Frank Newell. Isaacs, who had chronicled the fighting in China, India, and Southeast Asia in the 1930s and 1940s, was now covering another battle, one which to him represented the front line in the Cold War. Imagine, marveled Newell, who now sold insurance: a foreign correspondent in Little Rock! How, Isaacs asked him, did all the attention make him feel? "Embarrassed," Newell said. "Embarrassed and ashamed." "Newell used most of the key words: appalling, terrible, shameful, humiliating," Isaacs later wrote. For the next eight days he canvassed the local gentry. Years later, his remarkable unpublished notes of those self-lacerating interviews read more like something out of Spoon River than Little Rock.

Newell took him to the Little Rock Club, the favorite and extremely segregated watering hole of the squirearchy at 4th and Center, where, even on a Sunday morning, folks were drowning their shame in drink. Though they had little idea how wretched life was becoming for the Little Rock Nine—the newspapers reported next to nothing about it—they knew that both inside and outside Central, the segregationist rabble was winning. "Faubus

Harold Isaacs (Courtesy of Arnold Isaacs)

unleashed the idiots," lamented Harry Ashmore, the editor of the *Gazette,* who, as Isaacs put it, "stand[s] out like a monument in Little Rock, where nobody stands very high." Publicly, the city's most respectable figures conspicuously agonized; "handwringers and head-holders," Isaacs called them. But with the livelihoods of many of them dependent upon the bigots—they could always take their business to Memphis—they felt paralyzed. All felt too timid to speak out, except in their cups at the Little Rock Club to Harold Isaacs, a Jew who, had he lived in town, would not have been allowed to join.

"If you find any people with any decent convictions in this town, you'll find that they are also gutless. Gutless! Gutless!" a "Joseph Cotten–like" lawyer named Downey told him. A "half-crocked" businessman kept repeating the lyrics from *South Pacific*—"you've got to be taught, to hate and fear"—while his wife tried repeatedly to shush him up. "Compulsive talking" was a leitmotif, Isaacs learned: if they gabbed enough, people seemed to feel, maybe they could wiggle out of their predicament. Officially, Isaacs got only a few minutes with Faubus, but two hours later the governor was still yakking as Isaacs edged his way to the door. " 'Moderation' in Little Rock seemed to cover everything from a rather weary and non-virulent pro-segregation to a timid and covert pro-integration," Isaacs wrote. "It was not a banner to rally an army. It was rather a ragged shelter under which all sorts of people could huddle in the storm while doing nothing." Newell gave him the local definition of moderate: saying "Negro" rather than "nigger."

Isaacs did not limit his interviews to the "moderates." The lawyer for the segregationist Mothers League, thirty-eight-year-old Griffin Smith, vouchsafed that the restaurant in the Hotel Marion, Little Rock's finest, wouldn't serve blacks in his lifetime. "This is not what the goddamn niggers want," a cabdriver said while taking him to Central. "They want to go everywhere, the cafes and hotels and all. Pretty soon they'll push white people out of everywhere—they're too many of them." Wesley Pruden, a local pastor and another segregationist leader, told Isaacs that the NAACP was paying the black parents to keep the Nine in Central. "They'd take their children out in a minute if they could," he said. Isaacs learned that newsboys delivering the *Gazette* were terrified, and that because his daughter had said something favorable about integration, the bread made by a baker named Meyer was being thrown out into the street. Of the clergymen he interviewed, only the Rev. Dunbar Ogden, pastor of the local Presbyterian church and the sole white minister who, on that first day, had accompanied the black children to school, supported school desegregation. He found Ogden to be a tortured man, badgering, even begging, Isaacs to judge him. "I could not undertake to help Ogden wrestle with his soul," Isaacs wrote. "But I was relieved to find him struggling anyway. I wouldn't have wanted not to have met in Little Rock at least one preacher of the Gospel who at least showed an awareness of what it called upon him to be."

The Jewish owners of the downtown department stores, politically moderate on most things, were running for cover, Daisy Bates told Isaacs. Having a Jewish reporter on the story, let alone one from the *New York Times,* let alone one who had publicly consoled one of the black girls, made them uneasy: "One of the Jews here called the *Times* and said, 'Why don't you send a white man down here to cover this story?'" she recalled. The South wasn't ready for desegregation, one Jewish merchant, Sam Strauss of Pfeifer's, told Isaacs. Isaacs asked Strauss how Jewish attitudes towards blacks in Little Rock differed from Hitler's anti-Semitism. "It's a question of color," Strauss replied. "Down here, we have our own customs. . . . The more this kind of thing gets stirred up, the more anti-Semitism you get."[1]

One night at the Dunbar Community Center, Isaacs met seven of the Nine, including Elizabeth—"smaller than she looked in those historic photographs," he noted. "I looked around at them and thought them lucky," he wrote. "However each assimilated the experience, he or she was having at this early stage a chance for a finest hour. They had written themselves into history." Elizabeth told him of the letters she'd been receiving. "I've gotten many trying to apologize for what happened," Elizabeth said. "I'd say two-thirds are from the United States and about a third from all sorts of foreign countries."

It had rained torrentially for much of Isaacs's stay in Little Rock, giving the place an almost biblical feel. One night at the Little Rock Club, he announced to his new acquaintances that this was in fact the Second Flood, and that this time Noah was a black man. "No one around me thought this was funny and, indeed, I hadn't meant it to be," he wrote. It rained still more on the day he was to leave—enough for him to worry he might not be able to flee what he called this "flat and ugly city." Before his plane finally took off, Isaacs scribbled a few last words in his notebook. "There are only nine heroes in Little Rock," he wrote. "It's a war of nerves, and the nerves are the nerves of the nine youngsters, sweating it out day after day inside Central High School. On their nerves, the whole issue hangs, and the issue is a great one."

TWENTY

S hortly before Christmas, the Nine would have an even more distinguished visitor. He was Dr. Kenneth Clark, the psychologist whose findings on the harmfulness of segregated education had buttressed the NAACP's case in *Brown*. As Clark explained to Daisy Bates, he and his family would be spending the holidays in Hot Springs, only a couple of hours away. "Needless to say, I could not be so close to Little Rock without coming by to talk with you and the nine youngsters who have so bravely fought our battles," he told her. In fact, the Southern Regional Council had commissioned him to investigate how they, and the black community generally, were holding up. He first met them at a Christmas party thrown by a black sorority, but he learned little there: "The students were having too good a time to talk with me about Central High School." So he met with them individually in the next few days. He found them in surprisingly good shape: centuries of oppression, he theorized, had endowed them with ample survival skills. In fact, to Clark their greatest danger was overconfidence; "some irresponsible fanatical hot head" might do something terrible to them when they weren't looking.

Clark put together appraisals of each, which were omitted from his final report. He'd been impressed with the three boys and smitten with Gloria Ray and Minnijean Brown. He had reservations about Melba Patillo, suggesting that she was a publicity hound.[1] With Elizabeth, who had joined him and his wife for dinner one night in Hot Springs, he was surprisingly detached and low-key, failing to note her role as the first, the most famous, and the most traumatized of the group. Still, his assessment was the most in-depth and expert of any taken at the time. It made clear that for all of the troubles it had brought her, integration had already fulfilled for Elizabeth one of its principal missions, which was to give her insight into another race.

Elizabeth Eckford gives the impression of being rather shy and somewhat introverted. As you get to know her and talk with her you are impressed with a depth, solidity, and maturity which seem extraordinary for a 16 year old. She, too, is calm and reflective as she discusses the tensions and deliberate cruelties which she has experienced in Central High School. She discusses, without passion, her dread of the jostling and name calling in the halls, in gym, and in the lunch room. She and Terrence are the more obvious stoics in their reaction to the systematic harassment which these nine students are required to experience in Central High School. She describes these cruelties in rather matter-of-fact terms. She faces her anxiety about them. She describes the whites who perpetrate these attempts at humiliation or physical damage as being "silly."

When I asked her what was the most important thing that she has learned as a result of her experience at Central High School, she answered in her deliberative manner, "When I used to go to Horace Mann School I thought that white people were different. When I saw the colored kids at Horace Mann acting silly or doing something that

I didn't think they should do, I said to myself that they did this just because they were colored. Now that I am at Central High School I see that white children do silly things too. Just like there are dumb colored children there are some dumb whites. There are some average colored and there are some average whites, and there are some smart whites and some smart colored. I guess what I have learned is that they are not so different and we aren't so different."

When her father suggested that maybe she was working a little harder on her school work than she worked at Horace Mann, she refused to accept this and insisted that she worked as hard as she could at Horace Mann and she is working as hard as she can at Central High School. She stated this with a firm, matter-of-fact conviction and her father had to accept her interpretation in spite of the fact that it did not agree with his.

Elizabeth, Jefferson Thomas, and Terrence Roberts were "quite disturbed at the cumulative cruelties which they have had to endure," Clark noted. For Elizabeth the worst class was gym, and not just because she was poor at sports; supervision there was spotty, so her tormentors could run amok. Girls put broken glass on the shower-room floor, or scalded her by flushing all the toilets simultaneously (everyone in the adjoining showers somehow knew just when to step aside), or threw flaming spitballs into the stalls. Minnijean had been a help, not only protecting but commiserating. "When things got really tough, Elizabeth and I would think of Jackie Robinson," she later said. "We felt if he could do it, we could too." With one exception, Clark concluded, the black students had reacted positively to the limelight. He did not identify that exception, but for those who knew the Nine, it wasn't really necessary.

TWENTY-ONE

The new year brought only more abuse, particularly as the troublemakers realized they risked little more than a slap on the wrist or a brief (and, often, welcome) suspension for any misbehavior. That, in turn, led the few school officials, teachers, soldiers, and students otherwise inclined to push back essentially to stop trying. School officials had some sense of which parents were behind the harassment—Mrs. Huckaby later claimed that the Central Intelligence Agency installed an agent in Little Rock that year, even finding his wife a job in a local beauty parlor to pick up gossip—but they were never reined in, either.[1]

Elizabeth continued to suffer disproportionately. Apart from being the most vulnerable, she was also the most symbolically potent: if only they could drive out the girl who had come to epitomize the Nine, the segregationists may have hoped, the others would quickly follow, and the whole integrationist edifice would crumble. January 10: Elizabeth shoved from behind on the stairs. "I was in a hurry and this li'l ole nigger was in my way," Darlene Holloway, who was suspended, explained. January 12: Someone spits on Elizabeth's hand. January 14: Elizabeth pushed down onto stairs face forward. Comes crying to Mrs. Huckaby's office. "It's a wonder she didn't pop her teeth out on the concrete and steel," a report states. January 22: Elizabeth spat on again. January 29: Elizabeth attacked with spitballs. January 30: Elizabeth asks to study in Mrs. Huckaby's office rather than attend pep rally. January 31: After girls serenade her with humiliating songs in gym, Elizabeth asks grandfather to take her home. "You mean you can't control these kids?" her incredulous grandfather asks. Not without community backing, Mrs. Huckaby replies. "It's hard to put these Negro children—the best-reared of their group—up against our near-delinquents," Mrs. Huckaby wrote her brother. "They couldn't retaliate even if they knew how, of course, being such a tiny minority."

These "near-delinquents" were easily spotted. Though there were exceptions, they were generally the ones with the leather jackets and ducktail haircuts from the poorer parts of town, who tucked Luckies into their T-shirt sleeves and smoked during recess. To Powell, hell-raising—"jumping on the fun wagon"— accounted for their misbehavior as much as bigotry. "These types don't especially hate coloreds, but they do enjoy attention," he said. After a good day's harassing, some went directly to *Steve's Show* to dance. It was all of a piece, all in search of a good time.

In history class, a boy named Charles Sawrie, with bad skin and a protruding Adam's apple, sat behind Elizabeth, muttering "nigger, nigger, nigger, nigger, nigger" at her daily, while more respectable classmates looked the other way. "I don't remember anything about [Elizabeth] except she was black and my job was to make it as rough for the blacks as I could and that's what I did," he recalled, with embarrassment, years later. Elizabeth never complained. She actually felt sorry for Sawrie, who clearly came from poverty himself. Along with race, both class and peer pressure were very much at work: marginalized whites made names for themselves by treating the even more marginalized blacks with as much conspicuous cruelty as possible. (Sawrie briefly became a folk hero by clobbering Ernest Green with a biology book as the principal stood nearby.) Their tormentors resented Elizabeth and the others because, for all the abuse they were taking, some people actually *cared* about them. As loathsome as their behavior was, there was also a kind of honesty and directness to these young people; one knew what they were about. For Elizabeth at least, they were preferable to the vastly larger group of "better" students who did nothing, who pretended nothing was amiss, who simply carried on and looked the other way. These students *could* mobilize when it suited them: for instance, the captain of the football team escorted Blossom's daughter between classes.

For some reason—perhaps tactical, perhaps some perverse form of chivalry—the rabble-rousers divided their tasks by sex; most of Elizabeth's tormentors were girls. Unlike Hazel, whose misbehavior had been ad hoc and short-lived, their actions were sustained and coordinated. When James Lawson of the Fellowship of Reconciliation, who had once instructed Martin Luther King, Jr., in nonviolence, met with the Nine, he advised them to protect their midsections. Elizabeth was way ahead of him; her loose-leaf binder had always doubled as a shield. But now, she enhanced her defenses. A houseful of seamstresses had plenty of extra straight pins, and she stuck them around the edges of her book. After that, she was hit from the front only once.[2]

The situation grew worse for Elizabeth in February, when Minnijean, who'd been reinstated a few weeks earlier, was finally expelled for calling one of her harassers "white trash." She would finish the school year in New York; along with the other black students, Elizabeth accompanied her to the airport, wishing she, too, could have boarded that plane. For her part, Minnijean worried about Elizabeth: what would happen to her now that her closest friend would no longer be around? She could easily have been speaking for Elizabeth when she described the world she was leaving behind: "I don't think people realize what goes on at Central," said Minnijean. "They throw rocks, they spill ink on your clothes, they call you 'nigger,' they just keep bothering you every five minutes." Around Central, little printed cards soon appeared. "ONE DOWN . . . EIGHT TO GO," they proclaimed.

February 4: Elizabeth has soda bottle thrown at her. February 13: Elizabeth unable to reach father's car when, as soldiers run for cover, nine boys throw snow-covered rocks at black students. (After her experiences on the first day, Elizabeth's parents had no longer let her ride city buses to school: either her father or her grandfather would take her, even though, for her grandfather, this meant closing his store. Oscar Eckford, Sr., loved money; to his granddaughter, shutting his place was the ultimate act of love.) At night, with her father at the train station, two neighbors, Mr. Brown and Mr. Bullock, patrolled around the Eckford house. Even before the school crisis, her mother always had a .45, and hearing something suspicious on several occasions, she opened the door a crack and shot outside.

Just about the only fate that did *not* befall Elizabeth was the one that Radio Moscow reported on January 25: that she'd been "brutally murdered." That gave the Voice of America a rare chance to chortle. "If the Soviet report was news to Americans as a whole, it was especially so to the supposed victim, who . . . merely laughed when informed of her violent demise," it said. That month, just around the time her father's union, the Dining Car Employees, awarded a thousand-dollar scholarship to Elizabeth, the press reported that she was about to quit Central. Several afternoons, in fact, she had left school vowing never to return, only to change her mind by morning. But as the year progressed, something descended on Elizabeth that never fully lifted. "She walked with her head down, as if she wanted to make sure the floor didn't open up beneath her," is how Jefferson Thomas described it.

To those inside Central who looked neither away from nor through her, there developed another indelible image of Elizabeth Eckford, this one uncommitted to film: a slight, solitary girl in modest but brightly colored handmade clothes, walking—solemnly, purposefully, warily—along Central's corridors, no one ever around her, books clasped tightly to her chest. Fifty years later, a Little Rock lawyer named Josh McHughes could still see her, plain as day: you wanted to approach her and reassure her, or say hello, or simply smile, but neither he nor anyone else ever did; you just got out of her way, and went about your business. There were taunts in the hallway—*"Good morning, nigger. Aren't ya'all gonna talk some of that coon jab you speak?"*—and days when students collectively stared at her, or walked on her heels. In assemblies the black students sat by themselves, listening to the rebel yells and choruses of "Dixie." Only the handful of Japanese-American students, children of families left over from the internment camps in Arkansas to which they'd been sent during World War II, were as isolated. March 7: Egg thrown at Elizabeth. Lands on her coat and books. Locker also broken. March 12: Elizabeth hit on back by rotten tomato. "She said that except for some broken glass thrown at her during lunch, she really had had a wonderful day," Mrs. Huckaby writes.

Over time she grew increasingly intent on going it alone. "Elizabeth is more anxious to be independent than safe," Mrs. Huckaby later wrote. Really, Elizabeth had little choice. Even had she been inclined to confide in someone, there was no one to whom to turn. She couldn't turn to Daisy Bates and the NAACP, which, she believed, thrived on the students' martyrdom and wanted to make desegregation work. She couldn't turn to her mother, who'd have yanked her out of Central had she known what was happening there. Or to her grandfather, because she'd not have wanted him to know how weak she felt she was. Or to her father, who paid little heed to her plight: "Just a little pushing and shoving" was how he later characterized it. Black America was at war, was how he saw it, and Elizabeth was doing her soldierly duty. Besides, he'd never seen any marks on her. His attitude anticipated some controversial comments made two years later by the philosopher Hannah Arendt concerning the proper role of children, parents, courts, and organizations in civil rights crusades.[3]

Elizabeth couldn't talk to the other black students; except in gym—where they were paired off—none were in her classes, and away from Central, Central was the last thing they wanted to discuss. Even had they wanted to talk, they sensed that Elizabeth didn't. "She was a real psychological mess," Terrence Roberts recalled. "I always had the feeling that whatever was going on, she was not about to say it to anyone. It was going to be hers alone." Despite facile assumptions (invariably by whites) that they were monolithic and intimate, the Nine were really not particularly close, either at Central or for decades afterward—no closer, really, than any nine people thrown together by circumstances would be. At no point during that year, for instance, did Elizabeth set foot in the homes of Ernest Green, Melba Patillo, Jefferson Thomas, or Gloria Ray. (Gloria had a party once and did not invite her.) Denied the chance at Central, some of the others participated in extracurricular events at Horace Mann, but Elizabeth's mother, ever eager to keep her close to home, would never have allowed that.

Elizabeth couldn't talk to friends; there were so few to begin with (most were really her sister's) and, hoping to avoid trouble, they steered clear of her. She couldn't talk to her minister, as some of the others—Ernest, Melba, Minnijean, Gloria—could. The goings-on at Central were rarely discussed at her church, whose pastor wasn't eager to rock too many boats, and never pulled her aside to comfort her. She couldn't talk to the local press; Blossom had instructed them not to, and Daisy Bates didn't want them to, either. "Everytime [sic] they print something about the kids, the kids have to face it the next day in school," she told the NAACP. And besides, the local press wasn't much interested. The *Democrat* sided with the segregationists. And while the *Gazette* was more progressive—it won two Pulitzer Prizes for its coverage that year—it largely ducked the story after the first few weeks.[4] One exception came in late November, when it put six reporters on the case. "Teachers, Students Say Central High Seethes with Myriad Undercurrents," the ensuing headline blared. But the story itself was timid, and ended on an incongruous and unconvincingly sanguine note: "A white girl in a gym class tosses a Negro girl's shoe out the window and the Negro girl cries. But then, it is common for white girls to throw other white girls' shoes out the window. Maybe it isn't such an unusual School after all."

None of the black schoolchildren were interviewed for the story, in part because none of the interviewers was black: a decade would pass before the paper hired its first black reporter. The Nine remained, as the former *Gazette* man Gene Foreman put it, "cardboard characters" in the paper, and all but invisible in the *Democrat.* Local television was even more skittish. When NBC staged a discussion between four white schoolchildren (some of them segregationists) and three of the blacks, its Little Rock affiliate wouldn't carry the program.

Those people who attacked Benjamin Fine were, in fact, on to something: it *was* the hated "Yankees" who wrote most penetratingly about life inside Central. "Technically, these are the most protected school children in the world," one of the most persistent of them, Stan Opotowsky of the *New York Post,* wrote from Little Rock that spring, noting that the Supreme Court, the army, and the local school board were behind them. "But in reality they walk alone. You see them move down the twisted halls of Central High in a quick, tense gait, eyes riveted to the floor, fearful and expectant." Opotowsky looked on as someone dropped a cup of water down a stairwell, and heard raucous laughter reverberate through the halls when the water landed on a black girl's face. One of the few sympathetic white students, Robin Woods, told him the blacks were in a state of shock. "They jump when you speak," she said. "The other day I smiled and said hello to Elizabeth Eckford and she looked so startled. She looked as though she were waiting for me to say something bad after I said hello."

"In the chatter and laughter of the corridors, this observer saw

Elizabeth, right, and Carlotta Walls often went to and from Central together.
(George Tames/*New York Times*)

no white student stop to talk or even smile with [the black students]," Gertrude Samuels of the *New York Times* wrote in March. It was "as though they were in a hostile land where no one spoke their language." Elizabeth told Samuels that she divided the student body into three groups: first, the majority, civil and courteous, "who might like Negroes if they had a chance"; second, those who attacked them verbally; and third, those who actually tried to hurt them. "I knew it was going to be rough," she said, "but knowing it, and experiencing it, are different things."

And here was the final, most important outlet unavailable to Elizabeth: she couldn't talk to the two thousand–odd students around her. Most of them wouldn't think of hurting her—if you were from a respectable family you'd *never* call anyone "nigger," or hit her, or trip her—but they didn't do anything good, either. It was an attitude neatly captured in the school newspaper, the Central High School *Tiger*. As Mike Barrier, the student who wrote most of the paper's few stories on the subject, later put it, the message from on high was to depict "a normal school year with a few hundred extra army personnel on the premises." When the subject of the black students *was* raised, it was done elliptically, or in code, and always understatedly. "To say that hostility is non-existent would not be true, but in many hearts there has never been any prejudice," went an article from November, which, to its credit, hinted at some of the teachers' attitudes. ("Reserving their personal opinions for themselves, they have never neglected their duties.") Having barely acknowledged any abnormality that fall, the *Tiger* suggested in January that normality had returned. "Negro students no longer draw stares as they walk down the halls," it stated. "As a topic of discussion, integration has become pretty thoroughly secondary." None of the Nine was ever interviewed, nor even identified, in the *Tiger* that year; an item detailing an award alumnus Will Counts had won for his now-famous picture of Elizabeth and Hazel managed to omit what that picture depicted. In fairness, the student journalists enjoyed little latitude: the paper's faculty adviser, Miss Edna Middlebrook, belonged—like Elizabeth's history teacher, Miss Penton—to the Daughters of the Confederacy.[5] Officially, then, all was fine at Central High School. "No child has been physically injured, no persons in town have been killed or seriously hurt, and no teacher has resigned his or her position," Jess Matthews told a group of educators that March. "Life within the school has been very normal."

Looking back on his ninetieth birthday in early 1958, W. E. B. Du Bois painted a bleak picture of life for American blacks, whom he characterized as bewildered and scared. "Only the children like those in Little Rock stand and fight," he wrote. That was little consolation to Elizabeth or her peers. But feeling that she couldn't let the others down, Elizabeth finished out the year. The last ten days or so, she didn't need to be at Central much, and she was grateful for the reprieve. Her class ring—it was onyx and gold, the school's colors— became one of the few tangible mementoes of her time there (and only until she lost it sometime over the summer); having been absent when her homeroom picture was taken (perhaps while Faubus kept her and the others out), her face appeared nowhere in the yearbook. It was as if she had never been there.

TWENTY-TWO

That summer, the Little Rock Nine, who had already proven to be potent fund-raisers for the NAACP, went on the road. Apart from a childhood trip to St. Louis that she couldn't remember, it was Elizabeth's first time away from home, and her first time in a plane. But that didn't matter: she was just excited to be out of Little Rock and the South. That June the group was feted for three days in New York, in a program organized by the local branch of the Hotel and Club Employees Union. After a tearful reunion with Minnijean at the airport, the Nine received an award from the union. Among those saluting them was Governor Averell Harriman. The next day, Mayor Robert Wagner met the group at City Hall, and, after a press conference, they toured the United Nations, where they saw Ralph Bunche and Dag Hammarskjöld. (Bunche doubted that he'd have shown their restraint; in his own high school days, he told them, he had been a "chip on the shoulder" type.) On Broadway that night, they watched Lena Horne and Ricardo Montalbán in *Jamaica,* then met with the stars backstage. Elizabeth collected signatures on an "autograph hound," a cloth dachshund that was, for her, a substitute for conversation. Then it was on to Times Square and a midnight snack at Lindy's. (What most amazed Elizabeth was that a fancy restaurant served sandwiches.) The next day featured the Empire State Building and Statue of Liberty (Elizabeth was too scared to go to the top of either) and Coney Island (she skipped the roller coaster), with a ride on the New York subway in between. There was church on Sunday before they left. In Chicago they collected an award from the *Chicago Defender* and met Mayor Richard J. Daley. (To Elizabeth, he looked like a Teamster.) In Cleveland they accepted the Spingarn Prize—it had previously gone to W. E. B. Du Bois, Marian Anderson, Jackie Robinson, and Martin Luther King, among others—from the NAACP.

All this time away was a balm for Elizabeth. From then forward, whenever she returned to Little Rock she left her bags packed, anticipating her next escape. In August the Nine went to Washington, where they toured the White House and were Johnny Mathis's special guests at a television show, produced in a local hotel. (When Mathis learned that the segregated establishment would not admit them, he arranged for them to sit separately onstage.) Outside the Supreme Court, they posed with Thurgood Marshall. (Never position yourself on the edge of a group picture, he counseled Elizabeth: you might get cropped out. Of course, that would have been fine with her.) Elizabeth's demoralizing experience at Central had snuffed out her plans to enter law, or any plans at all. But Marshall—funny, profane, the only man gutsy enough to talk back to Daisy Bates, the only lawyer representing the children who actually *talked* to them—well, she had a crush on *him!* In a parade sponsored by Washington's Negro Elks, the Nine appeared on a float, sitting at desks to which their names had been attached. Along with the others, Elizabeth received a thousand-dollar scholarship from the group. "Her 'I wish to

Elizabeth shakes hands with Governor Averell Harriman of New York as
Daisy Bates and others from the Little Rock Nine look on, June 1958.
(Photographer unidentified)

express gratitude' is nervously spoken, hurried and her slight
body trembles," wrote Mary Stratford in the *Washington Afro-
American,* adding that Elizabeth appeared no more comfortable
there than she had been amid the mob outside Central. "Elizabeth's self-contained reserved demeanor suggests a sign marked,
'Private. Do Not Enter,'" Stratford continued. "She has a great
capacity for quietness."

At summer's end, Birdie Eckford lost her job at the deaf and
blind school—retaliation, Elizabeth believed, for her role in the
Little Rock drama. Then, in the final paroxysm of the old order,
local voters decreed that rather than integrate, the city's public
high schools would close for the 1958–59 year. (Central's football
team nonetheless played a full schedule.) Most whites went to

With Thurgood Marshall at the Supreme Court, August 1958. From left:
Melba Patillo, Jefferson Thomas, Gloria Ray, Daisy Bates, Marshall,
Carlotta Walls, Minnijean Brown, Elizabeth (Bettmann/Corbis)

hastily-put-together private schools, or to public schools out of
town. Some northern institutions offered slots to the black students, but fearful that sending them away would render an on-
going court case moot, Daisy Bates had not accepted—to Elizabeth, another respect in which they were sacrificed for the cause.[1]
To Elizabeth, Bates was a self-promoter. Though the other black
students felt little affection for Bates, some thought that judgment unduly harsh, as Elizabeth's judgments of others tended to
be. There can be no doubt that Bates played a crucial role in
the desegregation of Central High School, and that she and her
husband—their lives and home repeatedly threatened, the newspaper they owned eventually forced to close—paid an enormous
price for their courage.

The Nine scattered. Ernest Green graduated. Terrence Roberts moved to Los Angeles and Gloria Ray to Kansas City. Minnijean Brown returned to New York. Elizabeth remained in Little Rock, studying algebra and English with a tutor, and French via an extension course from the University of Arkansas. When an official from the hotel workers union polled the Nine to find out how they were coping, Elizabeth expressed frustration. "However, I am keeping up on some of the reading," she noted. "Right now I am reading Shakespeare's 'Much Ado About Nothing,' and after that I think I will try 'King Lear.'" Shakespeare, she explained, was a requirement for twelfth-grade English. She also hung around her grandfather's store, listening to him when she wasn't reading books. That summer, the NAACP placed each of the Nine in "safe houses" in black neighborhoods in big cities away from Little Rock. Along with Jefferson Thomas and Thelma Mothershed, Elizabeth lived with Frankie Muse Freeman, a prominent NAACP lawyer in St. Louis. Her father's coworkers on the railroad made sure "Eckford's kid" was well cared for throughout the trip there. (She got to ride free on the Missouri Pacific; other lines charged her a penny a mile.) Perhaps the first person to whom Elizabeth spoke candidly about her experiences, Freeman recognized her fragility. She made sure Elizabeth did fun things—visits to a friend's pool, movies—but always within the black community, so that no whites, especially white reporters, knew she was in town. The others ventured out much more freely. It was during this summer that Elizabeth first tried to kill herself. It wasn't really premeditated; in fact, she had been having a good time. But one day, she swallowed a bottle of over-the-counter sleeping pills. There hadn't been enough of them, and she was never really in any danger; that she had even tried became apparent only from her grogginess the next morning. At the Freemans' insistence, she then saw her first psychiatrist, and she was never allowed to lock her bedroom door again.

When, after moderate elements in Little Rock finally prevailed, Central reopened in September 1959. The school's black population had been reduced to five, including two of the original nine, Carlotta Walls and Jefferson Thomas. Though still a few credits short of graduating—she never did collect a Central diploma—Elizabeth opted instead to attend Knox College in Galesburg, Illinois. Knox suited her desire for a small school and had been recommended by the National Scholarship Service and Fund for Negro Students. Still, when the school year began at Central, Elizabeth showed up, just to lend Jefferson some support. (Carlotta was still at summer school.) He would need it. Many of the segregationist students would also be returning; only the press would be gone. "I know how bad it was when there were nine of us," she told Ted Poston. "It would be ten times as bad if no one was with him."

When word came of fresh trouble brewing outside the school, Daisy Bates asked Elizabeth whether she was sure she wanted to return. "You didn't think I was going to chicken out at this last moment, do you?" Elizabeth replied. Elizabeth and Jefferson rode to the school with Carl Rowan, then a young reporter with the *Minneapolis Tribune*. As the police held back another jeering crowd, Elizabeth went inside Central for a few hours. "I don't think they'll stay after the way they were treated today," one student said afterward. "[Elizabeth] sat there in the middle of the room, and no one spoke to her." "I'm glad and I'm proud, although I've been thanking God she didn't have to go back to Central," Birdie Eckford said afterward.

Knox College is a small liberal arts institution with a proud abolitionist background; it was one of the first schools to give a black woman a degree. When she arrived on the campus, accompanied by Daisy Bates, Elizabeth was one of twelve black students. Scholarships paid her way, covering even her books. Initially she felt liberated; Knox was the first place in which she could really express her feelings. After so many years in the cocoon of Little Rock, it became a kind of wonderland for her: suddenly, there was so much to acquire, taste, know. It marked the first time she had seen snow so deep (she went outside and lay down in it), the first time she had eaten meat cooked rare, the first place she'd felt popular. She thought no one knew anything about her connection to the Little Rock Nine but that wasn't so, at least among the school's other blacks. "It was almost a part of her name," one recalled.

Elizabeth got involved with the theater group, working backstage in a production of Lillian Hellman's *The Little Foxes* and even appearing in it briefly—as a maid. Gradually, though, she came to realize something quite fundamental: she missed black people. Sometimes, she would wander nostalgically around Galesburg's small black neighborhood, drink at a local bar, and then, lest her house mother discover her slinking back after hours, spend the night in the ladies' room at the local train station. She grew disillusioned with the school when the fraternities and sororities would not admit her black friends. She had academic problems and lost her scholarship. Just around the time the NAACP magazine, *The Crisis*, reported that she was at Knox, it became clear that she would soon be leaving. She finished the year, then disappeared: a classmate heard from her only once after that, when she sent him a collection of famous poems that she had copied by hand. After writing "deceased" on some literature the college sent her, she lost touch with Knox.

In the fall of 1960 Elizabeth moved to Central State University in Wilberforce, Ohio, whose president Daisy Bates knew. This marked Elizabeth's first encounter with what she called "hardcore, northern ghetto blacks," and it was jarring: to her, they were predators, people who mocked her innocence and took advantage of her goodwill—the types to bum cigarettes off you when they already had their own. The small allowance Elizabeth got from her father (at Bates's insistence) covered only her laundry and her hair; for smokes, she ironed shirts for the other girls. On a couple of occasions she again attempted suicide, but in different ways: by putting plastic laundry bags over her head (very inefficient: you breathe and breathe and breathe, and nothing happens) or, even more implausibly, by hitchhiking far from campus, half hoping that someone would pick her up and kill her. At this Central, as at the last, she endured for a year—hiding in the library, skipping classes. She left little trace of herself. A school photographer took her picture for the paper, but it couldn't be used: it was in profile, and her teeth protruded too hideously. Finally, her father fetched her. She returned to St. Louis, selling driving lessons, doing bookkeeping, working at a department store. She told herself she wanted to teach; her grandfather considered that a woman's highest calling. But really, she was lost.

Around this time the United States Information Agency, seeking to counteract the images of church bombings and fire hoses coming out of the South, commissioned a film about Little Rock and its aftermath—a story it evidently deemed, at least in the sorry context of American race relations, to have had a happy ending. As the historian Melinda Schwenk has pointed out, it marked the first time the USIA focused on ordinary black people rather than on marquee names like Marian Anderson, Ralph Bunche, and Wilma Rudolph. Still, for the agency, then headed by Edward R. Murrow, making propaganda out of Little Rock was delicate: you had to concede the embarrassment of 1957, then pivot to the progress since (such as it was), but not too enthusiastically, lest you antagonize your segregationist congressional bankrollers. (Easing the effort a bit was that by statute, the film could be shown only abroad.) The writer and director, Charles Guggenheim, had to hopscotch around all these land mines, plus others. He dared not disclose, for instance, that four of the Nine had married whites. Nor could he fault Faubus, who was still governor.

Nine from Little Rock, which was completed in 1964, actually focused on just five from Little Rock—Jefferson Thomas, Minnijean Brown, Thelma Mothershed, Ernest Green, and Elizabeth. They became proxies not just for the others, but for all of America's blacks. Elizabeth was probably included because she couldn't be excluded; it was she whom people would remember best, and wonder about most. Apart from the familiar, martial images from 1957, the film is upbeat, showing an integrated Central that had moved beyond its agony. So, too, it suggested, had its first blacks. "I haven't counted all the victories since that first day we all went to school here," an earnest Jefferson Thomas, shown walking around the school in a coat and tie—actually, the voice was a stand-in, reading someone else's words—declares, "but I know there's been at least—nine."

Fitting Elizabeth's story into the inspiring superstructure required considerable legerdemain. As their own documents attest, the filmmakers were well aware of Elizabeth's problems: that she'd been sent home from Knox, where she "seemed subject to fits of apathy"; that at Central State (which they mistakenly called "Wilberforce College") she had spent the first month of her second year watching television in her room. They'd picked up that at three o'clock one morning, the police had found her wandering in a field ten miles from campus, with no idea how she'd gotten there. And that she had eventually dropped out, then failed to appear when she was supposed to have reenrolled, telling school officials she'd become a domestic in Dayton. In fact, the documents noted, her present whereabouts were unknown.

Guggenheim tracked Elizabeth down in St. Louis. But he told his viewers nothing about her setbacks. Instead, the film pretended both that she'd never been at Knox and that she had never left Central State. It depicted her as a typical coed, when in fact she had had to be brought back to the campus and given a handful of someone else's books. And there she is, checking a bulletin board for jobs, participating in a pep rally. Throughout, a voice purporting to be hers—it, too, belonged to an actor—read someone else's script. "The world is a big place, and when I go out into it, I want to be sure I go out in the right direction," "Elizabeth" says, neglecting to mention that she was out there already, directionless. As unthreatening as Elizabeth was, Guggenheim apparently felt that he had to neuter her still more, by criticizing her own people.

No race, this Elizabeth points out, had a monopoly on prejudice: some blacks also opposed integration, including at the historically black Central State. "The Negro is like most Americans, possessing no monopoly on tolerance, and hoping that the few—the uninformed—will not be confused with the rest of them," the ersatz Elizabeth concludes.

Never one to make waves, the original Elizabeth went along with the ruses. She flew up to the campus (making a side trip to Southern Illinois University, where the segment on Minnijean was filmed).[2] When she finally viewed the documentary, at a private showing in St. Louis, she disliked what she saw: it really had nothing to do with her. Also, the woman reading her lines had a voice thinner than hers, didn't enunciate as clearly, and had more of a southern accent. Given the slow pace of change at Central, the film's congratulatory tone seemed unwarranted, but its feel-good message surely helped it win an Academy Award (for best documentary short subject).[3] It was Elizabeth's last such venture for a time. When an Associated Press reporter attempted to speak with her in 1966, Birdie Eckford informed him that her daughter was "too shy to be interviewed."

Far more genuine than Guggenheim's film was another drama, also set in Little Rock, around the same time. Elizabeth, now twenty-one, was visiting home in the summer of 1963 when she received a surprising phone call. It came from someone she'd never heard of before—a young woman named Hazel Bryan Massery.

TWENTY-THREE

F uller High School was only seven or eight miles from Central, but they were about as different as two schools could be. It was utterly unknown, of no particular distinction, and very small—only about thirty students per class. All of them, of course, were white, and desegregation was far from their minds. For a time Hazel stayed in touch with Sammie Dean, who kept her apprised of events at Central. But those calls gradually became less frequent. Hazel came not to care; her life revolved around her new boyfriend, Antoine (pronounced ANtone) Massery. He hadn't a clue who Hazel was, or had been; his family didn't own a television set, and besides, mornings and evenings there were the pigs to feed.

Antoine graduated from Fuller in the spring of 1958, as Hazel completed her junior year. Her angelic image from that year's yearbook, as radically different from the famous photograph of her taken nine months earlier as two pictures could ever be, would be as close to a graduation picture as she would have, for her high school career would soon end. By that fall, the two were engaged. It wasn't a formal, bended knee kind of thing; she just wore his senior ring around her neck. This engagement stuck, even though there was unhappiness on both sides. Hazel's church frowned on

Hazel and Antoine, spring 1958 (Courtesy Hazel Bryan Massery)

marriages to Catholics; the Masserys, too, had religious misgivings, and for a time, Antoine's father walked out of the house
whenever Hazel walked in. There were practical considerations,
too: Hazel wasn't big-boned, and therefore was ill-suited for
farm work. One night in November 1958 they married, in Hazel's
church. There was no wedding party or photographer; there were
people in the pews only because the preacher had asked the congregation, there for the normal Wednesday night service, to stay

Hazel Bryan, Fuller High School (Courtesy Hazel Bryan Massery)

on. Only one-fourth of their parents—Hazel's mother, who was in church anyway—was there. Hazel was sixteen.

School rules, designed to discourage such early unions, required brides to stay away for the next six weeks; Hazel never bothered going back. Sammie Dean's father got Antoine a job with the Rock Island Railroad. It didn't pay much; during that first winter, Antoine drained the water from his car nightly because he couldn't afford antifreeze. Sammie Dean married the following year—the two girls were always vying with one another—and for a short while the couples rented adjoining apartments in a neighborhood not far from Central. Hazel and Antoine then moved into a trailer on some land his family owned off a gravel road in West Pulaski County, about fifteen miles from downtown. The couple had two sons, the first in November 1959, the second in July 1962. Money was still tight. Unable to afford beds and mattresses, Antoine built some frames from plywood, then bought foam.

Despite her cousin's admonition that she should hold on to something so historic, Hazel had long ago tired of the mint green dress from the photograph and gotten rid of it, probably bequeathing it to another relative. She had saved all those harsh letters from 1957 (it was the packrat in her more than any sense of history or desire for reflection), and they had landed in her mother-in-law's barn. But cleaning up one day, she had burned them all, along with all the old love letters from various suitors (Antoine wasn't happy about them) and other teenage souvenirs. If it was meant as an exorcism, it failed. The Kennedy era had begun, and the civil rights movement had intensified. Night after night there were stories on television, from places like Oxford, Mississippi, and Birmingham, Alabama, giving events a vividness and immediacy they'd never had in print, especially if one didn't take the papers. Hazel watched it all, on the portable Philco with rabbit ears her father had bought her. Working in Memphis, Antoine was home only two nights a week; alone with her children, surrounded by forty acres of woods, without a car or, for a time, a telephone (the lady across the street had one), Hazel had plenty of time to ponder the racial turmoil, and her small but distinctive contribution to it. Her situation fostered in her a growing independence and sense of introspection; from the high school conformist she had been, she was becoming almost a contrarian.

Several years passed before she thought of Elizabeth at all. She was too busy being married and tending to her sons. But something—maybe a report about Martin Luther King, maybe seeing black protestors fire-hosed: she could never remember— touched her. She hadn't marked the time, but some night in 1962 or 1963, when she was around twenty years old, Hazel found herself lying awake, thinking about Elizabeth, and about her own legacy. She wanted to be for her sons the role model on racial tolerance she'd never had herself. To put it more brutally, she didn't want either of them to become the bigot she had been. Part of that, she believed, required her to get her own house in order. Spontaneous by nature—that was, after all, how she'd gotten into this fix in the first place—she was suddenly seized with an idea, one she didn't discuss with Antoine or her pastor or anyone else: she would track down Elizabeth, then call her and apologize. By now the Masserys had a telephone, so she could do it in the privacy of her own trailer.

She was emotional about it, but not nervous; once she had resolved to do something, she never was. She dialed the first Eckford she found in the Little Rock directory. A man answered. Hazel introduced herself, explained who she was, and asked to speak with Elizabeth. Elizabeth remembered things slightly differently; the call came to her grandfather, with whom Hazel had left a message. Elizabeth wasn't sure which of the girls in the picture Hazel was; far from studying the photograph, she had always avoided it. She certainly had never focused on the people in it, or bothered to separate the grown-ups from the teenagers or the teenagers from one another; Hazel was just one piece in the

mosaic of white hostility that day. Left to herself, Elizabeth probably would not have called Hazel back. She wasn't especially curious about her, nor sociable generally. But she always had considered her grandfather a fine judge of character, and he urged her to
return the call. Then the stories, Elizabeth's and Hazel's, converge.

"I'm the girl in the picture that was behind you yelling at you,"
Hazel explained when they finally spoke. ("Pitch-er" is how she
would have said it.) There was really no other way to introduce
herself. Hazel then said she was sorry—that what she had done
was terrible, and that she didn't want her children turning out like
that. She was crying. Elizabeth didn't say much, but she was gracious. She accepted the apology, not just because her grandfather
and father wanted her to but because this woman sounded sincere, and so clearly craved forgiveness. Even though she had no
children of her own yet, Elizabeth could empathize. Besides,
though she still wasn't sure which of the kids Hazel was, she knew
that she wasn't one of those who had harassed her all year in
Central, some of whose names she remembered, none of whom
had ever apologized. The entire conversation lasted five minutes,
if that; there was really little else to say. There was no talk of
meeting: this was still the South.

But in a way, the newly fortified bond, though fragile, persisted.
Henceforth, Elizabeth felt protective of Hazel, just as she did of
Ann Williams and Ken Reinhardt, the two students who had befriended her in speech class. White people, she knew, still paid a
price for extending to blacks even the most rudimentary cour-
tesies. So she protected her anonymity: whenever asked to identify
the white girl with the hateful face, she declined. (Before long she

had forgotten anyway—first the last name, then the first.) But the picture kept reappearing, especially as the anniversaries got bigger. After fading for a time, it was becoming famous again, this time for keeps.

Hazel and Antoine had a third child, a daughter, in 1966. The television repair and satellite business they'd begun—after taking a class in accounting, Hazel did the bookkeeping, and often climbed roofs to do installations—did well, and they built themselves a home where the trailer had been. Hazel wanted it to look organic, as if it had grown out of the ground, like a mushroom. The Arch Street Church of Christ consumed much of their sparse spare time. Antoine had converted, and had become a deacon. Three times a week there were services; if they didn't show up, someone called to ask why. On still another day, Hazel taught teenage girls about love and marriage, urging them to move a bit more deliberately than she had. Twice a year there were revivals, which meant church every single night. Theirs was a strict, fundamentalist faith: no dancing, swimming, drinking, gambling. Do any of them and you'd burn forever. For a free spirit like Hazel, it wasn't easy. Though few people around Little Rock knew much about Doctor Lamaze, she insisted upon having her third child naturally, read books on yoga, wore pants and short skirts. Increasingly, she felt smothered.

TWENTY-FOUR

D espite the occasional interview, Elizabeth usually lay low. But in August 1963, at twenty-one, she had joined several others on a bus from Little Rock to the March on Washington. It was a long trip through the South, and, two years after the violence visited on the Freedom Riders, fear stirred in her at every stop. When she reached the capital, she was just another face in the throng. She was awestruck and heartened by the numbers and variety of the people, as well as by their temperament: so many friendly white people, and black folks who, unlike those back home, were not afraid. But she could never escape her past completely. Certain sights or sounds—mobs leaving a football game, too-boisterous church choirs, blaring sound systems—triggered old anxieties. She had panic attacks in crowded elevators, especially with people behind her. Watching a production of the play *In White America* one night in St. Louis, she heard her own words: unbeknownst to her, an account of her walk that she had once given had been incorporated into the script. She jumped up, ran into the bathroom, and cried.

In 1964 an image like hers—of a black schoolgirl dressed in white and walking a gantlet—appeared anew, on the cover of *Look,* becoming so famous that, in many minds, it merged with, or even superseded, the original. But this was a painting (by Norman Rockwell) rather than a photograph and depicted not Elizabeth but Ruby Bridges, the six-year-old girl who had integrated an elementary school in New Orleans four years earlier. It was an altogether friendlier image, more fit for a family magazine, with little of the menace of Counts's photograph. There were no hectoring white students, only the word "Nigger" scrawled on the wall behind Bridges and tomato splotches nearby. Bridges, moreover, wasn't alone, but escorted by four federal marshals wearing armbands. No wonder Rockwell could place so innocent and tranquil an expression on her face.

While Elizabeth faded from view, her image continued to inspire. For many people—men and women, white and black, in grade school or high school or college—the photograph supplied a spark, inspiring them to march along southern highways, sit in at segregated lunch counters, hit the law books. Blacks quietly blazing new trails—like Andrew Heidelberg, who helped integrate the public schools of Norfolk, Virginia, or Raphael Cassimere, the first black to enter the New Orleans campus of Louisiana State University—often, in their minds, took Elizabeth with them. So did Lew Zuchman, a New York high school student who became a Freedom Rider. Seven years after watching Elizabeth on television, Arlene Dunn of Boston was registering voters in Arkansas for the Student Nonviolent Coordinating Committee. Deborah Mathis, the first black editor of the Central High School *Tiger,* learned of Elizabeth from the box of yellowed clippings her mother kept under a bed, which she had pulled out after Lyndon Johnson signed the Civil Rights Act of 1964. Not everyone found the picture so inspiring. When C. Fred Williams began teaching Arkansas history at the University of Little Rock in the late 1960s, departmental officials almost barred him from using a textbook in which it appeared.

In the fall of 1963 Elizabeth moved back to Little Rock. For a short time she was engaged to a young man named Anthony Honeycutt, whose mother, the treasurer of the state NAACP, was the hairdresser who had made the girls of the Little Rock Nine, Elizabeth among them, look so pretty. Honeycutt gave her a ring, and the two celebrated their engagement with a trip to see the fall leaves in northwest Arkansas. But concerned that Honeycutt wasn't college-bound and that marriage would hinder Elizabeth's own prospects, Birdie Eckford nixed the relationship. Her mother's interference, plus her own failure to graduate from college or find a teaching job—the school official doing the hiring in rural Marianna, Arkansas, got cold feet after realizing who she was—left Elizabeth in a bad state. When she spotted an army recruiting station in September 1967, something dawned on her: with one bold move, she could simultaneously escape her birthplace, her parents, and her past. For a young woman like her, enlisting was the safest way to run away from home.

Her timing was good: it was the middle of the Vietnam War, when an army swollen with draftees represented a broader cross-section of the country than usual, less dominated by poor southern whites. She survived her initial interview when, asked whether she could obey orders, she responded with Longfellow's admonition: "Be not like dumb, driven cattle." Over the next five years she was stationed in Indiana, Georgia, Washington State, and, for eighteen months, Anniston, Alabama. (Remembering the beating some Freedom Riders had taken there, she spent only one hour off the base.) She worked as a pay clerk, then wrote news copy. Whenever her past threatened to rear its head, she took pains to hide it. She tried eluding *Ebony* when it came looking for her, but didn't completely succeed; it included a photograph of "Spec. 5 Elizabeth A. Eckford" in a "Whatever happened to . . ." feature on the Nine in February 1972. The others were shown with spouses and children; Elizabeth was described as "single, with no marriage plans." The others looked at, and smiled for, the camera; Elizabeth looked away. She made sure that a copy of the *New Yorker* containing a story on the Nine and what had happened to them all did not circulate around the base. She won herself a good-conduct medal, and it made her proud: in that lockstep culture, it was hard to stay good. She was so eager to get out that although the army would have paid to have her teeth fixed, she couldn't wait. She quit in 1972.

She went back to Central State and completed her degree, in history. In the spring of 1973 she moved to Los Angeles, where two of her younger brothers lived, and took a job with the water company. The next year, she flew to New York for ceremonies marking the twentieth anniversary of the *Brown* decision, and when they were over, she decided on a whim to return to Little Rock. It was a matter of both resignation and defiance: other places, she had come to realize, weren't necessarily any better; they were just other places. And now, she could confront whatever had led her to flee.

She moved back into her old house, which her mother had gotten when her parents had finally divorced. Some of the old neighbors were still around, but the place had changed, had grown more dangerous. The simple, snug old home now had an alarm

Elizabeth during her army days (Courtesy Elizabeth Eckford)

system and window bars. Elizabeth found work in the state unemployment office. On a couple of occasions, she tried to learn to drive, but after plowing into a hedge she gave up; every day, she took a bus to and from work. She had little luck with, and low expectations of, men: she warned them in advance that if they hit her, she would press charges. In October 1975 she turned thirty-four. She was determined to have children, and because of the experiences with Baby Brother, she wanted to do so soon, before the odds of retardation rose. She just had to find a father. In part because she liked some of his poetry, she selected Thaddeus Honey-cutt, the older brother of her former fiancé. There was no question of marriage; and since he had gone to jail for failing to support the two children he already had, she knew he wouldn't interfere in her child rearing. In 1976, the year she bought her mother's house (for $13,900) on a no-interest Veterans Administration loan, she had a son. She named him Erin Alexander, after two boyfriends who had treated her nicely.

When Roy Reed of the *New York Times* tried to reach Elizabeth in 1977, she did not return his call. But as leery of the press as she was, she believed that as the only member of the Little Rock Nine still in Little Rock, she was duty bound to speak with reporters, at least whenever she could stomach it, and she agreed to meet with Steele Hays of the *Democrat,* whose story on her was splashed all over the front page. Living in Little Rock was now "tolerable," she told him, but for black people, the place hadn't changed much. Only she was different: she expected less. "Someone's done a good PR job for Little Rock," she told him. "There are some things I encounter every day that make me say 'When are these folks going to get some sophistication in their racism?' People I work with still refer to adult black males as 'boys.' That's kind of stupid." Elizabeth insisted she was "basically optimistic"—"I'm here, aren't I?"—and noted that blacks with college degrees could now be more than teachers and mailmen. But lots of places still discriminated—because, she theorized, "they haven't been sued enough." No way, she said, could blacks feel truly secure. "No matter what you have in terms of economic security, no matter what you have in terms of self-confidence, if you are black, you are vulnerable—vulnerable to losing everything you have," she said.

Her time at Central had made her hate whites, she told Hays, but those sentiments had since softened. She complained of feeling oppressed as a woman in addition to being black. And she began talking about motherhood, only to muzzle herself because it was "too personal." Besides, her son was crying in the next room. But as Hays prepared to leave, she made one last point. "I want you to understand why I came back," she said. "I came back because I felt I was chased away and because I thought it was cowardly and I wanted to prove I could live in this situation. . . . I don't intend to be driven out." To Hays, she appeared on the brink of a breakdown.

Still, in 1978, she had a second son, named Calvin. Here, too, marriage was out: this boy's father, a stonemason named James Oliver, was married. Feeling overwhelmed, she briefly put the two children into foster care. That two officials from the child welfare agency handling her case had been classmates at Dunbar and Horace Mann made it even more humiliating. But she quickly retrieved them and found, surprisingly, that having children helped her integrate into the larger community, at least in her own mind. She no longer felt, as she had from the very beginning, so damned different from everyone else.

Many of her tormentors at Central were still around town. But because she didn't remember faces, she didn't recognize them. Sometimes, out shopping or on the bus, she would see a woman about her age with short light hair, and she would wonder whether it was Hazel. (For some reason, she thought of Hazel as a blonde.) Generally, she avoided conversations about those days; people wanted the five-minute, *Reader's Digest* version of her story, and that annoyed her. But when big anniversaries came around, the topic was hard to escape. Her rare interviews became barometers of her emotional state. "Well, this is a kid whose life problems weren't solved by going to an integrated school," Eric Engberg of CBS News thought to himself after speaking with her in 1977. In one interview Elizabeth mentioned Hazel's apology, but it obviously didn't register and was never reported or explored.

In January 1980 Elizabeth, now thirty-eight years old, quit work and went on nonservice veterans' disability for recurrent depression. She began taking medication and getting therapy. With none of her doctors did she ever bring up who she was, or had been. Only when she was hospitalized later that year did a psychiatrist recognize her name and make the connection. He diagnosed her with posttraumatic stress disorder.

Slowly but steadily, Elizabeth fell deeper into an abyss. She rarely went out, except to shop or do laundry; by the third or fourth of every month, after paying the bills and buying groceries, she would be broke. She signed up for a free upholstery class once only because it came with a small stipend from the Veterans Administration. She constantly toted things up in her head to make sure she would have enough at the checkout. She would declare "soup-and-casserole months" to buy primitive toys for her boys. Until they were old enough to feel ashamed, she bought them only secondhand clothes. She learned the tricks of thrift stores: buying winter clothes in spring, for instance, and several sizes at once. One time, Elizabeth was scared enough by a shabbily dressed man approaching her and her boys to cross the street. "But Mama, he's dressed like me," Calvin told her. She earmarked her first disability payments for insulating the house, thereby cutting the cost of heat. So accustomed did her boys get to turning off lights in empty rooms that they would do it in other people's homes. Erin was diagnosed with obsessive-compulsive disorder and placed on medication. Elizabeth couldn't stand to be around her children— all that noise and bickering!—and resented it when they brought friends home. They felt alone in their own house.

Long gone were the elegant clothes she had handmade for school, fashioned from the fine fabrics her mother had taught her to savor. To avoid people, and dry cleaners, she bought mail-order wash-and-wear items out of the Sears or Montgomery Ward catalogues. Invariably, that meant polyester—always black, which went with everything and, she was convinced, better masked her poverty. "Cheap don't scream so loud in black," she liked to say. (But never black *and gold*. These were Central's colors, and she could not handle them. In the army once, someone had given her some black and gold towels, and though they were far nicer than the frayed ones she had, she had gotten rid of them.) She had two serious outfits: one for the PTA, the other for funerals.

Wherever possible, she purged her past. The "autograph hound" was long gone, and at some point she had thrown out all her letters from 1957. Fire hazards, she told herself, before burning them, just as Hazel had done, in the barrel in the backyard. For hours at a time she would lie on her bed, her face to the wall. Or sleep, sometimes for sixteen hours at a stretch. Or watch soap operas, though she barely followed the plots. Or sitcoms, though they never made her laugh. Or the televangelists, though she never bought what they sold. (She did feel religious stirrings sometimes, and even prayed occasionally—never for *things,* but for strength and peace.) Even her grandfather was scant comfort to her. Over the years, they had grown less close: he was candid, and she feared his criticism. He died in 1982, just shy of eighty-seven. Whatever image she retained of him was strictly from memory; the old sepia-toned portrait of him in his army uniform that had belonged to her father had vanished, and there were no others.

Sometimes, she would plan her own demise, or pretend that it had already happened. "Tell them I'm dead," she'd have the boys say to reporters when they called. (But that, she quickly realized, wasn't such a good idea: the papers might actually believe it and run her obituary.) Never could she get herself to tell her sons what had happened to her at Central; that forced them to pick it up and piece it together from watching documentaries or from overhearing her occasional interviews. Erin and Calvin came to resent these strange intruders who visited their home from time to time, asking questions that made Mama cry, then disappearing. But they were among the few men around. Erin's father, as Elizabeth once put it, "didn't give him the eye water to cry with." He saw Erin only a handful of times. (The last time, Erin didn't recognize him and wouldn't let him into the house.) Calvin's father, by contrast, visited regularly. He loved children and brought them toys. But he died when Calvin was only five. One thing remained constant: the house. Though it was gradually falling apart, Elizabeth cherished it. She knew its every sound—the way it whistled on windy nights, the rattle of the loose tiles in the hallway. She also knew that that house was all that separated her and her boys from the projects, which for her would mark the very end. Even in the worst of times she managed to hold on to it, never buying anything on time, somehow scraping together the small payments— $127 a month—that staved off foreclosure.

TWENTY-FIVE

H ow, nearly twenty-five years after Central was de-segregated, do you place a help-wanted advertise-ment in the Little Rock newspaper declaring that "no blacks need apply"? Or parade around what had by now become a largely black neighborhood with signs shouting "Niggers Go Home!"? Small wonder that the casting director for *Crisis at Central High School* had his work cut out for him. In fact, he very nearly had a nervous breakdown.

Hollywood had finally discovered Little Rock. In 1981 Mrs. Huck-aby's recently published memoirs became a made-for-television movie, with Joanne Woodward in the starring role. School offi-cials were portrayed much more heroically—or, in the case of "Grinning Chicken Jess" Matthews, more benignly—than they deserved. Knowing that Elizabeth's walk was perhaps the most memorable moment in the story, the director, Lamont Johnson, insisted that it be added to the script. Johnson was struck after-ward by how enthusiastically the extras had re-created the scene: they *loved* baiting the black girl and were delighted when he or-dered a second take. Elizabeth hadn't been involved in the pro-gram, except for requesting that her real name not be used. Hazel, who was not contacted at all, became a plump and particularly

unattractive girl named "Billie." They'd picked the name, she figured, because it sounded like white trash, and like "bully."

When seven of the Nine gathered in New York in May 1982 to
celebrate the twenty-fifth anniversary of their entrance into Central, Elizabeth didn't attend. She was under a doctor's care, the
paper reported. On the real anniversary that September, she told
People magazine that she lived like a hermit, and she would not
let herself be photographed. "I've got to get to the point where
I can talk about this," she said, dabbing her reddened eyes with
a dish towel. "Until then, it will never be over for me." A former neighbor of Elizabeth's, Morris Thompson, returned to Little
Rock in 1984 after several years away and was shocked at Elizabeth's poor state. She seemed adrift—on good days, friendly and
relatively talkative, but more often morose and antisocial. Her
sons were more subdued than boys their age should be; her house
was in disrepair. Thompson and his wife bought her groceries,
and clothes, and things for her home, like a bunk bed for the
children. It angered him that a hero had fallen so low, and that so
many who had profited from her courage, including the more
prosperous among the Nine, had let this happen.

Relations within the group remained surprisingly superficial.
But by the thirtieth anniversary in 1987, they had begun to co-
here a bit. Carlotta LaNier even proposed that Alex Haley, the
Arkansan who'd written *Roots,* do a book about them, devoting
a separate chapter to each.[1] Elizabeth, though, remained reticent.
She "prefers not to be asked about the 1957 desegregation crisis,"
the *Gazette* reported. Those she spurned included the makers
of *Eyes on the Prize,* though the widely watched documentary
naturally included the familiar footage of her. Word reached some

old admirers, like Roger Wilkins, that Elizabeth was in very bad shape, and it troubled them deeply. But few people reached out to help.

That thirtieth anniversary year, the Nine really had something to celebrate: Bill Clinton, the man who so freely acknowledged his debt to them—who said, essentially, that they'd saved him from becoming a redneck—was now governor. He took special pleasure inviting them to the governor's mansion—the "command post," he noted, from which Faubus had thwarted them in 1957. (At seventy-seven years old, Faubus was still very much alive.) The NAACP was having its annual meeting that year in Little Rock, and it was the first time the Nine had returned there as a group. The city had changed, at least superficially: a black woman, Lottie Shackelford, was mayor, and a young black man was president of Central's student body.

Clinton proved an amiable host, showing them around the mansion, barbecuing hamburgers. Elizabeth kept her head down and said little, evincing scant interest in the proceedings. When she did talk, she was impolitic, telling Clinton of her resentment toward the NAACP; when she said it, she thought she saw Hillary Clinton's jaw drop. (Elizabeth had a long memory for injustice: years after Coca-Cola had refused to give a small raise to its delivery men, nearly all black, who lugged around those heavy wooden crates, she still wouldn't drink the stuff.)

Though she never felt particularly welcome there, Elizabeth returned to Central periodically for various commemorations and programs, and had gradually acclimatized herself to the place. The corridors, which had seemed so wide when she was getting slammed into lockers, had somehow narrowed. She was all right there, as long as she wasn't crowded. But it was clearly a mistake for her to reenact her walk for *Super Chief,* a documentary on Chief Justice Earl Warren made by Judith Leonard and Bill Jersey. The result was almost too painful to watch. "I thought they were there for my p-p-p-protection," she stammers, tears streaming down her face, as she describes the Guardsmen. (In the shadows, one can make out a hand reaching out to comfort her. It belonged to Daisy Bates.)

With the release of *Eyes on the Prize* in 1987, Elizabeth inspired a whole new generation. One was the poet Cyrus Cassells. He identified with Elizabeth; his father and uncle had served in an army still emerging from segregation; his father had helped integrate the dorms at West Point. The image of Elizabeth percolated within him until 1991, when he wrote "Soul Make a Path Through Shining," which he dedicated to her.[2] Hazel, too, made an appearance in it, as a character from Greek mythology.

> *Thick at the schoolgate are the ones*
> *Rage has twisted*
> *Into minotaurs, harpies*
> *Relentlessly swift;*
> *So you must walk past the pincers,*
> *The swaying horns,*
> *Sister, sister,*
> *Straight through the gusts*
> *Of fear and fury,*
> *Straight through:*
> Where are you going?
>
> I'm just going to school.

Here we go to meet
The hydra-headed day,
Here we go to meet
The maelstrom—

Can my voice be an angel-on-the-spot,
An amen corner?
Can my voice take you there,
Gallant girl with a notebook,
Up, up from the shadows of gallows trees
To the other shore:
A globe bathed in light,
A chalkboard blooming with equations—

I have never seen the likes of you,
Pioneer in dark glasses:
You won't show the mob your eyes,
But I know your gaze,
Steady-on-the-North-Star, burning-

With their jerry-rigged faith,
Their spear of the American flag,
How could they dare to believe
You're someone sacred?:
Nigger, burr-headed girl,
Where are you going?

I'm just going to school.

TWENTY-SIX

Hazel's family kept her very busy. As she liked to say, there was always someone being hatched, matched, or dispatched. Her children grew, married young (though not quite as young as she), and in some instances, remarried young, too; by procreation and acquisition, she amassed a slew of grandchildren.

Her family filled the void left by the church from which she had strayed, gradually at first and then decisively. Though she still read the Bible (and could rattle off its books in order), she came to wonder whether it was all made up. When prayers began with "Our Father," she wanted to pipe in "Our *Mother*." She questioned her church's racial attitudes: nothing she'd seen in Scripture talked about separating people by color. She also questioned its hypocrisy, especially after one prominent churchman ran his finger up the back of her leg while purring about how pretty she was. Later on Hazel had trouble remembering the names of her fellow parishioners—her memory was sometimes selective, especially for unpleasant things—but they certainly remembered *her*: emotional, exotic, erratic, erotic Hazel. They remembered potluck dinners at her house, where she had painted a rainbow (actually, some abstract colored swirls) on the wall, kept a Buddha on the floor, and had them sit on pillows rather than in chairs.

Periodically Hazel stopped attending church, only to come back, seek forgiveness, then quit again. Her growing skepticism threatened her marriage, not just because Antoine continued to go there with the children, but because such rebellion—anything that might embarrass her husband—was something no upstanding southern wife was supposed to do. As she grew disenchanted with the church, the church grew disenchanted with her. At some point in the late 1970s she was "disfellowshipped," excommunicated. She felt liberated, but very much alone. Still craving some sort of spirituality, she began exploring New Age alternatives: Shirley MacLaine, Earl Nightingale, Tony Robbins, Wayne Dyer. Wanting to dance, and to slake her interest in foreign cultures, she began studying belly dancing, traveling to Memphis, Austin, and Oklahoma City for workshops. To rehearse, she covered up those colored patches on her living room wall with mirrors.

To pay for all the exotic costumes, all those hand-sewn beads, she began doing singing telegrams. Several times a week, she would don top hat, vest, black bow tie, black satin shorts, fishnet hose, and stiletto heels, and, for fifteen to twenty dollars a pop plus tips, she would perform. On Valentine's Day there might be eight or nine stops. Other times, there were luaus, in skimpy tropical getups. Most recipients loved it, though some, like the police chief of Benton, were not charmed. The more straitlaced people around her were appalled, and Antoine probably wasn't thrilled, either, though, characteristically—he'd learned long ago that Hazel had to do her thing—he never said much about it. For adult birthdays, she would always begin with "You Must Have

Hazel as a belly dancer, sometime around 1987 (Courtesy Hazel Bryan Massery)

Been a Beautiful Baby." For children, she became Posy the Clown, making balloon animals and performing magic tricks.

She stopped voting automatically for whomever Antoine supported, usually Republicans. She became increasingly political, branching out into peace activism and social work. One program focused on self-esteem for teenagers. She urged that the subject be taught in the state's public schools, and, to that end, joined a delegation which, in 1990, met with Governor Bill Clinton. She took black teenagers who rarely had left Little Rock on field trips, climbing Pinnacle Mountain (some refused, for fear of falling off) and picking strawberries. And, putting her course work in child psychology to use, she counseled young unwed mothers,

Hazel with participants in Teen Outreach Program atop Pinnacle Mountain, Arkansas, June 1991 (Courtesy Hazel Bryan Massery)

many of them black, on parenting skills. One was a twenty-six-year-old named Victoria Brown, who was about to have her sixth child. Hazel helped Brown, whose children were temporarily in foster care; she was, Brown thought, one of the few whites who didn't assume she was bad because of her situation. Long after the class ended and Brown's children had been returned to her, they kept in touch. On Brown's birthdays, Hazel brought her presents; when one of Brown's children died, Hazel and Antoine brought food to her home.

All this do-gooding with blacks, Antoine joked, was really her way of atoning for the picture. And maybe he was right. Her whole outlook toward black people had changed. At the Barnes and Noble in Little Rock, she perused the sections on black history. She bought Juan Williams's companion book to *Eyes on the*

Prize and Gordon Allport's *The Nature of Prejudice*. She read David Shipler's study of black-white relations in America, *A Country of Strangers*, a book Elizabeth herself had, without ever knowing it, helped inspire.[1] And, after the syndicated columnist George F. Will praised it, she bought a book by the black author and commentator Shelby Steele. She also picked up the souvenir book of front pages from the *Democrat* and *Gazette* during the schools crisis, including her appearance in both papers. Sometimes, this created friction with her family. When Hazel's mother called some relatives who had been romantically involved with blacks "nigger lovers," Hazel objected. "Well, Mother, are we not supposed to love 'niggers'?" she asked. "Well," the older woman replied, "you're not supposed to *marry* them." "Why not?" Hazel replied. Her mother grew flustered. "Well, b-b-because we're better than them." "Why are we better than them?" The older woman grew more flustered. "Because our skin is white," she finally said. Hazel didn't press the point; she'd picked up what she'd set out to learn. Hazel also had it out with Antoine, who, she felt, had retained vestiges of racial prejudice himself.

Hazel maintained few ties with her past. In Dallas for an ice skating competition in the mid-1980s, she had run into Sammie Dean Parker, who had invited her and Antoine to the home she shared there with her second husband.[2] They'd had fun together, talking in the easy way that only old friends can, but it did not rekindle the relationship. The two had taken very separate journeys. Sammie Dean admired Hazel's adventurousness, but *bellydancing?* And while Hazel had lost her faith, Sammie Dean had discovered hers, dedicating her life to Jesus Christ. Hazel, in fact, had few real friends. Her life was her family, and even there, she had no soulmates or confidantes. Those intellectual adventures and spiritual journeys she took, she took alone. Isolated physically, provincial by background but worldly by temperament and aspiration, Hazel didn't really fit anywhere.

She had setbacks. In 1990 she had been carjacked, forced at what she thought was knifepoint to drive her assailant until she purposely crashed and fled. She began locking doors, staying home nights, checking bathroom stalls before entering. Like Elizabeth, she came to hate elevators, especially when someone stood behind her. She felt less inclined to help people. Several times she testified at her attacker's parole hearings, trying to keep him behind bars. But generally, life was good. With some money inherited from Antoine's family, in 1987 the couple invested twenty thousand dollars in an Arkansas company—Wal-Mart—and as its stock split and split again, they had begun to provide for their eventual retirement.

Hazel still wanted to make the world a better place. When *Murder, She Wrote* became popular, she decided to try and sell a program called "Love, She Wrote," collecting clippings from *Parade* and *Reader's Digest* on great acts of human kindness. (She thought of contacting Jane Fonda or Ted Turner with the idea and, after taking a five-week screenwriting course, maybe putting something together herself.) Her civic involvement deepened. Surely no one concerned with the Little Rock schools crisis noticed in March 1990 when a local newspaper reporter wrote about the chairwoman of the subcommittee on recycling of the Solid Waste Study Citizens Advisory Committee, one Hazel Massery, chastising a local official for neglect. But it marked the first time that Hazel, now forty-eight years old, had appeared in print for thirty-three years, and the first time ever for something besides attempting suicide or badgering a black schoolgirl or decrying desegregation. A year later, the paper published its first picture of her since 1957, taken at a luncheon at the governor's mansion honoring volunteers for the Centers for Youth and Families.

Occasionally, Hazel would tell people she was *that* girl, always appending how ashamed she was of what she'd done. They'd invariably gasp: so archetypal had that face become that it was hard to believe it belonged to anyone, let alone to her, let alone evolved. Like Elizabeth, Hazel did not discuss the photograph with her children, nor was there any call to. It wasn't on television much when they were young, and once it was, her children weren't particularly interested. "That's my mama!" Hazel's daughter, sixteen years old at the time, had exclaimed in school when it popped up during the twenty-fifth anniversary celebrations, but her daughter hadn't been upset or embarrassed: the woman she knew had always taught her tolerance.

As for her apology, no one knew about it, nor, it seemed, would they. Hazel wasn't about to broadcast it. And while it would have been nice if someone had reported it, that never seemed to happen. The press seemed content simply to run the picture over and over, without wondering who that angry white girl was or what had ever become of her. Will Counts, who had quit newspaper work in 1963 to teach photojournalism at Indiana University, never did try tracking Hazel down. "The rest of the world didn't get the apology, I'm afraid," Hazel told Tom Wagy, a professor at Texas A&M University who interviewed her for a book in 1991. Elizabeth continued to say nothing about it. Once again, Hazel thought of contacting her; she knew that an Eckford

—Elizabeth's stepmother—taught at a nearby school, and called her. When Mrs. Eckford wasn't reachable (she was on medical leave) Hazel shelved the idea.

Sometime around 1990 Hazel became involved in Peace Links, a group of women agitating against nuclear war. She read extensively on the subject, hiding the books under the bed so Antoine wouldn't think she'd become a Communist or something. Through a local political activist named Jean Gordon, she met Sara Alderman Murphy, who was writing a book on the campaign to reopen the schools Faubus had closed in 1958. When Murphy interviewed her in June 1992, Hazel described her path from closed-mindedness to public service and racial healing. "You're doing some pretty neat things," Murphy told her. She also recounted her apology.

Murphy in turn mentioned Hazel to the local Associated Press reporter, Peggy Harris. *The girl in the picture? Really?* It was a terrific story, and Harris quickly arranged to interview Hazel. Hazel struck her as colorful, energetic, sincere, and contrite, racially enlightened in spite of her background. (On the subject of civil rights, Hazel told her, "My parents have come maybe *this far* since the fifties," holding up two fingers about a quarter of an inch apart.) Harris had an idea: how about reuniting Elizabeth and Hazel and writing about the two of them? But Daisy Bates told her Elizabeth was a recluse (an outcome for which Bates felt herself partly to blame); the reunion never materialized, and Harris didn't write up the half story she had. One reunion that did come off was for Central's "Lost Class" of 1959, the class to which both Elizabeth and Hazel had belonged; in 1994 it marked the thirty-five years that had passed since it *hadn't* graduated. Hazel attended with Sammie Dean. The two even joined in the group picture, the first time they had been photographed together since . . . well, that wasn't the kind of thing to discuss that night, or at any Central reunion.

TWENTY-SEVEN

For the final four years of her life, Birdie Eckford lived with Elizabeth. During this time Elizabeth came to realize that what people had always regarded in her mother as eccentricity was really mental illness. She heard voices and continued to follow her strange remedies, like rubbing anti-freeze on her face or writing things down on brown paper, then urinating in a jar. In January 1992, Birdie passed away. Though she was seventy-two, in one sense she had died too soon: Elizabeth had never thanked her for letting her go to, then stay in, Central. Only many years later did she realize the high price her mother had paid for that decision.

Birdie's proximity and decline only added to the tensions in Elizabeth's life. A few months after her mother's death, Elizabeth again placed her sons, now sixteen and fourteen, in foster care, ostentatiously threatening to hit Erin in front of a case worker when the office seemed disinclined to take the case. It was a desperate step, but she had her reasons. Her neighborhood had grown still more dangerous. Once, with her boys, she'd been mugged. No one made a big deal out of it; the police just treated Elizabeth like any other poor person. But after that, she and her sons carried small pieces of iron pipe. As she could detect from their sudden preference for red clothes, the boys had begun hanging around one of the notorious street gangs that had come to terrorize neighborhoods like theirs, and she wanted to get them away from that. She was also afraid she might hurt them. Over the next fifteen months they stayed in various places, including, for a time, with her sister Anna.

Neither of the boys ever attended Central; Erin preferred magnet schools offering courses in math and science, while school didn't interest Calvin at all. Even had they wanted to go to Central, Elizabeth would have been opposed; black boys, she believed, did not do well there. In any case, both skipped school so regularly that the juvenile court intervened. The case landed before Judge Wiley Branton, Jr. Here was another twist of history: Branton's father and namesake, one of the first black lawyers in Arkansas, had worked closely with Thurgood Marshall on the original Little Rock desegregation case. Now, as a family division judge, the younger Branton was dealing with the next generation of Eckfords, and the next generation of problems.

Branton instantly recognized Elizabeth's name and face: the picture had been with him forever. But he had never met or listened to her, and he was struck by how extremely intelligent and well-spoken she was. Normally, he would confront a parent with wayward children: you needed to shake them up, too. But Elizabeth, he knew, had already been confronted, and had suffered, enough. So rather than meet with the family as a group, he sent her out of the room and talked to the boys alone. Your mama is a hero, he told them. She had paid an enormous price so that they could get a quality education; the least they could do was to get off their asses and go back to school. But Elizabeth's sons were unmoved by her history. In fact, they found it irksome: because of it, people were forever expecting greater things from them. In fairness, their mother's struggles seemed remote: they, too, had to fight to survive. And could Erin have cared, even if he'd wanted to? For the first several months of his recent bout with foster care, he had been in a psychiatric hospital. Elizabeth knew her sons were indifferent to her story. When Calvin put up a poster of the Little Rock Nine in his bedroom, it was, she suspected, just to cover a hole in the wall.

As Elizabeth walked around town or waited for the bus, few in white Little Rock would have recognized her, or remembered what she had done. But in black Little Rock, they well knew who she was, and heroic as she'd been, she was also a cautionary tale. She personified for some the price paid for integration—a price, these people had concluded, that had been too high. Black people talked about her in hushed, pitying tones. Some seemed almost embarrassed by her, or perhaps embarrassed at themselves for allowing her to slip so far. "The people in town dubbed her as being crazy, weird," someone who'd long known her recalled. "People wrote her off as damaged, eccentric. But nobody came to her and said 'Elizabeth, is there anything we as a community can do for you?' That didn't happen. All I ever heard in the beauty shop or restaurant was *'I saw the Eckford girl today, I saw her walking down Main Street. She sure did look a sight.'* You heard the empathy. But you also heard the shame."

Then Annie Abrams came along. Abrams, a longtime local civil rights activist, was energetic and determined; it was hard to turn her down. She encouraged Elizabeth to speak publicly about her experiences; it would not just enlighten others, she argued, but help Elizabeth herself move forward. In June 1991 Elizabeth agreed to meet with some high school students from Toledo, Ohio. The session, arranged by Dr. Helen Cooks of the University of Toledo, took place at the Hoover United Methodist Church in Little Rock. Standing up in a pew, summoning her courage, maintaining her composure, Elizabeth praised the visitors for venturing into what she called "a strange land like the South." Then she told her story. For the boys and girls, who had studied the civil rights movement and met several of its luminaries (Coretta Scott King among them), hearing Elizabeth was profoundly affecting. Seeing her, though, was sobering. All of the others relished being icons, but Elizabeth was a living, breathing casualty: in her, the past lived on. "She wasn't assassinated or hung, but she was definitely bleeding," was how one of the students, William Davis, remembered it.

For years, Elizabeth had been on a regimen of medication and therapy designed, in large part, to keep her from killing herself. But when she switched antidepressants in 1992, her world began to brighten. Her emotional palette suddenly extended beyond the blackness of anger and despair. She could sense again when things were funny, and grew more tolerant of people. She started to read again, stocking up on books from the thrift store. Some—the novels of Charles Dickens; *Robinson Crusoe; The Call of the Wild*— she remembered from childhood; others, like the works of Plato and Aristotle, were new to her. They complemented the mysteries, true-crime sagas, and police procedurals she'd loved since she was young, and had begun picking up again as well.

In 1992 the organizers from Toledo persuaded Elizabeth to appear at a conference there. Her mother had died only a few days earlier, but Elizabeth wasn't deterred: for one thing, she needed the honorarium—$750—to help defray the cost of her mother's burial. (She took the money under the table so as not to jeopardize her disability payment.) Elizabeth spoke before a large and appreciative audience. Several of the Nine were there; one organizer was struck by how little attention the others paid to Elizabeth. Terrence Roberts spoke as well, and was startled afterward when Elizabeth lit into him for, at least as she saw it, discussing their trials so blithely. He had never realized how affected she remained by her experiences.

For many years, Ernest Green had been the most visible of the Nine. It was he who had been the first to graduate, the one most often interviewed, and, as an official in the Carter administration and, later, an executive at Lehman Brothers, the most conventionally successful. When the Disney Company came to town in 1992 to film *The Ernest Green Story,* Elizabeth agreed to work with it, though again, her reasons were pragmatic: her roof leaked. Once more, Elizabeth's walk was re-created. This time around, the locals weren't so eager to shout "Nigger!" at the actress portraying her; the word had become more taboo. The crowd around Elizabeth was also downsized; all those extras were expensive. To re-create the 1950s version of the neighborhood, many of the now-deteriorating houses along Park had to be given fresh coats of paint. The film premiered in Central's auditorium in January 1993; President-elect Bill Clinton attended. Elizabeth came, as usual, by bus and sat, as usual, alone and unrecognized, until she was about to leave. She was then brought backstage to meet Clinton and suddenly got tongue-tied. Fortunately, Clinton talked enough for them both.

Elizabeth soon resumed her reclusive ways. But in the fall of

1996, a tenth-grader in Uniontown, Kansas, named Heather Jurgensen learned of Elizabeth from *Eyes on the Prize*. Uniontown—population two hundred, zero blacks—was no Little Rock, but Jurgensen felt drawn to Elizabeth: she was fifteen, as Elizabeth had been in 1957, and also new in school. The theme for that year's National History Day competition, which Uniontown High School was entering, was "Taking a Stand in History," and Elizabeth's story seemed perfect. Elizabeth took her call warily; it helped, though, that Heather was a student and didn't act as if she knew everything already, the way journalists did. Working with Heather also offered Elizabeth a chance to teach, something she had always wanted to do. Within days Jurgensen was in Little Rock with her history teacher, Norm Conard, and two classmates, Jeremy Johnston and David Foster. They set up their primitive video camera, and began questioning Elizabeth. She told them that if she got emotional, to let her be; she needed to work things through.

And emotional she soon got. The youthful cameraman zoomed in on her well-rubbed eyes, which she began to rub some more. Soon, with a rustling sound, Elizabeth put down the microphone and walked off, leaving the camera focused on an empty chair. Elizabeth reminded Foster, who'd grown up on a farm, of an animal who had been whipped when young. But she quickly returned, and grew stronger, though, self-conscious as always about her teeth, she covered her mouth as she talked. She avoided sensitive topics, speaking instead about her two friends from speech class, Ann Williams and Ken Reinhardt. She had seen neither since Central; the two boys quickly tracked them down. As a result, in late May 1997 Reinhardt and his wife, who lived in Louisville, had an emotional reunion with Elizabeth at her home, in a part of town Reinhardt had always avoided as a boy. In June, Elizabeth went to Washington, where the History Day competition was held. She brought two outfits with her, each black and gold: she was enveloping herself in colors which, until recently, had repelled her. And she struggled through more interviews. "Even today she can't complete a sentence about her experiences without tears," Tara Mack wrote in the *Washington Post*. "Her single tissue is shredded before she gets to lunch."

Elizabeth let a few other outsiders in. Reading about how the Mennonite Disaster Service had recently repaired nearby College Station, Arkansas, following a tornado, she'd asked the group's local liaison, the Rev. Hezekiah Stewart of the Mount Nebo African Methodist Church, if it might heal her own beleaguered house, now overrun with mice. Soon, a team came by. "She is a very intelligent lady still bearing scars of 40 years ago," Vernelle Voth, whose husband was the crew chief, wrote afterward. "She becomes very uncomfortable when more than one or two people are around her." But that changed. Elizabeth even told the workers where she hid her house key, so that they could fix things when she was out.

As she slowly became more engaged, Elizabeth grew curious about the history of the schools crisis—how it had been written up, how widely available it was. In Little Rock's bookstores and libraries, she learned, there was almost nothing on the subject, and what there was was either incomplete or unreliable. The Nine themselves hadn't always helped. Ernest Green's recollections, Elizabeth complained, invariably came with a happy ending, a triumphant "topspin." He wasn't exactly fibbing; it was just that, in the process of becoming what she called an "acceptable Negro," he'd blocked out anything unpleasant. (In the *New Yorker* article she'd banished from her army base, Green described the early stages of the Central crisis as "a lot of fun" and "great.") Then, in her 1994 memoir, *Warriors Don't Cry,* Melba Patillo Beals had gone to the other extreme. By focusing on the Nine and highlighting the misery they'd all endured, she had filled an important hole in the literature. But she seemed to claim for herself the experiences and traumas of them all. Privately, several of the Nine considered Beals's account untrustworthy or worse, but, determined to present a united front, they never said so, at least out loud.[1]

When Oprah Winfrey brought seven of the Nine together with four white contemporaries from Central in January 1996, Elizabeth declined to join them. And she had to be coaxed into participating in the fortieth anniversary celebrations in 1997, even though they promised to be the most glorious yet: President Bill Clinton would preside. Ernest paid her way to Las Vegas, where the Nine met to plan for the occasion; later, when she called Elizabeth to talk about the program, Carlotta was forced to ask an elderly neighbor to walk over to Elizabeth's house and urge her to pick up her phone. Elizabeth gradually became involved, meeting with planners of the new visitor center the National Park Service planned to open in the old Mobil station near the school. And when one of several submissions for a garden honoring the Nine moved her to tears—it featured nine trees plus nine benches (an homage to the spot where Elizabeth's journey that day had ended)—that was the design selected.

Also involved in the commemorations was Elizabeth Jacoway of the University of Arkansas at Little Rock, who was writing a detailed history of the schools crisis, a task for which she was peculiarly well suited.[2] Jacoway had interviewed dozens of participants, including Elizabeth (in 1994) and Hazel (in early 1996, joined by Pete Daniel of the Smithsonian Institution, who was writing a book on the South in the 1950s). Having pondered Hazel's face for decades, Jacoway had been expecting an unregenerate, uneducated hick and was surprised by how articulate and remorseful Hazel was. So was Daniel, who was struck as well by the contrast between Hazel and Sammie Dean: Sammie Dean was out to erase or launder her past; Hazel was willing to exhume and explore. And repent.

Someone had suggested that an entire wall of the new visitor center be devoted to the photograph. The final version was only poster-sized, but it greeted everyone by the entrance. Surprisingly, it was not Counts's image that was selected but Jenkins's: it happened to be the first one the designer had located, and its shape—square—may have lent itself better to display. (Counts was gracious: Jenkins's picture also told the story, he said.) Jenkins would not be at the opening, though, assuming he'd have wanted to be.[3] But Jacoway had another idea: subordinating the original photograph to a contemporary picture of Elizabeth and Hazel together—one symbolizing the racial progress Little Rock had made. Hazel, she knew, would like nothing more. And while aware that Elizabeth made few public appearances, she thought that maybe Annie Abrams could persuade her.

Nothing came of that idea. But Will Counts was thinking similar thoughts. Newly retired from Indiana University, where he had nurtured dozens of journalistic disciples, he had returned to Arkansas to chronicle the changes at Central since 1957. He'd tried reaching Elizabeth, writing her (and getting no response), seeking assistance from Abrams, even going to Elizabeth's house once, all without success. Elizabeth never bothered learning who had taken the famous photograph, or the kind of man he was—to her, he was simply someone from the largely hostile local press. But as the anniversary neared, she had gone incognito to one of his presentations, during which he had praised her dignity and bravery. She had gone up to him afterward, and the ice was broken. Now Counts needed to find the white girl.

TWENTY-EIGHT

ots of students, black and white, identified with Elizabeth. Anyone who'd ever felt abused, or alienated, or lonely, or just different from everyone else—and who in high school hasn't?—would have. But Linda Monk, a young Harvard Law School graduate from Mississippi who had written on constitutional history and civil rights, was different. She also empathized with Hazel.

As a seventh-grader in 1970, living in the part of the state where Jefferson Davis had once raised cotton, Monk had tried to keep a black classmate out of a school play about Rip Van Winkle. How, she had asked, could blacks portray upstate New Yorkers of Dutch descent? She was haunted afterward by what she'd done, and many years later had called the black girl to apologize. So when she learned of Hazel—she had used the photograph in a book about the Bill of Rights—she grew curious about her. "I often wonder about Hazel Bryan," she had written in the *Baltimore Sun* in 1994, in a piece marking the fortieth anniversary of the *Brown* decision. "What became of her? Did her attitudes ever change, or will she take her bigotry to her grave? I ask these questions because there but for the grace of God go I."

Now, three years later, as a different anniversary loomed, Monk revisited those questions. After doing a bit of homework, she called various Masserys in the Little Rock directory and, upon reaching Hazel, said what Hazel so longed to hear: that she wanted to tell her story. Any misgivings Hazel harbored evaporated once Monk described her own brush with racism: here, Hazel concluded, was someone who wouldn't belittle or stereotype her. "There's more to me than one moment," Hazel told her. It was a good line; Monk asked whether she could quote her. "Please do!" Hazel exclaimed. They spoke for almost an hour.

On September 4, 1997—forty years to the day after Hazel had stalked Elizabeth—Monk's article about Hazel appeared in the *Chicago Tribune*. It described Hazel's efforts at redemption, including her phone call to Elizabeth. It marked the first time Hazel's story had been told, at least in a place where it would be widely read. Now that they'd been spoon-fed the information, all those journalists who had never managed to find Hazel, especially those in her own backyard, would surely clamor for her. But naïve about such things, Hazel and Antoine left for ten days in the Florida Keys just before it was published. Sure enough, when they returned, their answering machine was full. She spoke first to *Nightline*. After an inauspicious start—a black technician lit into her for, well, being *that* girl—Hazel got to tell her story. "We were just in the crowd and it was more like, 'Hey, this is fun, you know, it's exciting,'" she said. "I hope you get the part in there that I'm truly sorry and that I apologize for my behavior," she added as the interview ended. "It was uncivilized, and I have grown." That snippet was included, but the program omitted what to her was something equally important: that she'd apologized to Elizabeth *thirty-five years earlier*. Maybe that was why some viewers found her sincerity suspect. "Positive behavior evidently had no value to Niteline [*sic*]," she wrote afterward in the journal she occasionally kept.

Two days later, she spoke with Michael Leahy of the *Democrat-Gazette*.[1] Treading carefully, fearful that she might yet change her mind, Leahy did not bring a photographer. But he brought the photograph, and handed it to Hazel. She gripped it hard, Leahy wrote. But the real truth, he went on, was that the photo had a grip on her: it would not let her go. As they spoke, she scratched unconsciously at it, as if to rub it out. Leahy found himself staring at Hazel—staring at that mouth. It was surreal to see it now as a living, protean thing, and to hear the sounds of reasonability and conciliation coming out of it. It was even harder to connect the clenched jaw of the young girl in the too-tight dress and the pleasant smile of the middle-aged woman in denim sitting across from him.

Privately, Leahy thought Hazel a bit self-pitying. "I'd love to sit down with Elizabeth sometime," she told him. "That'd be wonderful, that'd be miraculous. But the press doesn't want that story. They want to keep me where I am in that picture. I've just about given up hope on that." And he thought her memory a bit selective. How could someone recall exactly what she wore one day forty years ago, but forget mouthing off to the cameras twenty-four hours later? Still, Hazel seemed to be doing her best, and she didn't duck. He thanked her for her candor. Soon, people all over Little Rock would know Hazel's story. Before that, she believed, there was one conversation she needed to have: with Victoria Brown, the unwed black mother from her parenting class. Hazel had never told her of her peculiar claim to fame, and she wanted the younger woman to hear it first from her, rather than stumble

upon it in the paper or on television. Brown was dumbfounded—
"*Hazel, are you sure you don't have a twin somewhere?*" she asked—
and chalked it up to immaturity: everyone does dumb things
when they're young.

Leahy also interviewed Elizabeth. He marveled at her intelligence, too, and wondered what she might have been—a college
professor, perhaps—had life treated her more fairly. As Carlotta
and Melba held her hands, Elizabeth also spoke to *Newsweek*. On
September 19 she was back in Central's massive auditorium, for
another presentation by Will Counts. "Don't let me go without
saying how delighted I am that this woman is in this auditorium,"
Counts told the crowd. "To me she is the real symbol of the civil
rights movement." The audience applauded. In the most famous of
Counts's pictures, noted the *Democrat-Gazette*, "a woman sneers
at Eckford behind her back." It didn't identify that "woman." Nor
did Elizabeth, but she did tell the gathering that the woman had
apologized.

The day before, while planting tulips, Hazel had mused to Antoine about how nice it would be to have a *second* picture of
her and Elizabeth, one that would supplement—and maybe even
supplant—the first. By putting ideas out into the universe, Hazel
believed, one could sometimes bring things to pass; in fact, nothing cosmic was required. Hazel was eager. Elizabeth was curious.
When Elizabeth cut the black and gold ribbon at the dedication of
the new visitor center on September 20 (she folded it up and put it
in her purse as a keepsake), Counts looked on. Afterward, Jacoway
gave him Hazel's number. Later that day, he spoke to both women.
They agreed to meet the following Wednesday. But why wait that
long? Perhaps someone else would have the same idea! So on

Sunday he called them back. Now they'd get together the following morning.

Counts took care to rent a van with Arkansas plates (so it wouldn't look at all conspicuous) and dark windows. He and his wife picked up Hazel at the new visitor center, then headed for Elizabeth's. The timing, Hazel felt, was propitious: it was her father's eighty-seventh birthday. The van entered Elizabeth's neighborhood, then turned left onto West 18th Street. The three of them got out and walked up the short brick pathway, past the last of that summer's irises and tea roses, to Elizabeth's front door. They were an odd-looking delegation, three middle-aged white emissaries from another world. They rang the bell, to the right of the iron bars. Forty years and eighteen days after their first encounter, Elizabeth and Hazel were about to have another.

TWENTY-NINE

For a moment, the two women faced one another. This rendezvous, unlike the last, would not be made memorable by their clothes. Elizabeth wore jeans and a sweat shirt; seeing her now, rounded out, even stocky, it was hard to visualize the slight and fragile girl of forty years earlier. Hazel had already dressed for the photograph, of course, in a beige pants suit beneath a jacket with a blue floral print. She wasn't crazy about the outfit, but she'd been too busy to find anything better.

Elizabeth greeted Counts and his wife warmly. Still imagining Hazel as a blonde, she was taken a bit aback to behold a brunette. "Hi, I've always wanted to meet you," Elizabeth told her. Hazel thanked Elizabeth for seeing her. The encounter was inevitably more freighted for her: as was her wont, she hoped for something grand, something symbolic, while Elizabeth was stoic, clinical, wary. "You're mighty brave to face the cameras again," she told Hazel as the three visitors entered the house. Hazel found the remark puzzling: Elizabeth seemed to be warning her of risks she herself couldn't foresee. Well, the papers had hinted at her prickliness. A line from the Dale Carnegie course Antoine had once taken popped into her head: if you see a fish on the wall, ask about the fish. When she brought up Elizabeth's flowers, it seemed to break the ice a bit. It was a sad house, Hazel thought: dark, with none of the pillows or bric-a-brac or pictures or wall hangings that decorated hers.

Elizabeth had saved up to buy two new outfits for the commemoration; the question now before the house was which of them to wear. As Vivian Counts remembered it, Elizabeth turned to both her and Hazel for guidance. Hazel recalled things differently: she felt excluded. Elizabeth, who had gradually restored colors to her wardrobe, ultimately opted for a navy blue pinstriped jacket, red vest, white blouse and a navy blue skirt. Then they hopped in the van, with Hazel and Elizabeth, like two teenagers being fixed up by their parents, thrown next to one another in the back. Elizabeth spoke animatedly with Will and Vivian Counts; again, Hazel felt ignored. Vivian Counts treated Elizabeth overprotectively, Hazel thought, as if she were made of glass. Only when Elizabeth asked Hazel where she lived did things thaw a bit. The whole way, in fact, Elizabeth was thinking, "lamb to the slaughter." While feeling no particular bond with Hazel, she pitied her: she was a naïf about to reenter the racial maelstrom; soon she would find herself in over her head.

At the visitor center, Counts ran into Skip Rutherford, a Little Rock public relations executive who was helping plan the commemoration. After swearing him to secrecy, Counts told him who was in his car and what was about to happen. Rutherford was amazed: here, he thought, was something the whole world would want to see. Counts had already scouted possible locations, including in front of Central's famous façade. But he started at the side, where competing newsmen were less likely to congregate.

The two women lined up, and Counts began taking his pictures. Elizabeth looked comfortable, even ebullient, her eyes narrowed, her right hand up to her chest, as if she'd just heard a good joke; to her left, Hazel also smiled, though more tentatively. The new photograph was static, lacking the drama of the first. And it would be in color, which would rob it of its documentary feel. But Counts couldn't have been happier. He was thinking not so much about making great art, but about making a point, about the power of human beings to grow, and to forgive. And these two women actually looked comfortable with each other; they weren't just putting on a show. Watching it was, for him, a near-religious experience, one of the most thrilling moments in his life.

Though she had parked by the school, Hazel accompanied the Countses when they took Elizabeth home, just so she could spend a few more moments with her. Hazel asked Elizabeth for pointers on how to handle the inevitable attention. "Screen all of your calls," Elizabeth advised. Again, Hazel told Elizabeth how much she appreciated the chance to be with her. It was, she said, a pity so much time had passed before she could offer the public apology she'd always wanted to make. Elizabeth recalled that she had long ago told interviewers about Hazel's change of heart—but that, lamentably, it had gone over their heads.

Before they separated, Counts asked each of them what they made of the meeting. Hazel quoted Einstein, on the difficulty of solving problems, and George Bernard Shaw, on passing on values to future generations. Elizabeth was more circumspect: she wouldn't presume to tell anybody what it all meant. To Hazel, though, she was more direct. "Don't make too much of this picture," she cautioned. Given the euphoria of the moment it was a deflating thing to say, but the original picture had appeared in countless places and, to Elizabeth's mind at least, little had changed; by lowering Hazel's expectations, Elizabeth thought she was doing her a favor, that she'd be cushioning any blows. But in this instance it was Elizabeth who was naïve. A community intent on burying its past was all but certain to seize upon the photograph. And did.

On September 23 the *Democrat-Gazette* gave over much of its front page to it. "40 years later, tormentor and target meet again," the headline declared. Alongside the new picture, and considerably smaller, was Counts's original photograph. Accompanying them were Leahy's profile of Hazel—"Prisoner of a photo: The private journey of Hazel Massery"—and an account of the reunion. "Hazel Massery beams," he wrote, "wondering whether at long last she gets to step out of one photograph and into another."

Some found the picture startling. Little Rock's mayor, Jim Dailey, knew Antoine and Hazel from a club of business owners to which they all belonged, but had never suspected she was *that* girl. There was skepticism, too: the anchors on one local news show debated Hazel's genuineness. But as a general matter, the picture bathed the commemoration, already blessed by a local boy turned president, in hope. If it didn't quite upstage Clinton's impending return, it sure came close. What better way to capture how far Little Rock had traveled? If such archetypal antagonists could reconcile, then *nothing* was impossible! Saddled with images from 1957 wherever they went, embarrassed to say where they were from, dismissed as racist yahoos when they did, many in Little Rock saw Hazel's reemergence and penitence, and Elizabeth's apparent acceptance, as signs that they, too, might finally be forgiven. Having

Elizabeth and Hazel, again on the front page, September 23, 1997
(Courtesy *Arkansas Democrat-Gazette;* Will Counts Collection,
Indiana University Archives)

once embodied Little Rock's original sin, Hazel had now given it instant absolution.

Some discussed the new photograph in epic, even apocalyptic terms. "The beauty of the God-made deep black skin of the one seems to enhance the same-made and equally beautiful ice-white skin of the other," wrote the Rev. Will Campbell, one of the ministers who had accompanied the black students on their abortive first day at Central. The rapprochement, he declared, was "the stuff of Scripture . . . a glimpse of the Promised Land." For forty years, wrote Deborah Halter in the *Democrat-Gazette*, she had assumed the Hazel of the picture to be an adult, and had loathed "this almost mythical character standing like an icon of Southern racial hatred." Now she realized that Hazel had been *fifteen years old*, an empty vessel into whom others—her parents? her teachers? her minister?—had poured all their prejudices. The hometown paper heaped praise on them both. "The apology came from the real Hazel Bryan Massery, the decent woman who had been hidden all those years by a fleeting image," it declared. "And the graceful acceptance of that apology was but another act of dignity in the life of Elizabeth Eckford."

Little Rock's congressman, Vic Snyder, carried poster-sized copies of both pictures onto the floor of the United States House of Representatives. "We learned from your courage in the past," he said, presumably referring to Elizabeth. "Today we learn from their wisdom, about the ability to forgive, move on and learn from the mistakes of the past." Quickly, people sought ways to extend the euphoria. Sensing its public-relations potential, Skip Rutherford decreed that the new photograph be enlarged into a poster.

A few people—Sammie Dean Parker, Victoria Brown, Joe Holland (the man with the smiling face behind her in the original picture)—called Hazel to congratulate her. And she got some encouraging mail. Jean Whitehead of Little Rock wrote to say that tears of joy had run down her cheeks as she read the article. To Diane Lyons, whose father had coached at Central, the story was the best part of the entire anniversary. After reading about Hazel, Sherrill Heerwagen wrote, it was *she* who was now ashamed—for misjudging Hazel on *Nightline*. "I am sure I am not the only one this morning to have a change of heart about you," she said.

Hazel got little reinforcement from her children. They seemed equally uncomfortable with both ends of their mother's story: what she'd originally done, and what she was doing now. They just wanted it to go away. Her mother's reaction wasn't so clear. Pauline Bryan took the paper, but for days afterward she said nothing to her daughter about what she'd just done. Finally, unable to stand it any longer, Hazel brought it up. Had she seen the new picture? Yes. Silence. Had she read the story? Some of it. More silence. Well, what did she *think* of it? She didn't know. Hazel finally dropped the subject. It hurt her that while so many people were proud of what she'd done, the person who mattered most evidently wasn't. Hazel's sister wasn't so restrained. She said that their father, who had died the year before, was rolling over in his grave. In fact, even metaphorically, it probably wasn't true: Sanford Bryan's racial attitudes had moderated toward the end of his life, and Hazel thought he'd have gotten a kick out of what she'd done. He usually had.

THIRTY

I t was June Shih's first big break. Only a few days before Bill Clinton was to speak at the fortieth anniversary celebrations at Central, the man assigned to write his remarks had an illness in the family and couldn't deliver. So the president's chief speechwriter, Michael Waldman, put Shih on the case. Befitting an epic occasion—Clinton reflecting on one of the formative moments in his childhood, one that had infused his attitudes toward race relations and helped shape his whole political life—Waldman would handle most of the job. But he asked Shih, who had joined the speechwriting team only a few months earlier, to come up with a beginning. It made sense, for before going to work for the Clintons, Shih, twenty-five years old at the time, had been a newspaper reporter. She knew how to write a lead.

Pretty much all Shih had learned about Little Rock she had picked up watching *Crisis at Central High,* the 1981 made-for-television movie featuring Joanne Woodward as Mrs. Huckaby and an anonymous actress as an anonymous Elizabeth stand-in. Shih remembered it well, especially a scene with a lonely black girl at a bus stop. But to help her brush up, a reporter friend from the *Democrat-Gazette* sent her some clippings, including one with the photograph of Elizabeth. Seeing it touched her deeply: three years out of Harvard, working in the White House, Shih didn't really know from discrimination. But as a first-generation Chinese-American, she did know about feeling different, and lonely. She, and Bill Clinton, would begin with Elizabeth.

"Forty years ago, a single image first seared the heart and stirred the conscience of our nation, so powerful most of us who saw it then recall it still," he would say, standing on the landing just below Central's epic entrance.

A fifteen-year-old girl wearing a crisp black and white dress, carrying only a notebook, surrounded by large crowds of boys and girls, men and women, soldiers and police officers, her head held high, her eyes fixed straight ahead, and she is utterly alone. On September 4th, 1957, Elizabeth Eckford walked to this door for her first day of school, utterly alone. *She was turned away by people who were afraid of change, instructed by ignorance, hating what they simply could not understand. And America saw her, haunted and taunted for the simple color of her skin, and in the image we caught a* very *disturbing glimpse of ourselves.*

Shih's remarks survived the flight to Little Rock on September 24, during which various Clinton advisers pored over the draft. But later that afternoon, there was a problem: Clinton himself. It wasn't the sentiment, with which he entirely agreed. The problem was Elizabeth. He remembered her fragility and worried that all the attention might cause her pain, or throw her off stride. Shih blanched: all those beautiful words, and now they might not be used! But Clinton's secretary of labor, Alexis Herman, volunteered to find out whether Elizabeth would mind, and apparently satisfied herself that she would not. The story of Elizabeth survived a second meeting around three in the morning on the 25th, between Shih, Waldman, and Clinton at his mother-in-law's condominium in Hillcrest, not far from downtown. Amid the papers strewn about the place, Shih noticed, was the *Democrat-Gazette* with Elizabeth and Hazel on the front. That, she presumed, accounted for a line Clinton had tacked on himself. "With their innocence," he would say of the Nine, "they purchased more freedom for me, too, and for all white people—people like Hazel Bryan Massery, the angry taunter of Elizabeth Eckford, who stood with her in front of this school this week as a *reconciled friend.*"

A few hours later, Hazel and Antoine were among the hundreds standing outside Central awaiting Clinton's speech. Standing in the midst of the crowd, somewhat back from the speakers, Hazel was only a stone's throw from where the original picture had been taken. Forty years wasn't that long, she thought, and all of the changes amazed her. The whole city seemed jubilant, and her emergence, she knew, was partly responsible. She was excited to meet Wolf Blitzer—she had agreed to go on CNN afterward—but was hoping no one would recognize her in the meantime. She heard Clinton praise Elizabeth, though only barely: much to Shih's frustration, some AIDS activists nearly drowned him out. Elizabeth handled it all with no visible difficulty. Then, much to Hazel's surprise, Clinton had praised her, and the crowd had applauded.[1] Though the president did not refer to Elizabeth again directly, implicitly he might have been. "Reconciliation is important not only for those who practiced bigotry but for those whose resentment of it lingers, for both are prisons from which our spirits must escape," he said. If Nelson Mandela could invite his jailers to his inauguration, he noted, "then each of us can seek and

give forgiveness." Who was seeking forgiveness, and the burden
on her, was plain. But Clinton had also set a lofty standard for
those called upon to dispense forgiveness, including Elizabeth and
the rest of the Little Rock Nine.

When he had finished, Clinton and the governor of Arkansas, Mike Huckabee (whose own daughter attended the school),
wended their way up Central's staircase. The Nine followed, this
time with Elizabeth near the rear, and walked through Central's
monumental doors, held open by the president and the governor.
Clinton was struck by how much healthier Elizabeth seemed than
she had been at that reception in the governor's mansion ten years
earlier. Privately, though, Elizabeth remained her usual pessimis-
tic self. "It's a good thing I'm here because I won't live to the
fiftieth," she told one of the event's organizers, a real estate executive named Rett Tucker.

When the speeches ended, Hazel was spotted by a member of
the Mount Nebo African Methodist Church, whose pastor, the
Rev. Hezekiah Stewart, had arranged for the Mennonites to fix
Elizabeth's house. Stewart worked hard for racial reconciliation—
he had attended the day's proceedings with parishioners from two
white churches—and when he was introduced to Hazel, he was
greatly moved. Hazel's presence that day, he felt, was providential,
and he told her so. Members of the three congregations then lined
up for Hazel and, one by one, they hugged her.

THIRTY-ONE

No one paid much mind to the two middle-aged women, one white, one black, sitting in the front seat of the burgundy 1990 Toyota Camry as they embarked upon their latest field trip, making their way to some flower show or country garden around Little Rock or heading down I-30 toward Hot Springs, talking continuously and animatedly all the way. By the spring of 1998 the sight of a white woman and a black woman together wasn't all that odd. But had the other motorists known just who these particular women were, they might well have driven off the road.

When the anniversary commemorations ended in late September of 1997, Elizabeth and Hazel prepared to go their very separate ways, just as they had after their first two encounters. Neither expected anything more. Elizabeth's curiosity about Hazel had apparently been sated. And Hazel had her own life, and family, to tend to. But as time passed, Hazel realized that she wasn't quite ready to let go. It was that missionary spirit of hers: Elizabeth seemed to be a good person; perhaps she could help her out, cheer her up, distract her from her unhappiness, infuse her with some all-important self-esteem. This time, a phone call would have been too forward. So, three weeks later, she sent Elizabeth a note. Much of it was small talk, about settling down after all the excitement and doing things around the house, bringing in the plants before the weather turned cold. She looked forward to spring, she wrote, when she could visit the large iris farm near her mother's home; walking through all those flowers in bloom, she felt she was in paradise. Just thinking about them would help sustain her through the winter. Then she grew bold, then bolder still. "I would like for you to go with me this coming spring," she wrote. But must they wait that long? She'd heard that Reverend Stewart's congregation was visiting Elizabeth soon; could she possibly come along? "I have so much I would like to discuss with you," she concluded. "Please call or write or let me know soon." She included her phone number.

She never heard back.[1] But Elizabeth did call in early November, after the National Conference of Christians and Jews announced plans to honor the two of them for illustrating "the strides which can be made in race relations." They had a long and pleasant conversation about the award, and about what they would wear when they signed the new poster at the visitor center shortly before. "I felt very happy," Hazel wrote after they'd spoken. "I went to sleep with a smile on my face." In mid-November, Hazel invited Elizabeth and two of her sister Anna's grandchildren to her house. Then, later that month, came the poster signing. A large crowd showed up, including Congressman Snyder. As for the poster itself, Hazel thought the original picture was too small: as much as she hated it, she believed it couldn't and shouldn't be hidden. Elizabeth had a different problem with it: she thought the title—"Reconciliation"—overstated; there was a big difference between that and forgiveness. But no one had asked her about it and, characteristically, she did not complain. In fact, she used the term when she and Hazel inscribed a poster for Will Counts. "Thank you so much for your wonderful support to make this event possible," was what Hazel wrote. "What a difference 40 years can make!" "Thank you for making it possible for us to close the circle," Elizabeth added. "Reconciliation helps us to look forward to a hopeful future."

Afterward, Hazel proposed to Elizabeth that the two have lunch together sometime. So in early December, they ate, then went to the Salvation Army together to look at secondhand books. Throughout, they spoke about families and recipes and enjoyed some plain girl talk. A week later came the NCCJ luncheon. Elizabeth was late, having come there, Hazel was shocked to learn, by bus. The program included the familiar grainy footage from 1957, accompanied by a loud soundtrack—just the things that upset Elizabeth. When she began to tremble, Hazel reached over, and held her hand.

Their encounters gradually became more frequent, almost routine. Over the next several months, they went to a home and garden show, and bought daylilies and irises together. They shopped for fabrics together. They heard Maya Angelou read poetry together. (Hazel insisted on going backstage to see her—she thought Angelou would want to meet them—and was crushed to find her standoffish, without the slightest idea who either of them was.) Elizabeth visited Hazel at her home, and they grilled hot dogs together. They went to Little Rock's Riverfront Market and ate barbecue together. They discovered some sweet peas growing wild on a vacant lot together, digging them up furtively and giggling over their petty theft together. For Elizabeth's birthday, Hazel bought her daffodil bulbs.

The two also enrolled in a seminar on racial healing offered by Little Rock's racial and cultural diversity commission. Discussing race relations in a group of twenty every Monday night for twelve weeks was a revelation to each: Elizabeth had never realized how paralyzed by anger and hate she had been, and hoped to leech some of that rage. It seemed to work, and she came to look forward to each session. As for Hazel, she was naïve about how bitter and resentful some blacks were; here was a problem one couldn't simply wish away, or eliminate with soothing words or good intentions. She was also amazed by how little race history she knew: after one class, Elizabeth mentioned "Strange Fruit," the anti-lynching song Billie Holiday had made famous, and, much to Elizabeth's astonishment, Hazel knew nothing about either the song or the subject. Clearly, she had some homework to do. The picture itself was never discussed. But their classmates were tickled to be sitting alongside two such famous antagonists and, week by week, watching them bond.

In February 1998 the two made the first of many joint speaking appearances—this one at the University of Central Arkansas at Conway. With Elizabeth unable to drive, Hazel always supplied the transportation. She had become Elizabeth's chauffeur, she joked. Hazel paid for everything, though either being treated or spending her own money was awkward for Elizabeth, who had a hard time explaining to people just how poor she was. Once, during a visit to Elizabeth's house, Hazel learned that Elizabeth didn't own a can opener—she'd had to borrow one from a neighbor—

and she went out and bought her one. After some visits, Hazel would sit down and write about what they had just shared and what she thought it meant. Then she would go over what she'd just written with a dictionary at hand, circling and correcting whatever she had misspelled.

Something strange, inconceivable even, was afoot. It was one thing to pose for a picture together. But now, out of the public glare, Elizabeth and Hazel were becoming friends. Slowly but steadily, they realized that more than fate had bound them together; they really had a good deal in common. True, Elizabeth was better educated, better read and better spoken, far more cerebral than Hazel, while Hazel was better adjusted, led a more balanced and stable life, and was more practical than Elizabeth. But each was, in a sense, self-taught. Each was far more introspective and inquisitive than those around them, more inclined to pick up a book than to turn on a television. Each craved good conversation. Each was a loner, with few real confidantes. Neither quite fit in anywhere, whether in their communities or their families: Elizabeth joked once that she'd been switched at birth. That was literally impossible in Hazel's case: she had been born at home. But sometimes it sure felt like it to her as well.

The two confided in each other about the most intimate things, like their children. And they gave each other advice. Having scraped by on her own, Elizabeth couldn't understand Hazel's dependence on Antoine—what would she do if anything ever happened to him?—and urged her to find some sort of livelihood. Hazel, in turn, buttressed up Elizabeth. Folks always thought Ernest Green was the most important of the black students, she told her, but when people thought of Central, it was the picture that immediately came to mind; besides, Ernest hadn't made the sacrifices she had. Upbeat, enthusiastic, rarin' to go, with a turn-lemons-into-lemonade personality, Hazel feared she was too much for her taciturn and somber companion. She wanted to get Elizabeth out of her house and rut, make her discover life beyond West 18th Street and 1957. Elizabeth called her Pollyanna; Hazel considered that a compliment. "Hazel, you can't make her happy," one of her colleagues from the parenting center cautioned her. She disagreed. Elizabeth was her grandest project yet.

Hazel wanted to up the ante, and soon had her chance. Every spring, her mother prepared poke salat, a green that grew wild in the Arkansas countryside. One morning in April 1998, Pauline Bryan called to say she was cooking up a batch, along with some pinto beans, fried potatoes, and corn bread. Could Hazel come by around three for some? (It was Friday, when Hazel's mother and stepfather danced at the senior center. They'd have already eaten, and would leave shortly after Hazel arrived.) Hazel and Elizabeth were set to visit Hot Springs the next day—they'd tour a garden and stop at McClard's for some barbecue—but the forecast called for rain; why not reschedule, and have her meet Mother instead? En route, they could stop at that iris farm she'd mentioned to Elizabeth last fall.

As Hazel dialed her mother, her heart raced. She made her proposal, then closed her eyes as she awaited a response. "Bring her on," her mother replied. "A smile came across my face and a sigh of relief and a feeling of immense joy that my mother had accepted this unusual visit so graciously," Hazel wrote. She hurriedly called Elizabeth—as if, were she to hesitate, the chance might be lost, or she'd wake up and realize she was dreaming.

Elizabeth asked if her mother was expecting her. Never before, Elizabeth figured, had she ever served a black person in her home, and Elizabeth wanted to make sure the coast was really clear.[2] The iris garden was closed; the two had to settle for gazing over the fence. But one of the irises in her mother's yard—a Saint Helen's Wake, with white ruffled petals and a yellow beard—was in bloom. Elizabeth gasped, then walked over and cupped it in her hands. "I smiled as I felt our commonality for the beauty of this flower that had played its part in mine and Elizabeth's budding relationship (friendship)?" Hazel wrote later.

Hazel's mother greeted them at the door. Soon, lunch was ready. Elizabeth fixed herself a plate but held back: this was the South, and she'd assumed Hazel would say grace. "Oh, no, I'm not religious!" Hazel replied, and the two realized there was one more thing they shared. Dessert was lemon meringue pie, made with fresh lemons Hazel's mother had brought back from Arizona. (So impressed was Elizabeth with Pauline Bryan's flaky pie crust that she asked for, and got, the recipe.) Hazel's mother served her guests, but did not join them. Hazel hadn't mentioned her dance date; Elizabeth assumed she was purposely staying away.

THIRTY-TWO

Though Elizabeth allowed few people into her life, she made an exception for students. Young people, she believed, were still untainted by racial prejudice, and less likely to exploit her. Now, thanks to a persistent high school history teacher from northern California named Jeff Steinberg, her sessions with them became a regular occurrence. For a program he called *Sojourn to the Past,* Steinberg, who had long taught about the Little Rock schools crisis, hoped to bring some boys and girls to Central in 1998. When he telephoned Elizabeth to ask whether he could, she was noncommittal. But when 150 of his students wrote her letters, she almost had to relent. Besides, she thought the session might provide her a kind of therapy, helping her to overcome her posttraumatic stress disorder. She consented to see them the following February, but with one stipulation: that Hazel, too, take part. Steinberg happily agreed.

Coming to learn of Elizabeth's sensitivities, Steinberg devised a code of conduct for his students: no hugging or crowding around her, no loud noises, no picture taking. (That last item was Elizabeth's idea: after all, she thought herself ugly.) Elizabeth developed her own rituals. She would never eat or drink beforehand. She would always keep a lined wastebasket and paper towels nearby, just in case she got sick. She wouldn't wear her glasses, so she couldn't make out any disapproving faces. Reading off cue cards, her hands visibly shaking, she would describe Jim Crow Little Rock, her family, her decision to attend Central, her experiences there. She'd speak of the two students who befriended her, and encourage small acts of kindness. She would speak fast, the better to exit quickly.

Hazel, too, enjoyed children (and grandchildren, and, as of 1997, great-grandchildren) but talking about her past also presented a challenge. She had to overcome other people's skepticism (or hostility) and maintain her composure. From one of her self-help books she'd picked up some "affirmations" that she'd review beforehand: "Perfect wisdom is in my heart." "I am dynamically self-expressive." "Communication is a contact sport." "Goal of communication is to become: 1) RELAXED 2) AUTHENTIC 3) CONFIDENT 4) PERSUASIVE." "Be your natural self." "Make emotional contact: be honest-natural-likeable-believable-credibility-trust-smile-winning manner connects to people." She'd write out cues for herself: "Why did I do it?" "What made me change?" While Elizabeth was historical, Hazel focused more on the future. She'd quote Lincoln and Martin Luther King. She'd stress the importance of listening. Often, she would end with a parable: a coal mouse sits on a branch, counting snowflakes as they fall on it. Soon there are 3,471,952 of them. Each weighs nothing, but when just one more lands, the branch breaks. Perhaps, the coal mouse tells a white dove, the world works this way as well: with just one more voice, peace can come.

In June 1998 Elizabeth and Hazel went to Mobile, Alabama,

where, as part of Little Rock's submission to the All-America City competition, they read a script on racial reconciliation. In effect, the city was putting them on display. An even more exciting project was the book they now planned to do. The force behind it was Linda Monk, the lawyer from Mississippi who had identified with Hazel, then written about her. No one seemed better equipped to braid their stories together: Monk could empathize with Elizabeth, too, for she had relatives who struggled with depression. And she had long been interested in racial rapprochement. The topic was timely: Bill Clinton had just created a presidential commission on race and called for a national conversation on racial reconciliation. Hazel initially hesitated—her motives would surely be doubted—but she soon signed on. Together, she and Monk worked on, and wore down, Elizabeth. Monk proceeded gingerly with her, hoping to make her feel safe and strong enough to tell her story without inhibition.

Putting it all together, Monk warned, would not be easy. The two women would have to go to what she called "the depths of the depths together," starting that candid conversation about race that most Americans avoided. Hazel was ready to go. Elizabeth said that as long as she took her medication she could proceed, but she had a couple of caveats. First, nothing could preclude the children's book she hoped one day to write. And second, the book could not be a tearjerker. "I don't want to be crying in it like Tammy Faye Bakker," she declared, referring to the disgraced televangelist. "Her crying was tiresome." ("Well, you don't have the mascara," Hazel noted.) As for the proceeds, Elizabeth had it all worked out: thirty-three percent each for Hazel and Monk, and thirty-four percent for her. (Given all she'd been through, she thought she deserved a bit more.) Generally, she was upbeat. "For me, things are a whole lot better," she said. She'd become more tolerant. She wanted to live.

Over that Fourth of July, Monk came to Little Rock. Like everyone else, she needed to convince herself that Hazel was sincere (that part proved easy) and that Elizabeth believed in racial healing (which was harder). But Elizabeth, she could tell, was clearly emerging from the darkness. At Hot Springs the three women took mineral baths and massages together, a tradition for white Arkansans maybe but experiences Elizabeth had never had. (She seemed afraid of the water, climbing into the tub very timidly; Hazel and Monk helped her. Then each massaged one of her feet.) Monk returned over Halloween, when they cooked hot dogs and toasted marshmallows together around a bonfire outside Hazel's house. Watching the flames illuminate these two famous faces, then reach skyward, Monk felt something almost supernatural in the air.

She fashioned a collaboration agreement and book proposal. As she saw it, Hazel's apology to Elizabeth was only the start of their story. "With fear and trembling," she wrote, the two had now entered the thicket of race, and were committed "to developing an authentic relationship of reconciliation, not papering over differences or ignoring conflict." Once they had embodied racial strife; now they could inspire racial harmony. The book, she continued, would appeal not just to activists but to optimists. The pair would be available for school appearances, conventions, television, corporate retreats, training sessions; companies seeking diversity could order the book in bulk. Their tale was "a natural" for Oprah Winfrey, addressing "the themes of triumph over adversity and redemption out of suffering that Oprah finds so compelling." All they had to do now was write their story. And, before that, to live it.

In November 1998, as he signed legislation making Central High School a National Historic Site, Bill Clinton signed a second document, awarding the Congressional Gold Medal to the Nine. (A formal presentation would be held the next year.) Along with the others, Elizabeth came to the White House for the signing ceremony; afterward, she was invited to fly back to Arkansas with the president on Air Force One. She was far too flustered to say much to him in the few minutes they had together, and she felt bad about it: the Monica Lewinsky scandal was then engulfing him, and, she thought, he could have used a boost. Things had progressed with Hazel to the point that when Elizabeth had happy news, she wanted to share it with her as much as with anyone else, and Hazel was among those she called from the plane. Hazel saved the message, and played it for her grandchildren.

For Hazel, the benefits of the relationship were immediate: an enormous weight had been lifted from her shoulders; the world could begin to see what she had become rather than who she'd been. She had made herself a new friend, and found herself someone else to help. For Elizabeth, it was just one component of something larger, something she came to call (and she was hardly given to overstatement) her "renaissance." In the spring of 1999 she took an even more dramatic leap.

THIRTY-THREE

—————

J
udge Marion Humphrey of Pulaski County Circuit Court in Little Rock had a problem on his hands. One of his probation officers had had a fling with a probationer, and the matter had hit the papers. He needed to hire a replacement fast, someone who would help dispel the stench, someone of instant impeccability. He thought of Elizabeth Eckford. To put it mildly, it was an unconventional choice.

By this point, after all, Elizabeth had not held a job in twenty years. She had toyed periodically with returning to work, but had never gotten past the interviews: too much baggage, potential employers presumably concluded. And as a probation officer? Aside from the problems with her sons, she had no experience in criminal justice. She knew nothing about computers, and her typing skills, such as they were, had atrophied. And of course she had more than her share of problems. Hiring Elizabeth, whom Judge Humphrey had never met, was a risk.

But he had his reasons. Elizabeth embodied for him the old-fashioned values and pride he found lacking in so many of the young black defendants passing through his court. He felt, too, that he had a debt to discharge. As a black boy in Pine Bluff, he had followed the fortunes of the Little Rock Nine, then followed in their footsteps. Elizabeth had opened doors for him and lots of people like him and, he felt, was owed far more than she had ever received. Humphrey was a religious man—he doubled as pastor of the Allison Memorial Presbyterian Church—and the same second chances he often bestowed on the men and women who came before him on the bench he now wanted to give to Elizabeth.

He checked with several people about her—Rett Tucker, the real estate developer who had worked with Elizabeth on the anniversary observances; Morris Thompson, the neighbor who had helped out her and her boys; Annie Abrams. All thought hiring her was a wonderful idea. Why, she asked Judge Humphrey when she came in to be interviewed, would he ever consider her? Not because he felt sorry for her or was doing her any favors, he replied, but because *he* needed *her.* So thrilled was she at the prospect of working again that she never asked what the job paid, or balked upon learning that it wasn't very much. Instead, quietly, unobtrusively—in the ten years she was to spend at the court, the *Democrat-Gazette* never thought she warranted a story—she went to work.

Elizabeth's coworkers were pleased to have someone of her fame alongside them, but also a bit perplexed. They, too, had seen her around town, always alone, head down, seemingly in her own world, and they thought her, well, a bit *off.* To them, she remained what she'd been for forty years: a lonely figure at a bus stop. And suddenly here she was, counseling others. But she quickly impressed them with her conscientiousness and intelligence. Like Judge Branton, they were amazed that someone who had always been so mute was so well-spoken. (As she talked, one coworker surreptitiously scribbled down some of the big words she used, so she could look them up once Elizabeth wasn't around.) Forgoing the bus and treating herself to cabs, Elizabeth spent much of her discretionary income getting to and from work. But with whatever was left over, she started to treat herself with respect. She began wearing eye shadow and lipstick; the court officers and bailiffs complimented her on her appearance. Boxes began piling up outside the chambers: Elizabeth was ordering clothes, from Appleseed's and Chadwicks and other places with plus sizes. She moved from polyester to blends and even, occasionally, to linen or wool. (When she changed her mind about something or it didn't fit, she'd give it to a probationer she liked, whose closet was soon filled with her castoffs.)

Elizabeth's clients were almost always poor, often semiliterate, in trouble for passing bad checks or credit-card fraud or taking or selling drugs. They were usually young; for a time Elizabeth dyed her hair (and tried wearing a wig) so that she wouldn't remind them of their grandmothers. Many couldn't afford lawyers; few were hardened criminals. She could be compassionate—keeping peanuts around for prisoners who had missed breakfast, letting them make toll calls to their mamas, giving them bus fare home. But she could also be harsh. "Aren't you ashamed to show your underwear?" she might ask. Or, to someone sporting gold teeth, "How are you going to get a decent job looking like that?" She would ask someone wearing drooping, beltless pants whether he was practicing for prison. Or she'd tell a scantily clad woman to go home and put on some clothes. Such comments sometimes made her colleagues wince. They were bothered, too, by her willingness to send probationers back to prison, recommendations Judge Humphrey might diplomatically ignore. But they understood her thinking: she had endured, and surmounted, so much herself that she had little truck for the weaknesses of others. Woe betide anyone telling Elizabeth, who had taken buses all her life, that he couldn't work without a car. If a probationer was especially handsome, though, she might cut him a break. Coworkers knew to steer such "eye candy" to her.

To get the job Elizabeth had to learn how to shoot a gun, which did not come easily to her. Handling a computer was even harder —so hard, in fact, that she'd had the new terminal on her desk removed so she could still do everything by hand. But for all the adjustments, she cherished the job. Though she had begun at an age—fifty-six—when people contemplated retirement, she told people they'd have to carry her out feet first. Few of the probationers realized who she was. But every once in a while, after a documentary aired or the picture appeared somewhere, someone would exclaim, "Miss Eckerd, I didn't know that was *you!*" Treat her as they always had, she'd tell them.

THIRTY-FOUR

For most of its existence, Little Rock had appeared on few travel itineraries. But its days of shame had made it a tourist destination, and not just for busloads of teenagers retracing the civil rights movement. From all over the world they now came. Signs for the "Central High School Natl Historic Site," its National Park Service brown standing out amid the Interstate green, directed motorists to what was, at least until Bill Clinton's presidential library was built, the main local attraction.

Before or after standing in front of the school, visitors would study the exhibit on display in the converted gas station down the street. One day an Indian tourist named Parimal Mehta got a bonus. He'd already seen the famous, familiar photograph when he heard his young daughters calling him. "They are here! Elizabeth and Hazel! Please come!" they shouted as he prepared to leave. "I turned, as if in a dream," he wrote later in an Indian newspaper. And there they were, the two women in the picture. It was, he recalled, as if Abraham Lincoln had walked out of one of his portraits and shaken your hand, or Mahatma Gandhi had climbed off some pedestal and touched you with his walking stick. The girls were grown now and, miraculously, the best of friends!

He bowed, then asked to shake their hands. He asked Elizabeth how she had felt, then and now. "Frightened then; hopeful now," she replied. And Hazel? "Confused then," she said. "Now . . . relieved and joyful."

Quietly, though, some considered the rapprochement, however lovely in principle, a triumph of sentimentality, wishful thinking, and marketing over reality. They saw something artificial and strained in it. They wondered how deep it went and how long it could last. Some of that skepticism bled into overt hostility. In some segments of her own community, Elizabeth stood accused of what she had laid at Ernest Green's feet: whitewashing reality. "I have been surprised with the vitriol that some young blacks approach me," she told the BBC. "They feel like I'm saying that what happened, it's all over with and there are no repercussions. . . . They feel like I'm wiping away the past." There was flak from black activists and coworkers. Her sons, too, were skeptical. "These people weren't your friends before. . . . How come they're your friends now?" Calvin asked about Hazel and Linda Monk. He thought he detected hatred in Hazel's eyes, and considered the relationship, as he later put it, "fake from the get-go."

With Elizabeth at least, the skeptics were few, and black. With Hazel, they ran the gamut. It was something that Paul Greenberg, the contrarian editorial page editor of the *Democrat-Gazette*, had anticipated. Simply for apologizing, he had written the next day, Hazel was a woman of valor. But would she be accepted? "Once again, in 1997, a despised and rejected minority presents a test for the majority," he wrote. "Now it is those who resisted integration in '57 whose voices are muted, who go unrepresented in the official history, who have become unpersons."

After her initial enthusiasm, Hazel worried a bit about her sudden conspicuousness. "After 40 years of being just a face in a famous picture . . . I now had a name," she wrote. "I had become a real person some would accept but not all." Some of her fear, which her family shared, was physical: maybe someone unstable— a white supremacist or some black holding a grudge—would want to harm her. Elizabeth had been right: she *had* been naïve. Some blacks doubted her genuineness and gave her the cold shoulder. When Hazel approached Lottie Shackelford, a former mayor of Little Rock (and the first black woman to hold the position) at a reception, Shackelford rebuffed her. "We're tired of excuses!" she snapped. While Hazel's children were courteous to Elizabeth—her younger son had hugged her when they met; her daughter had installed a computer in her home—Elizabeth's sons had been rude and hateful to her, ignoring her when she came around.

Some of the Nine were frosty, too. At the reception following Clinton's speech at Central, none had spoken to her. Then, at a signing a couple of days later, Melba Beals had fulsomely inscribed a copy of her memoirs to her—To "a warrior, a spiritual partner growing along her God-perscribed [*sic*] journey"—but her goodwill had clear limits.[1] Others, unaware of Hazel's first apology, assumed that the second was atonement on the cheap, a quick, belated attempt to assuage her conscience or, worse, to cash in. Some shared their skepticism with Elizabeth. Why had Hazel appeared only now, Carlotta asked her. Where had she been all these years? "Are you extremely gullible or are you just very, very forgiving?" asked another. Ernest Green found Hazel amusing. "We kind of joked about it: here she is, framed forever with her mouth spewing out whatever she was spewing out, and no matter what she does in life she can't erase that photo," he recalled. Only Terrence Roberts, whom the Little Rock school system had hired to help implement another round of court-ordered desegregation, got to know Hazel a bit—because she had asked him to lunch while he was in town—and he'd been struck by her sincerity.

Magnanimity and open-mindedness and forgiveness are also forms of bravery; perhaps it was unrealistic to expect such things from Elizabeth's comrades-in-arms, who had already shown so much courage of the more conventional kind. More surprising to Hazel, and more upsetting, was the reaction she got from Little Rock's whites, especially those who had gone to Central. To them, she was a tick who had burrowed under their skin forty years earlier, and would simply not let go. In fact, she was only getting bigger.

Hazel's old confederates, the ones who had marched and heckled with her that September morning, and her successors, who had afflicted the Nine once school got under way, were silent about her now. Sammie Dean congratulated her over the reconciliation picture, but privately she found it puzzling: what, after all, had they really done wrong? Had the Good Lord thought that she, Sammie Dean Parker, had acted improperly that morning, He surely would have told her, but He never did. No one else from Central ever came forward to say that they, like Hazel, had sinned, and that she shouldn't have to take the heat by herself. Meanwhile, the great silent majority of Central students, who felt then and still felt that they were not only blameless but maligned, fumed. Representing them as always was Ralph Brodie, the student body president then, now a lawyer in Little Rock. He had spent a lifetime attempting to cleanse Central's sullied image, with a single-mindedness that even those who agreed with him publicly privately found striking.

Though still maintaining that he had seen nothing untoward himself, Brodie had long since come to acknowledge what the Nine had endured. He had praised them at a twentieth anniversary commemoration in September 1977 that Elizabeth, along with Ernest Green and Carlotta Walls LaNier, had attended. A picture of him and Carlotta smiling at each other appeared on the front page of the next day's *Gazette,* prompting an anonymous phone call. "Who'd you sleep with last night?" the caller asked. "Your wife or a nigger?"

But Brodie's mission remained unchanged. If history were fair, he'd tell anyone who would listen, the world would know that most of the students inside Central that year could hold their heads high because, as he put it, "we were just plain good kids." No doubt terrible things had happened, but that was only a small and very unrepresentative part of the story. For visitors and the folks coordinating anniversary events and National Park officials alike, Brodie had *other* photographs at the ready, including that picture of Elizabeth talking to her classmates during the bomb scare on the first day of school. He'd discovered it only decades later, while going through some clippings put aside by his old Sunday school teacher. And he had been thrilled: in fact, for someone out to prove that a couple thousand hearts that year had really been in the right place, it was, as he put it, "gold." "The Relaxed Elizabeth," he came to call it. *This* picture captured the *good* instincts of most Central students, before events turned nasty. *This* picture was actually *more* revealing than that other one, for it showed *real* Central students, not some fly-by-nighter

To Ralph Brodie, this photograph of the "Relaxed Elizabeth" vindicated what he'd been saying all along. (Photographer unidentified)

who quickly left the school. *This* picture should be displayed alongside *that* one, and just as big. But wouldn't you know, *this* picture, which did not fit neatly into the conventional civil rights "narrative," the one that demonized anyone white and canonized anyone black, had been misplaced or forgotten or maybe even suppressed: why else would it have vanished for fifty years? Brodie paid a copyright lawyer thousands of dollars to track it down, then procure publication rights to it, but, alas, she never could.[2]

Even once things turned sour, Brodie argued, these were isolated incidents, whose severity, one couldn't help but infer—it was never said explicitly—had been exaggerated; without the goodwill and level-headedness of most students, matters would have been much, much worse. Surely the ninety-five percent who had done nothing wrong that year were more important than the five percent who had; they, too, deserved praise.

Twenty-five years after their encounter, Brodie happened to run into Mike Wallace in a restaurant in Forrest City, of all places. Much to his chagrin afterward, Brodie had been polite with him, dredging up none of his lingering resentment over their interview. But the image with which Brodie believed Wallace had tried to saddle him and, by extension, all of Central's white students, that first day of school in 1957 had, in fact, taken hold; the world preferred seeing them all as bigots. Even people he might have counted on to set things straight, like Mrs. Huckaby in her memoirs, hadn't defended them, and he thought he knew why: all she had heard that year had been complaints from the Nine—as someone who had no children herself, she had taken a maternal interest in them—and nothing positive about anyone else. Brodie had read her book twice, and it sickened him; as loyal as he was to Central and everything about it, he never spoke to her again. And what she wrote promptly went into the movie version of the book, despite Brodie's entreaties to its producers and director. "In this day of political correctness," Brodie wrote, "no white person in 1957–58 can be allowed to be shown with any redeeming qualities, lest the halo of the Little Rock Nine be tarnished or not shine with the same intense brightness."

And who personified this unfairness? Hazel! In every history book and documentary and newspaper article, and on each and every anniversary, Hazel's hate-filled face popped up. Now, naturally, it was the first thing you saw at the visitor center. "Civic masochism," Brodie called it. Hazel had called herself "the poster child for the hate generation," but to Brodie, she had become the poster child for Central's 1957–58 student body as well. And it was all so unfair! With lawyerly precision, Brodie set out to document how marginal Hazel had actually been, retrieving old school records to show that she had in fact withdrawn only a few days into the school year. Hazel had gone away then, but she hadn't gone away ever since. In fact, now she had come back, more conspicuous than ever. And by apologizing, she had implicitly suggested that others should apologize, too.

Brodie was hardly alone. Almost from the outset, Hazel encountered hostility from whites. Some doubted her sincerity; more resented it. She felt people avoiding her, not looking her in the eye, acting awkward. After one television appearance, she found a bouquet of dead flowers on her driveway. Even those from whom Hazel might have expected support were reticent. In a restaurant, she had run into another figure from the picture: the fellow with the striped shirt, just behind (and partially obscured by) Elizabeth. When Antoine asked him why he, too, hadn't come forward, he said that it would hurt his business. The mayor's wife, whom Hazel had met a few times, gave her the cold shoulder. So did some of the Parks Department officials running the visitor center. As the official face of bigotry, she was useful to them; her coming forward as a changed woman complicated things. Like young Elizabeth before Central, Hazel had assumed that as people came to know her they would like, and maybe even admire, her. But it wasn't so.

Soon, and most serious, tensions developed with Elizabeth. Novelty and companionability, excitement and relief had propelled them along for a time. But strains soon surfaced. The source was Elizabeth, and it was predictable, for she was always the harder sell. Her usual wariness, vigilance, and perfectionism could be kept at bay only so long. As the two shared more time and platforms, Elizabeth spotted what she perceived to be gaps and discrepancies, inconsistencies and evasions, in Hazel's story. As Hazel grew more comfortable with her, Elizabeth thought, she would dig deeper into herself, wrestle with her racist past, and come fully clean, but that wasn't happening. Hazel seemed unable, or at least disinclined, to bare that part of her life. Like the prosecutor she might have been, Elizabeth began assembling a bill of particulars against her. She never wrote anything down, but in her mind, these were some of the counts:

• *Hazel always said that she had known right away, practically even as she marched behind Elizabeth, that what she'd done was wrong. In fact, she had made* additional *offensive comments over the next few days. There hadn't been just one aberrant "moment," as Hazel maintained.*

• *When they watched* Eyes on the Prize *together, and that old footage of Hazel talking about the rights of "Nigras" had come up, Hazel hadn't acknowledged that that was she!*

• *Hazel conveniently forgot that her mother,* as well as *her father, had been outside Central that morning. More generally, Hazel refused to blame her parents for her intolerance, insisting that bigotry had been "in the air" rather than instilled at home. Hazel was a loyal person, and her first loyalty was to them rather than to the truth.*

- *Hazel was impossibly vague about the events of September 4, unconvincingly pleading "amnesia" about it all. How could she remember so little about something so inherently memorable, about which Elizabeth remembered the most minute details?*

- *Hazel claimed to have known nothing about what had happened inside Central after she had left the place. But wouldn't her pal Sammie Dean, who was at the center of all the trouble, have kept her informed?*

Hazel had become perhaps Elizabeth's closest confidante, helping her to open up and to lift the omnipresent veil of sadness around her. She had kept her company, and made her laugh. She had treated her with great respect, even reverence. She had tried her damnedest to make amends. Was it not worth taking her as she was? But Elizabeth had always been a stickler. She saw things keenly and remembered things precisely, and assumed that only bad faith or selective memory could explain someone who did not. This was so even though her own memory could be selective, and selectively harsh.[3] But if she still harbored resentments against Grace Lorch and Daisy Bates—people whose intentions were good—how charitable could she be to someone whose weren't?[4]

Maybe Elizabeth was more comfortable, or accustomed to, feeling embattled, or manipulated, or misled, or simply being by herself. (Even Minnijean, who had moved back to Little Rock in 2001 after many years in Canada, kept her distance, remarking once that she knew Elizabeth "well enough to leave her alone.") And so maybe she sabotaged things. She convinced herself that Hazel's father had been a Klansman. She came to believe that Hazel's grandmother had been the biggest bigot in Sheridan,

Arkansas, when the woman had never lived there. Carrying a bouquet of balloons to Elizabeth's office for her birthday, Hazel noted that all of Elizabeth's coworkers were black; wasn't this, too, she asked, a form of discrimination? And Elizabeth mistook Hazel's curiosity, and eagerness to engage on the issues, and ham-handed naïveté—for bigotry. And the more Elizabeth got back on her feet, the more judgmental she became. In this sense, Hazel was the agent of her own undoing. Knowing herself as she did, shouldn't Elizabeth have foreseen that this would reach such a point? Maybe she'd been carried away by her curiosity. Or maybe she, too, had been naïve.

Elizabeth initially kept her doubts to herself. Publicly, she continued to praise, and protect, Hazel. When reporters or students pressed her understandably embarrassed counterpart to repeat what she had shouted outside Central that day, Elizabeth would cut them off: you don't have to oblige them, she would tell her. Some reporters, Elizabeth explained, actually *want* to see you cry: it made for good copy, or footage. For them, Elizabeth advised, she had crafted what she called the "nickel and dime" version of her story, something quick and superficial enough to sate their shallow curiosity, and she urged Hazel to do likewise. Hazel was often dissatisfied with her answers, and Elizabeth helped her hone them.

Cheery and positive by nature, Hazel failed at first to detect the undercurrents. Getting to know Elizabeth, doing interviews, going out afterward—she found the whole routine exhilarating. "EE made the comment she and I could get very good at this," she wrote after one session together. While Elizabeth approached interviews warily, Hazel was thrilled. "I don't know when it will air, maybe all over Europe!" she wrote after talking to the BBC. She gave herself more homework, buying audiotapes of Cornel West (she had seen him on "Oprah") and Angelou: perhaps she would gain some insights she could share with Elizabeth. She was also excited when the mayor of Little Rock asked the two to take part in a "Unity Walk" through the city's racial landmarks. "Yes!" she wrote. "Another opportunity for Elizabeth and I to walk together!" For Hazel's birthday in January 1999, Elizabeth bought her a nice black and white dress with a blue jacket, but what came attached mattered much more. "The card she gave me moved me with such joy to know she considers me her friend," Hazel wrote. "It is immensely pleasing. A treasure to keep and cherish."

But the fissure was painfully apparent that March, eighteen months into their relationship, when Linda Monk returned to Little Rock to work on the book. She recorded some of their sessions, and those taped conversations capture how Elizabeth's mood had changed. "After you saw [Counts's] pictures in the paper, *you don't remember how you felt or what people close to you talked about?*" she asked Hazel incredulously at one point. "There wasn't much conversation about it, really," replied Hazel. What she'd done that morning had been so banal—"just hamming up and being recognized—getting attention"—that it hadn't been worth remembering, she insisted. Maybe she had a block; perhaps hypnosis would help. But Elizabeth wasn't buying it. No way could Hazel have considered it so insignificant, and since it was significant, she couldn't have forgotten it; it *had* to be deliberate. Then again, *if she really didn't remember anything, and hadn't talked to her parents about it, and wasn't used to examining her life, how much could she contribute to any book?*

Elizabeth had forgiven Hazel, but that forgiveness, she concluded, had been obtained under false pretenses: Hazel hadn't fully owned up to her past. For her part, Hazel felt under assault. "It's very hard for me to sit there and listen to you, Elizabeth," she said weakly. "It's very hard for me . . . and if there's anything I could give you . . . If I could take it back . . . If I could . . ." She began to sob. She asked Elizabeth if it was all right if she touched her, and Elizabeth said it was—that it was actually helpful—and Hazel thanked her. That much of a connection remained.

Inevitably, though, Hazel began collecting her own grievances. Elizabeth kept saying that nothing had changed, but that clearly wasn't true: Little Rock had had a black mayor, for God's sake! Elizabeth wanted Hazel to call her parents bigots, to say the Bryans sat around devising ways to torture black people, but it wasn't so. Elizabeth wanted her to disown her father, but Sanford Bryan hadn't been a Klansman and besides, Hazel loved him and could not and would not turn on him now. Elizabeth was constantly negative. She didn't like Hazel's proposed book title—"Getting to Know You," just like the song—and that snowflake story that Hazel so loved, Elizabeth considered saccharine. Hazel felt patronized, belittled. She had always introduced Elizabeth respectfully, mentioning her army good conduct medal and various other honors. "Humorous, giving and caring, I present my friend, Ms. Elizabeth Eckford," she would say. But introducing Hazel once, Elizabeth asked the audience to picture a woman in fishnet stockings and a top hat. She meant it admiringly: it illustrated Hazel's zaniness. But when two people don't understand each other, everything's a potential misunderstanding; Hazel felt she had been depicted as a cheap exhibitionist. When Hazel said something that annoyed her, Elizabeth sometimes seized the microphone. That struck Hazel as rude.

As long as Linda Monk was around to encourage and mediate, the friction remained in check. But in April 1999 a traumatic divorce forced her to abandon the book project. A fragile friendship, already bending under the strain, had lost its strongest advocate.

It is here that I step into the story.

THIRTY-FIVE

———————

Elizabeth was positively giddy.

We were at a barbecue joint on the outskirts of Little Rock, with Hazel and Antoine. On the table were piles of denuded ribs and chicken bones in spicy brown sauce, along with half-finished glasses of sweetened ice tea. When the check came, Elizabeth insisted on picking it up. When I resisted—I'd invited them, after all—she gigglingly explained why. She had just gotten her first credit card—it was one of the perks of having a job—and she wanted to see whether it worked.

In the spring of 1999 I traveled to Little Rock on another project. While there I made a pilgrimage to Central High School, a shrine I'd long known about but never seen, then to the visitor center. There, for sale in the gift shop, I first saw the "reconciliation" poster. I was amazed. Could these iconic antagonists, people whose faces I well knew, really have made up? How had it happened? Why hadn't I read about it? *This* was a story. I learned of Lynn Whittaker, the literary agent who had been handling Monk's book project, and quickly contacted her. She arranged to get us all together; I arranged for the barbecue.

Afterward we went to Hazel's house and talked some more. It was, I thought, a friendly chat. Elizabeth did not let on that she and Hazel were having problems; the two of them were "very close," she said. They talked a lot, she went on, maybe once a week. Other blacks had criticized her for their friendship, but she had brushed them aside; "I tell them the questions they're asking are racist, that I choose my own friends, and that I believe she's sincere," she explained. Hazel was a bit more forthright about where things stood between them, but still oblique. "I think she still at times ... we have a little ... well, the honeymoon is over and now we're getting to take out the garbage," she said. Our conversation continued at Doe's Eat Place, a Clinton hangout during his presidential campaigns. There, due to what I think was a misunderstanding, any chance that we would all work together—on an article, that is; I hadn't contemplated writing the sort of book Linda Monk had envisioned—evaporated. In their own ways, both Elizabeth and Hazel had been naïve; it turns out I was, too.[1]

Most of Hazel's critics in white Little Rock, particularly whites who had attended Central, kept mum. Defending themselves, they had concluded, was a sucker's game; why put themselves out there, only to be dismissed as bigots? But sometimes their hostility broke through. That July, Hazel was treated to a letter in the *Democrat-Gazette*.

> *I read with interest another news item about Hazel Massery, the repentant harasser turned friend of Elizabeth Eckford, both students at Little Rock Central High School in 1957.*
>
> *When President Clinton and the national media used this tragedy for their own gain, I recall they also used Massery, who was more than anxious to publicly confess and repent of her past despicable sins.*

It is always good for one to repent of bad behavior, even if it is for notoriety and recognition.

This lady was a member of a small minority of the student body who either did not listen to their parents or were never taught that everybody they met deserved politeness and courtesy.

Like many others, I became Eckford's friend in 1957 in Miss Mc-Galen's [sic] speech class at LRCHS, not because she was black, or for any publicity, but just because I liked her.

The majority of us were fortunate enough to have learned that if you were in school with someone you did not want to befriend, you left them alone; you did not torment them.

I applaud and compliment the vast majority of my classmates who 40 years later do not have to apologize to our nine black classmates because we were good citizens then as now.

I would like to tell the media, the president, and the country that the strength and stability of this nation are not headline-grabbers like the president and Massery.

In a couple of weeks, if you care to peek in on our 40th class reunion, you will find several people whose names you will recognize, not because they have ever made headlines apologizing for their sins, but because they have been good citizens who have contributed in a positive way to our culture.

R. W. Ross[2]

Van Buren

Ross hadn't known Hazel in 1957, nor would he have, coming as he did from the other side of the tracks. But he was saying, in effect, that Hazel hadn't changed; whatever she did, she did strictly to get attention.

Both Hazel and Elizabeth had been invited to the reunion Ross mentioned, and planned for a time to go together. "That should be interesting," Hazel wrote in her journal. Characteristically, Elizabeth eventually opted out; equally characteristically, Hazel did not. That was unwise. Many of the others on hand believed Hazel owed apologies not just to the Eckford One and the Little Rock Nine, but to the Class of 1959 Five Hundred, the Central High School Twenty-two Hundred, the Little Rock Hundred Thousand, and the Arkansas Two Million: she had sullied them all. Some were annoyed or indignant that she had shown up, and derisive, too. "*She's* the one who was in the picture!" a woman at Hazel's table (who'd also admitted to being one of those who'd jumped out the window when the black students entered Central) explained with a laugh to a table mate. A man Hazel had known both from Central and from church looked poised to say something unpleasant, only to muzzle himself.

All this galled Hazel. Everyone was acting as if only she had misbehaved. She had been made a scapegoat, she believed, and for her it was more than a metaphor: she remembered the story from Leviticus about the goat that was made to bear the sins of an entire people. Only as she left that night did someone say he admired her for what she'd just done. Hazel spent many sleepless nights wondering why she had agreed to talk publicly about any of this.[3]

THIRTY-SIX

A *Life Is More Than a Moment.*
That was pretty much what Hazel had told Linda Monk when they first spoke over the phone. And it was what Will Counts decided to call his collection of Little Rock photographs, which was published in the fall of 1999. Counts and his wife marked the occasion in Bloomington, Indiana, where they now lived in retirement. Naturally, Elizabeth and Hazel were invited. While in town, they scheduled a series of events, including a talk with students and an interview at a local radio station.

Even before the activities began, Hazel detected frostiness from Elizabeth. Before a packed house at Indiana University, some saw discomfort in their body language. The tensions burst into the open during an interview with a local radio host named Shana Ritter. When Hazel told Ritter that her parents had pulled her out of Central for her safety, Elizabeth suddenly interjected. "Every time you say that I'm puzzled," she said. "Who did they expect to harm you?" Hazel fumbled. Some people—L. C. Bates; Elizabeth's father—had had guns, but Hazel didn't want to say that on the air; it might embarrass Elizabeth. Anxiety simmered until Ritter asked for some closing thoughts. When Hazel spoke about "dialogue" and "understanding," Elizabeth's frustrations boiled over.

"There's a southern saying about some people peeing and calling it rain," she said. Hazel wasn't quite sure what that meant, but she knew it wasn't friendly.

Vivian Counts, who had been in the studio with the two, felt like crawling out of the room. By now, she, too, was souring on Hazel—or, to be more precise, Hazel and Antoine. Over dinner one night, Antoine had complained to the Countses that everyone had made money from the picture but Hazel. It was, Hazel knew, his way of describing the pain it had caused her, which he had now witnessed, with growing impatience and frustration, for forty years. But it was certain to be taken as an attempt to cash in, and it was. Relations between the couples quickly soured; and when word of the remark reached Elizabeth (by which point Antoine's comment had grown even balder), her own mounting skepticism was fortified. Elizabeth might be the probation officer, but it was Hazel who, for whites and blacks alike, was on perpetual probation. Returning from Bloomington, Hazel was discouraged enough to seek out Reverend Stewart. The relationship with Elizabeth wasn't working, she told him. She wasn't sure what to do.

Nor, for that matter, was Elizabeth. In November 1999, only a few hours after Daisy Bates was buried in Arkansas, the Nine collected their Congressional Gold Medals at a White House ceremony. Some fifty people from Little Rock attended; Elizabeth invited her sister Anna, Judge Humphrey, Ken Reinhardt, Annie Abrams, and others responsible for her "renaissance." (Neither of her sons came.) She knew that Hazel also belonged in this group, but did not invite her: some of the other eight might object. As one of them put it, "We're the Little Rock Nine, not the Little Rock Ten." Oblivious to all this, Skip Rutherford provided Hazel's name

Elizabeth receives a Congressional Gold Medal from President Clinton, November 1999. (Bettmann/Corbis)

to the White House, and she eagerly accepted the invitation. Sure enough, there was static. Walking through the White House gate, Hazel spotted the least public of the Nine—Gloria Ray Karlmark, who lived in Sweden—a few feet ahead of her. "Hey Gloria!" she shouted, then walked up and introduced herself. Karlmark gave her a wilting stare. "Hah! I should have known!" she said, then walked off. Hazel was mystified. Should have known *what?*

Elizabeth with President Clinton at the White House. Also pictured are Hazel, fifth from left; Judge Marion Humphrey, fourth from left; Annie Abrams, sixth from right; and Elizabeth's sister, Anna Goynes, sixth from left.
(White House photograph, courtesy of Hazel Bryan Massery)

The medals were handed out in the East Room. Hazel beamed as Bill Clinton summoned Elizabeth to the podium. "Come here, girl!" he'd said cheerily. Friends had never seen Elizabeth so happy. She saluted the president—civilians weren't supposed to, she knew, but she just got carried away—and he saluted back. Then they hugged for a long time. As they did, Elizabeth told him how bad she felt for not consoling him more on that flight last year back to Arkansas. Elizabeth did ask Hazel to join her guests when they posed with the president in the Oval Office. She felt sorry for her; she was in town by herself. Now there was a *third* picture of the two. Elizabeth didn't keep a copy, or a complete one, anyway. Periodically, people asked for her head shot; now she had one, once she had clipped away everyone else. The medal, worth several thousand dollars, instantly constituted her life savings. Once she got it home, she tried donating it to the Smithsonian; it would spare her the cost of a safe-deposit box. Then, for a time, she kept it in the closet.

Having quickly reached her capacity for people and ceremonies, Elizabeth did not attend the reception that night at the Library of Congress. But Hazel, dauntless or clueless or needy or naïve, did, and it was a redo of her class reunion. When she asked Ernest Green for his autograph, he seemed bemused. Convinced that Hazel was out only for publicity, or to show everyone that she was a "new woman," Gloria Ray Karlmark gave her the brush-off. Only Minnijean was really friendly; her son Isaiah asked Hazel to pose with his mother and siblings in front of Counts's original photograph. Hazel happily obliged.

THIRTY-SEVEN

On a stage in Chicago, the technicians scurried about, getting things just so for *Oprah*—and for Oprah. Nearby were some of the day's other guests, each a figure out of a famous photograph from the dying century: the mother of the schoolteacher-astronaut killed on the space shuttle *Challenger;* the husband and wife who had embraced amid the mud of Woodstock; the crying Vietnamese girl burning from napalm. Sitting nearby, in the front row, were Elizabeth and Hazel. Neither watched *Oprah* often, and as they followed the preparations, they were more clinical than star-struck. Hazel took note of how pampered Oprah was, with functionaries catering to her every whim. As for Elizabeth, she had never lost her seam-stress's eye. The sleeves on Oprah's pale gray knit dress, she noted, were a bit too tight for her arms.

With a book deal still in the offing, the two had agreed to go on the show. En route from Little Rock, Elizabeth once again kept largely to herself. They had expected Oprah to speak with them before the taping began, perhaps to set them at ease, but it hadn't happened. And once the cameras began rolling, it became apparent why.

Reconciliation and redemption were Oprah's things, but this

particular happy ending was apparently too much even for her. Something about it, and them, appeared to offend her, and once on the air, she did not conceal her displeasure. The picture flashed on the screen. "When we come back, how this shocking image of racism sparked a friendship, *if you can believe that,* forty years later," she teased. "If you can believe that": Elizabeth knew the relationship had its skeptics, but no one had ever been quite so vocal about it. The program resumed. "Elizabeth met Hazel for the first time two years ago in Little Rock, and now . . . they are *friends,*" Oprah said incredulously. "They . . . are . . . friends. They are friends." She sounded both indignant and resigned.

She turned first to Hazel. What had gone through her mind as Elizabeth showed up at school that morning? Integration, Hazel replied: her parents and everyone she knew opposed it. Elizabeth, who covered up the photograph with a tissue whenever she inscribed it, suddenly beheld it on a massive screen, and grew distracted enough to jump when Oprah turned to her. "Do you still find it difficult to look at that photograph? Obviously you do," she said, answering herself before Elizabeth could. "It still causes a great deal of emotion. *Why?*" Her tone was brusque. "Because I am in that moment," Elizabeth mustered. Again, Oprah moved on fast. And what did Hazel feel? "Remorse. Regret." Embarrassed? "Yeah." "'Embarrassed,'" Oprah repeated. "So what we want to know is how you all got to be friends after a photograph like that?" She affected a folksy southern accent: "y'all," "*FRAY-ends.*" The two described their first phone conversation. "You called her because you wanted to say—what? 'I'm sorry'?" "'I'm sorry,'" Hazel replied. "Yeah, 'I'm sorry,'" Oprah repeated. "Thank you both." That was it. She couldn't wait to get rid of them.

Oprah had gone out of her way to be hateful, Elizabeth felt. She forever talked about "standing on the shoulders of giants," but she had been as cold as she could be. Maybe, Elizabeth thought, she had reminded Oprah of something ugly in her own story; after all, she had grown up in Mississippi. Or maybe it was her appearance: she had heard Oprah say once that bad teeth made her uncomfortable. (Before long, she took care of that: at an age when people generally started losing their teeth, Elizabeth finally straightened hers out. It cost her several thousand dollars; for one of the few times in her life, she went into debt to do it. Now that she was more often inclined to smile, she more easily could.) Oprah stepped off the stage and greeted her guests. She hugged Elizabeth, who was crying, but she merely shook Hazel's hand, saying nothing. The two left the studio feeling equally abused. For estranged friends desperate for something to share, it could have been a godsend. But Elizabeth said little and Hazel was afraid to say anything: if Elizabeth wouldn't knock a black person, Hazel sure wasn't about to. When they got back to Little Rock, it was raining; rather than letting her take a cab, Antoine insisted on driving Elizabeth home. She seemed surprised that the Masserys would be so kind. Hazel was surprised by her surprise.

Shortly thereafter, the two had another speaking engagement. Despite the remote location, Elizabeth insisted on taking the bus rather than having Hazel fetch her—another bad sign. Customarily, Hazel let Elizabeth decide which of them spoke first. The uncertainty sometimes rattled Hazel, and when she rose this time, she dropped, and scattered, her notes, forcing her to talk off the cuff. She spoke about her kids, and their friendships with black children—like Larry Bailey, who had once given her young son a pair of his homemade boxer shorts. Bailey later drowned; years later, long after her son had married, Hazel found the shorts in his dresser—an indication, she surmised, of how close the two boys had been. She talked, too, of the black girls her daughter had befriended while captain of her high school drill team.

Of the two, Elizabeth had the more compelling story to tell, and invariably garnered more applause. This time, though, Hazel got a standing ovation, and afterward, Elizabeth seemed subdued, even resentful. And she was. Stories like Hazel's, about children innocent of prejudice, irritated her. Lots of white people could tell them, she thought, but by age ten or so, all these angelic, tolerant children were calling black kids "niggers." Elizabeth had said once that she was competitive—that she liked to win; now, she acted as if Hazel had beaten her. "How does it feel to steal the show?" she asked.

So now, it was Hazel's turn to ask questions. Had Elizabeth really told anyone of her apology, as she had claimed? Had she ever really wanted to protect her? Or did she, too, prefer to preserve her as a bogey-woman? Why was she forever impugning her motives? Why was she so determined to prove that she was a bad person? Why did she look so unhappy in all of the pictures of the two of them together? Maybe Elizabeth was sending her a message, the same message young Elizabeth had sent Grace Lorch: that she didn't need or want her. Maybe she was telling her, too, to get off the bus.

THIRTY-EIGHT

arly in 2000 Cathy Collins, the sociologist who had
conducted the racial healing seminar Elizabeth and
Hazel had attended, invited them for catfish at a local
restaurant. Collins planned to write her dissertation on
the two of them, and wanted to discuss the project. She had picked
up no bad vibes that evening, but Elizabeth had: Hazel seemed
very much on edge. Her instincts were sound. Hazel had had
enough.

From one of the self-help books she had taken out of the library, Hazel had learned that before making any crucial decision,
Benjamin Franklin had always prepared a chart, listing the argu-
ments, pro and con. So, sitting on her bed, yellow legal pad in
hand, Hazel did just that. "Do I want to continue to participate
with Elizabeth in presentations, a book, Cathy Collins pHD ect.,"
she'd written on top of the first page. She then drew a line down
the middle, with "Why" on one side and "Why Not" on the other.
She started with the why nots.

1. *The prejudice I have encountered in the past 2 years [from] blacks
   + Whites.*

   A. *she just wants attention and to write a book*

B. Was she sincere [or] just wanted attention (many have errone-
ously [assumed] I just apologized in 1997 not 42 [sic] years ago
make judgements with few facts).

2. I want to be happy and dealing with this issue does not make me
happy

3. the time involved to prepare reading pondering = participating
that I could be spending with my family (what's important to me)

4. lack of Common goal with Elizabeth.

    A. The realization at 58 We don't have but maybe 15 years of good
        health left to do what we want to do

    B. This time subtracts from time spent on preparation for retire-
        ment

5. EE's attitude from the beginning "don't make too much of this
picture" she had her mind made up from the beginning to create a
negative out come (Will Counts)

    + "The book would not have a happy ending" How could she
know? Unless she was determined for it to be so?

    + "She has no hope."

    Her hateful behavior toward me in Indiana and Chicago

    the sour look (picture) as if a smile or to be happy

    would betray the suffering of a victim

    "I want to lead"

    "How does it feel to steal the show?"

    "pissing and calling it rain"?

    Snatching the microphone both times . . .

6. I do this by choice

    I don't HAVE to

7. If there is no hope why bother?

That filled four pages. Then, she turned to the "Why" side of the ledger. And she could think of nothing to write.

There *were* reasons, of course, but she had become too embittered to see them. So now she made another call to Elizabeth. Like the first one, it didn't last long; it didn't have to. She just said she didn't want to do any more programs together. As she remembered it, Elizabeth was surprised. "Oh, was I rude?" she asked. Hazel said nothing: she felt Elizabeth already knew the answer. Having effectively engineered the breakup, Elizabeth didn't object when Hazel completed it.

Hazel took down the "reconciliation" poster, which she had framed and hung in her library. (Elizabeth had also gotten one, but had long ago given it away.) She also concocted an alibi, in case anyone asked for an explanation. She would blame it on her family, hinting they were unhappy with what she'd been doing. Better, even, she concluded, for people to think her marriage was shaky, or that her husband and children were intolerant, than to be labeled a racist yet again. At the very moment of their rupture, there emerged two more traits they shared: each was proud, and stubborn. With neither prepared to pick up the phone, the break became more complete than either had probably imagined, or intended. Not only would they do no more programs together; they would no longer see each other. Quietly, unceremoniously, their great experiment in racial rapprochement was over.

This time, there were no stories, no pictures, no posters. In fact, almost no one noticed. In the next couple of years, Collins interviewed various movers and shakers around town for her dissertation; repeatedly, they praised a relationship that was, in fact, defunct. Oddly, among those saluting their friendship was Elizabeth: Hazel, she told Collins, had helped give her a new life, and she was glad they'd met. But such thoughts were interred in an academic paper; Hazel never saw them.

The few people who knew about the rupture came up with their own postmortems. To Collins and Monk, Elizabeth and Hazel wanted fundamentally different things. Elizabeth sought to focus on the past, Hazel on the future. Both were necessary; neither sufficed. To Annie Abrams, Elizabeth's sin was that she was not Nelson Mandela. Mandela's uncanny ability to move on had been nurtured by decades of leadership and activism, experiences Elizabeth had never had—and, given her mental makeup, never could have had. She had Mandela's intelligence but neither his wisdom nor his magnanimity. As for Hazel, Abrams believed she had been thrown into a situation for which she was utterly unprepared, exploited by people who turned her into a symbol, then dropped her as things got tough. All this was a pity; how many pairs of people have such extraordinary symbolic potential?

"The two unfortunately just didn't get along," said Skip Rutherford. To Vivian Counts, the hurdles Hazel faced were simply insurmountable. "It's hard to say 'I was wrong, I was a racist, I'm so sorry, I wish I had never done it,' and she had to say it over and over and over," she said. "She couldn't take it anymore because no one believed her. People look at that photo and they can't believe the person in it can change."

THIRTY-NINE

H azel didn't have much time to miss Elizabeth: among other things, she was busy with her new great-granddaughter. But relationships of such intensity don't just die; more than a year after they'd last seen one another, Hazel was trying to patch things up.

Only once in her life had she ever flown anywhere by herself, and never before had she set foot in New England. But in September 2001 she hopped on a plane to Hartford, then headed by car to Sheffield, Massachusetts. That was where the Option Institute, an organization she had learned of through her self-help explorations, held weeklong workshops. The group, founded by a man named Barry Neil Kaufman, posited that through sheer will, one could improve one's destiny. The hilly, wooded terrain en route reminded her of rural Arkansas, though in New England there were fewer rusted automobiles strewn about.

Coretta Scott King had endorsed the program, and Hazel hoped that maybe she, or Kaufman, could reach out to Elizabeth and revive their relationship. Maybe Elizabeth could come back with her at some point, she thought, and Kaufman could mediate. She brought the poster with her, and was set to meet Kaufman on September 12. But first came September 11. Alone in a remote place, without televisions and with only spotty cell phone coverage, Hazel grew so frightened by the events of that day that she called Elizabeth, and the two spoke briefly. She also called Antoine, who promptly drove up nearly nonstop from Little Rock to retrieve her. She and Kaufman never did meet.

Less than a month later Hazel and Elizabeth spoke again. This time, it was Elizabeth calling, to report that Will Counts, who had been battling cancer, had died. Elizabeth went to his memorial service in Bloomington; the picture of her and Hazel hung alongside other Counts photographs in an anteroom of the church. Dozens of Counts's disciples attended; one of them, Michel duCille of the *Washington Post*, who had won three Pulitzer Prizes, gave the eulogy. He was amazed that, as he spoke of Elizabeth, he could look out—and there she was. Hazel didn't attend, but in a note to his widow, she described Counts as someone who had "touched so many lives both personally and professionally." Who would have known this better than she? In separate interviews, the two related how Counts had brought them together. "In no time we were old friends," Hazel told one reporter, revealing nothing about what had happened since. Elizabeth and Hazel had communicated for the last time. But it was not the last time one of them tried.

FORTY

In the fuzzy video, a young man in green pants and a white T-shirt sits on a stone wall in front of a burned-out home. In his hands, lengthwise across his lap, is something that looks like a rifle. His legs dangle over the wall, his feet— black shoes, white socks—swinging nonchalantly. Almost casually, without holding up the rifle or taking aim, he fires a shot into the street, then another. Then there is a siren, the squawk of a police radio, another shot, some more smoke. "Put the weapon down," someone—obviously southern, obviously a policeman, obviously protected from any stray bullets—says through a loudspeaker with practiced calm. *"Put . . . it . . . DOWN!"* another voice shouts far more urgently. *"DOWN!"* a third voice commands.

The young man, looking amused but disconnected, ignores the orders. "Put the weapon down," the first voice repeats. "Drop the weapon on the ground!" Instead, the young man stands up. The rifle in his right hand hangs alongside his leg, like some forgotten appendage; he waves his left hand, as if greeting some friend. "Put the weapon down. Put the weapon down." An object flies into view, bouncing harmlessly off his shoulder: a bean bag, designed to distract deranged people brandishing guns long enough to subdue them. The young man pays it no heed. In the corner of the screen, below the numbers "01-01-2003," the seconds and milli-seconds race by. Elizabeth was no longer the only Eckford on a fateful piece of film.

Erin Eckford had never shaken his demons. In eleventh grade he was hospitalized for four months for depression. Though gifted at science and math, he had dropped out of college, stopped work-ing, and been placed on medication that he often neglected to take. He also had a minor criminal record, and was jailed briefly for selling marijuana. Once, Elizabeth made him sell two guns he had acquired. In 2000 he had moved back into his mother's house, and, convinced that she had become the enemy, had done what-ever he could to drive her out. He also made embarrassing, disrup-tive visits to her office, where he would ask for money or food or just simply sit there, acting strange. After he left, Elizabeth would cry. Her coworkers half worried that one day he might just come in and shoot them all. Because she didn't want her children fighting over her home should she die (though she was barely sixty at this point, dying was always on Elizabeth's mind), she transferred title to him—for five dollars—and moved into an apartment in a high-rise nearby. Erin promptly let the house and grounds deteriorate. Annoyed that they interfered with the lawn mower, he poured weed killer on Elizabeth's flowers and shrubs. He grew progres-sively unhinged.

Around a quarter past four that New Year's afternoon, Erin left the house on West 18th Street carrying an SKS military-style semi-automatic rifle—one of several weapons he had apparently se-creted in the attic, not far from where the white skirt had gone. Then he began firing the rifle into the air. The Little Rock police soon caught up with him, about six blocks away. Oblivious to the

Erin Eckford, seventh grade (Courtesy Elizabeth Eckford)

orders, Erin repositioned himself within the stone steps. For an instant—and to all appearances inadvertently—his rifle pointed toward the street, toward those officers. So they fired at him, at least thirteen times. Six times they hit him, his body convulsing, his back rising, from the impact. Three policemen then rushed in, though now he no longer posed a danger to anyone.

Elizabeth, who had been in her apartment, heard about the shooting from Annette Gilbert, her colleague in Judge Humphrey's chambers. When she and Gilbert reached the scene, they learned an ambulance had already taken Erin to the hospital. Though his liver had been cut to ribbons, the doctors thought that some extraordinary clotting serum might stanch the bleeding, and that he would pull through. But they didn't find all the bullet holes in time, and he bled to death. He was twenty-six.

When a son of one of the Little Rock Nine, especially of this particular one, dies violently, especially at the hands of the police, it is news, and Erin's death made the national papers. Hazel got word the next morning, when Antoine spotted the story and woke her up to tell her about it. The two sat on the edge of their bed, crying. How, Hazel worried, would Elizabeth respond? Would she simply unravel? After lunch, they drove to Elizabeth's building. Told she wasn't there, Hazel wrote out a short note, saying they'd been by and how sorry they were. The woman on duty promised to give it to Elizabeth. Hazel considered attending the funeral, but three years had passed since she had last seen Elizabeth, and she wasn't sure she'd be welcome. Besides, she feared it would turn into some kind of political rally, the sort of thing where the Rev. Al Sharpton or some other rabble-rouser might appear. Instead, she and her husband sent a more conventional card, which this time they simply signed. (Among others sending condolences was Lee Lorch.)[1]

The night before the funeral, there were visiting hours at the mortuary to which Erin, his shattered jaw patched up by the embalmer, had been taken. The editor of the *Arkansas Times,* Max Brantley, went, partly to pay his respects, partly for fear that if he didn't, no other whites would. In fact, so many people came to the funeral, at Judge Humphrey's church, that some were consigned to an overflow room. Erin's father recited one of his poems, and Elizabeth read the familiar passage from Ecclesiastes: "To everything, there is a season." Because Elizabeth wanted no loud gospel music, Minnijean's sister, Phyllis Brown, made other selections: some protest songs, some numbers by the a cappella group Sweet Honey in the Rock. Erin's cousin Jackee Johnson sang the Lord's Prayer. Even in the church, there was anger and resentment over Elizabeth's refusal to turn Erin's case into a cause, to claim police misconduct and sue the city. But Elizabeth believed Erin had wanted to die—"suicide by cop," she called it.

Thanking Vivian Counts for her note, Elizabeth acknowledged deriving comfort from what was, for her, an unlikely source. "I know that I do not bear this burden alone," she wrote. "Last summer for no reason at all I surrendered to God. There was no precipitating event—yet there was a need that could only be filled by prayer." But the handwritten note Hazel and Antoine left for her was never delivered, and when Elizabeth received their bare card, with nothing on it but their names, she was deeply hurt. A breach that was already approaching irreparability was now deepened by yet another misunderstanding.

Friends feared that Erin's death might finally tip Elizabeth over the edge. Instead, she seemed to draw strength from it. For one thing, it prompted her to move back into her house. Now *it* was in need of a renaissance. Calvin had been living in it, and it had fallen into even further disrepair: the kitchen counter was burned and, because he had begun raising puppies inside, part of the floor had rotted and a carpet needed to be replaced. Slowly, Elizabeth began bringing it back to life. She started by dumping a couple of loads of loam on the front lawn and planting new shrubs and bulbs. Blossoms began to reappear. Lecture fees helped pay for a new heating and air-conditioning system and awnings.

Elizabeth still devoted herself to her job, but with a somewhat chastened spirit: coworkers noticed that her tragedy made her a bit less judgmental. On Hazel, though, her position only hardened. The "reconciliation" poster was popular enough to warrant another printing. Minnijean told Elizabeth that it was a lie, and that she should repudiate it. Elizabeth let them go ahead; it was her way of supporting the place, something she couldn't otherwise have afforded. Now, though, she insisted that it carry a caveat, one she devised herself. Soon, a small sticker, resembling the surgeon general's warning on cigarette packs, appeared in the upper right-hand corner. It was gold, and relatively inconspicuous, particularly against Central's ochre bricks:

"True reconciliation can occur only when we honestly acknowledge our painful, but shared, past."

—Elizabeth Eckford

The message puzzled Hazel, who had not been consulted about either the reprinting or the disclaimer. As far as she was concerned, "acknowledging the painful but shared past" was just what she had been trying to do. She'd have liked to have had her own sticker, one that said, *"True reconciliation can occur only when we honestly let go of resentment and hatred, and move forward."* But that was only a thought; she never pressed for one.

The phrase soon popped up again, this time in cast iron. Before a couple of thousand people in August 2005, individual statues of the Nine, with Elizabeth, her binder held close to her chest, lead-

Elizabeth with statue of herself, capitol grounds, Little Rock, 2005
(Photo by Gary Crallé)

ing the way, were dedicated on the grounds of the state capitol. John Deering, the sculptor who designed the statues with his wife, Kathy, said that of the Nine, Elizabeth caused him the most concern: people remembered how *she* looked. (Her figure posed no difficulties; even in the photograph, her posture was statuesque.) As for her face, Counts had given him whatever he needed. But convinced that he could not capture Elizabeth's mix of stoicism and trauma with her sunglasses on, he gave her clear lenses instead. Seeing Elizabeth's eyes is not just disconcerting but demystifying: in her inscrutability that day had lain much of her power. Still, even while it sat in the foundry, a visitor from Sweden looked at the statue of Elizabeth and began to cry. Elizabeth thought it a good likeness—she had never realized that she had her grandmother's cheekbones—and was impressed that the Deerings had somehow captured the mix of hesitancy and resolve she had felt. Of all the tributes she received, this one made her proudest, though she questioned the wisdom of honoring living people; after all, they could still mess up! Most pleasing to her was the location: visible from the governor's office, not far from the monument to Confederate soldiers dedicated a century earlier, and another, dedicated in 1913, to their wives.

Every statue was accompanied by a phrase of the subject's choice; Elizabeth's was the same stern language she had stuck on the posters. Thus, even on the capitol grounds, Hazel was still alongside her. Otherwise, the topic of Hazel didn't come up often, and when it did, Elizabeth was dismissive. A journalist named Amanda Robb, writing on forgiveness for *Oprah* magazine, asked Elizabeth how she had been able to forgive Hazel. Elizabeth gave her the name of her antidepressant.

FORTY-ONE

Hazel had helped coax Elizabeth out of her shell, but she had also been a crutch. Without her around, Elizabeth's renewal intensified. She now went on television by herself, including on *Today*. Her appearances before students grew more frequent, on behalf of organizations like Facing History and Ourselves as well as Jeff Steinberg's groups from California. Partly with some tough love from Minnijean—"For God's sake, get rid of those cards! This is your story! You don't need them!" she told her—her fear of public speaking slowly eased. Still, it was not easy for her, as I saw for myself in 2006, when she spoke to students at a restaurant near Little Rock. First, they lined up to be photographed with her, and to have her sign their books. "Oh, my gosh! I can't believe that's you!" one girl gushed. "I'm sorry. I'm so emotional now. I'm about to cry." Elizabeth remained mostly stern, only occasionally yielding a semi-smile. Before the end of the line reached her, her increasingly fragile legs gave out, and she had to sit.

Talking to the group, Elizabeth spoke very formally, enunciating every word. Only intermittently did she sound southern: like a train picking up stray seeds, she absorbed accents wherever she had been and from whomever she had met, even from a Kenyan exchange student she once knew. Her remarks followed her usual pattern: some history of Little Rock, race relations there, her family, herself. (She described Central, saying that her only protection there was "fleet feet." She didn't graduate *cum laude* but "*thank you, lordy.*") Then came the admonitions. What mattered wasn't whether your teacher liked you; study for yourselves. Even a shy person can develop steel; even the most ordinary can do extraordinary things. Stand up for the most defenseless among you. Reach out to someone being harassed; you might help save a life.

Then came the questions. A student who had seen Elizabeth before remarked on how much more social and open she'd become. In fact, with each question Elizabeth grew more tense. People hemmed her in on all sides, and that always rattled her. Suddenly, she put down the microphone and quickly left the premises. "Get me out of here," she told the driver. A puzzled murmur filled the room, capturing that mixture of uneasiness and titillation schoolchildren feel whenever adults go off their scripts. "I do apologize, but she is having an episode," a group leader told the students. "You have to expect that. She relives the experience every time she talks about it."

With me, too, Elizabeth sometimes balked. Once, a day after we'd had a long phone conversation, she left me a message. She had to discontinue such interviews, she said; they were creating "some backwash" in her life. But she persisted, and over time I, too, could see changes. I was with her the following year when she spoke to one of Steinberg's groups at Central. (She had never felt especially welcome there, even under a black principal; unlike Ernest Green, she'd never spoken at commencement.) Steinberg reviewed the usual ground rules, then reminded his students that they were about to meet an icon. "Ladies and gentlemen," he shouted, "it is my pleasure to introduce to you Miss Elizabeth Eckfooooooooooooooord!" And Elizabeth strolled onto the stage, the stage on which she had delivered Portia's courtroom speech so many years earlier. As she approached the bare black plastic chair, the students in the auditorium, black and white, quietly rose, raised their arms, and, without making a sound, started waving their hands wildly. It was sign language—for a standing ovation.

FORTY-TWO

———

Elizabeth had grown claustrophobic during the crowded reception and, taking a break, looked out the windows of the Rainbow Room. It was after dark, and in all directions from Rockefeller Center there were spectacular panoramas of glistening Manhattan. She pointed toward a nondescript, generic apartment tower, somewhere around 56th or 57th Streets, just south of Central Park. Was that the Chrysler Building? she asked.

In April 2007, five months short of the fiftieth anniversary of the events in Little Rock, the Nine came to New York to be feted by the African American Experience Fund of the National Parks Service. Elizabeth had heard it all before, and despite the featured attractions (the professional power broker Vernon Jordan was to be the latest to salute them), she became restless during the umpteenth round of speechifying. She was visibly relieved when the evening ended. She was getting up in only a few hours—at 4:30 the following morning—to catch the plane back to Little Rock: she wanted to put in a day's work at the courthouse. Besides, this was really just a dress rehearsal. The real celebration would take place that September.

Elizabeth's wasn't the only case of commemoration fatigue. By this point, truth be told, many whites in Little Rock had had quite enough of the Little Rock Nine. They wouldn't say it aloud, but they felt the black students had been honored—and the white students trashed—long enough. Whenever the topic came up, they would tune out; when stories appeared on television, they would reach for their remotes. As usual, Ralph Brodie captured it best: "There was the fifth anniversary, the tenth anniversary, the fifteenth anniversary, the twentieth anniversary, the twenty-fifth anniversary, the thirtieth anniversary, the thirty-fifth anniversary, and the fortieth anniversary. Now there's the fiftieth anniversary. It gets real old," he said.

This time at least, Brodie wouldn't have Hazel to worry about: she was sitting this one out. The man who had put her on the poster, Skip Rutherford, feared that her absence would be glaring, and much commented upon. Hazel wouldn't dare *not* show up, he predicted; that would only prove that the last time wasn't for real. In fact, to Hazel, that hardly mattered. She had learned her lesson. Folks would surely ask all over again what she was doing there, why she wanted the attention, what was in it for her. So when the reporters left messages, she didn't return their calls. When I tried contacting her through an intermediary, she said she was "out of that loop," and never going back.

Naturally, she could never be entirely absent. The commemoration would include the dedication of a new, enlarged visitor center, replacing the one at the gas station; what Brodie called "the negative picture of Elizabeth" would, for all his complaints, be even bigger. Also, writers—like this one—remained interested in the white girl in the picture. "I don't really know how to say this but I wish you could get over your obsession with Hazel," he wrote me. "Too much has already been made over that young woman. Ignoring her may really be all she deserves." On another occasion he added, "we are all a bit paranoid about that picture and Hazel."[1]

Elizabeth would gladly have stopped giving speeches long ago had she not needed the money. She also would have happily skipped the anniversary events could she have gotten away with it. Annie Abrams had wanted Wal-Mart to mass-produce her original outfit for the commemoration, so that on September 4, 2007, schoolgirls everywhere could wear replicas, in admiration and solidarity. Elizabeth was dubious—why, she asked, would anyone want to wear *that thing?*—and nothing ever came of the idea. As for the original, someone finally ventured into Elizabeth's attic, where Elizabeth had always assumed it sat in mildewed tatters, and discovered that it wasn't there. One of her sons, who periodically and rather unselectively cleaned house, had probably dumped it in the trash.

Fifty years earlier, Grace Lorch had told the angry mob surrounding Elizabeth that in six months they'd all be ashamed of themselves. There was little evidence that she was right. Apart from Hazel and Mary Ann Burleson, who had apologized on *Oprah,* no one in the photograph or in the crowd that day or in the mob inside Central that year had ever come forward.[2] For some, like Olen Spann (the man in the hat and pressed khakis) or Richard Stinnett (the boy in the striped shirt just behind Elizabeth) or Lonnie Ward (the boy behind Hazel), it was too late: they had died. Richard Boehler, Frankie Gregg, Kenny Vandiver, and all of the others whose names pop up in Mrs. Huckaby's disciplinary files, had led their lives, some in Little Rock, never to be heard from on this subject again. But to Hazel, *they* were the smart ones. No one ever gave *them* grief.

On September 23 the latest anniversary extravaganza got under way. All of the well-practiced and increasingly elaborate rituals were again reenacted, bigger and bolder than ever. But the revisionists were ready, too. The *Democrat-Gazette* reported that the consensus among a gathering of Central graduates from fifty years earlier was that only "a handful" of students had misbehaved and that the Nine had generally been embraced. A former Central teacher insisted that the press had exaggerated what had been "routine misbehavior, not uncommon in any high school of the time." Much of white Little Rock quietly agreed.

What was different on this anniversary was a newly assertive Elizabeth. She, too, had read these claims, and at a press conference the next day, she called them "very, very annoying." A handful of students *did* stand apart, she agreed: the handful who had treated the black students like human beings. Among the nine of them, she speculated, they had encountered maybe five whites who fit that description. She made the same point even more strongly when she spoke at the dedication of the new visitor center.

Carlotta LaNier, who parceled out the assignments, had selected Elizabeth for that task because of her love of history. But Elizabeth had warned that LaNier might not like what she would say. The newly created Little Rock Nine Foundation, which was to provide scholarships for needy students, was holding a fundraiser that night; with hopes high for donations from the white community, this was no time to reopen old wounds. But the article, Elizabeth felt, had to be addressed. "I stand before you as a once shy, submissive child," she began. Then she departed from that role. "I was very dismayed when I read in yesterday's paper that the student body 'welcomed us.' I didn't feel it," she said. Scattered nervous laughter rippled through the crowd. "Or that there was only a 'handful' of students that harassed us. Each of us was followed from class to class by an organized group who assaulted us daily. And 'harassment' is a very, very mild term. I'll tell you what it was to me. It was to be scalded in the shower. It was to be body-slammed against the wall lockers every day. And my only protection was my binder that I held close to my chest." By this point, her eyes were red. She spoke of the pins she had placed around the binder. "Very soon after that a girl reported to the vice principal that I had scratched her," she said. "*Meek, mild Elizabeth scratch someone?* No. No. Didn't happen."

The next day, four thousand people gathered in front of Central for the main event. Several of the Nine reached their seats either in wheelchairs or by clinging to the railing, a reminder that, as Elizabeth put it, some of them would soon start slipping over the hill.[3] For the first, and last, time, at an anniversary commemoration, each of them spoke. The tone was generally upbeat. When her turn came, Elizabeth talked about forgiveness, and the burden it lifts from the forgiver. But one had to ask, she said, whether an apology was real. "I know the difference between an apology and someone who is just trying to make themselves feel good," she said. "If you can't name what you did, it's not an apology."

As the crowd dispersed, Peggy Harris of the Associated Press spotted Elizabeth walking away—on the same sidewalk she had trod fifty years earlier, once again alone. Elizabeth looked straight ahead, resolute and self-contained, just as she had the first time around. You could see how far Elizabeth had come, Harris thought, but also the fifteen-year-old girl she'd been. Harris weighed approaching her but quickly thought better of it.

The festivities were widely reported. One listener told National Public Radio that after hearing a segment about Elizabeth's walk, he had pulled over his car to weep. A second listener asked whether the white girl in the famous picture had ever been identified, or expressed any remorse. Yes, he was told, her name was Hazel Bryan Massery, and yes, some years afterward she had apologized, and yes, her apology had been gracefully accepted. Two weeks later, in another public radio interview, Elizabeth complained about Hazel's "amnesia" and suggested, mistakenly, that she had remained close to segregationist students inside Central even after she had left. Talking to others, Elizabeth was harsher still. Hazel was in this for herself. Hazel craved money and fame, and when she didn't find them, she wanted out. Hazel really had nothing to say or teach. Hazel was jealous of her. Hazel was physically repulsed, maybe even allergic, to her. Hazel wanted her to be instantly, magically cured, just so she would no longer feel guilty. Hazel was a liar, a show-off, an exhibitionist: Hazel thought *she* was famous, when in fact only the picture was.

Elizabeth's feelings grew more extreme because they festered; with even the slightest resistance, she would back off. (For someone raised prejudiced, I pointed out, going to a spa together—undressing and bathing together, massaging each other's feet—was surely significant. She hadn't thought of that, Elizabeth said. Hazel really had come a long ways! My goodness!) Perhaps she didn't entirely believe what she was saying, or even want to. She admitted missing Hazel, especially at certain times of the year, like during the annual flower shows. Were she to see her again, she said, she would embrace her—not to rekindle their relationship necessarily, but because that was how she would feel. She wished she could tell Hazel how much she had helped her, but she wouldn't, or couldn't, or shouldn't: after a lifetime of deference, she had grown "uppity." When she talked about Hazel, Elizabeth's head would droop, and her eyes would begin to water. But she would not let herself accept Hazel. To Elizabeth some things, like principles, mattered more than love. As hard as she was on Hazel, she was even harder on herself.

Similarly isolated, Hazel's heart similarly hardened. Whites weren't ready for desegregation in 1957, and blacks weren't ready for reconciliation now. Elizabeth didn't want reconciliation; she wanted revenge. She, and people like her—like most of the Little Rock Nine—could not accept that most white people aren't evil; they want white people to suffer, too. Maybe Elizabeth wasn't *that* vulnerable: maybe some of it was for show. And maybe she hadn't even soured on her; maybe she had been hostile from the very beginning, agreeing to the second picture only because disagreeing would have been disagreeable. Elizabeth might still be stuck in 1957, but there was no way that she, Hazel, would sit around forever in sackcloth and ashes.

But some of her anger, too, was clearly for show. She still thought of Elizabeth on her birthday every October, and on New Year's Days she thought of Erin. The more she read up on her history, the more she understood why black skepticism, and bitterness, were so deep. If she were black, she would feel the same way. These things would take years, or decades, to abate; she had just tried to speed things up a bit. She never did throw away the poster. When she talked about Elizabeth, her eyes teared up as well. Never would she reach out again as she had. But would they ever see each other again? Well, the story wouldn't really end until one of them died.

The poster continued to hang in the office of Central's principal, Nancy Rousseau, though more as an ideal to be sought than a reflection of reality. It was all heartbreaking to her. "I just had hoped that I could show this picture and say, 'This happened, and that happened, and now . . .' and there is no 'now,'" she said. "And that makes me sad. It makes me sad for them, it makes me sad for the future students at our school, and for the history books, because I'd like a happy ending. And we don't have that."

FORTY-THREE

Little Rock had early balloting during the presidential election of 2008, and Elizabeth voted as soon as she could on the morning of the day the polls opened. She never thought she'd live to vote for a black presidential candidate, though the pessimist in her believed that Barack Obama couldn't possibly win. Hazel vacillated between the candidates but eventually voted for John McCain. She found herself a reason—Obama would give away too much money to too many unworthy people—but really, it was bitterness, and a broken heart. Obama seemed like a fair and intelligent man, plenty presidential. But *they* hadn't treated her fairly; *they* hadn't given her a chance, so why should she give one to them? She felt silly about it afterward, especially when, on Inauguration Day, her mother confessed something to her: she had voted for a black man herself.

Before the swearing-in, Elizabeth gave a number of interviews, usually to foreign reporters she could count on never to bother her again. Then, all at once, it dawned on various people that when the nation's first African-American president took office, Elizabeth Eckford should be nearby. The rest of the Little Rock Nine would be, sitting with the Tuskegee Airmen. When Elizabeth told the *Washington Post* that she couldn't afford the trip, offers poured in to help foot the bill. She turned them down. Traveling had grown too strenuous for her, and she still feared crowds. Her confreres knew better than to push her. So she watched it all in her house, on a small, snowy television that seemed nearly as old as the house itself.

She continued to put a cheerier face on the place. She had never hung mementoes—she hadn't wanted to turn it into a shrine to herself—but now, a few of them began appearing on the walls. Her home was now replenished with Eckfords: her sister Anna moved in with her, and for a time, so did her father, and so did Calvin, back from the Coast Guard. Outside, the daffodils, irises, and roses filled up nearly every square inch of ground, a glorious burst of color in a neighborhood of drab greens and browns. People drove by to take in the blossoms, then turned around to see them again.

Sixty-seven years old on January 20, 2009, Elizabeth still had mortality on her mind. She was slowing down. She had diabetes, and tired easily. Someone who had become immortalized while walking could no longer walk far. She had always spoken bluntly, and sardonically, about death. (She didn't fear flying, she told people, because a plane crash offered the best death imaginable: fast, with funeral costs and debts covered.) With a mixture of resignation and mordant humor, she began planning for the next big family function, one she would miss herself. She already had the right crystal goblets for iced tea, and had found the perfect punch bowl, but she still lacked a twelve-cup percolator. She warned colleagues in Judge Humphrey's chambers that the pickings would be slim, so no one should show up just for the food.

Elizabeth had once said that when it came time to quit work, they'd have to carry her out feet first. Then she set a date that sounded very far off: June 30, 2009. But by that spring, she realized she couldn't wait that long. One morning in May, her coworkers arrived to find messages on their answering machines. It was Elizabeth, announcing she was through. It was effective immediately; they couldn't even throw her a party. From now on, Elizabeth would get by on her Social Security, plus a tiny pension from her job, plus fees from her speeches. But she knew how to be poor; she had been that way before.

The photograph—known to the archivists at Indiana University, to which Counts bequeathed his negatives, as "the scream image"—still appears all over the world. There is a rush for it around various Little Rock anniversaries, as well as during every Black History Month. It remains a staple of history textbooks. But as Elizabeth's burdens lifted, so, too, did the weight of the photograph itself. It had actually been a good thing, she came to believe, something that opened doors to her, helped her overcome her shyness. Jim Crow America, her traumas at Central, her uneven and interrupted education, her emotional history—all had narrowed the possibilities a woman of her intellect would normally have enjoyed. But the picture had helped her, relatively late in life, to find her voice. And for someone who cared so deeply about history, it had a wonderful irrefutability to it. It could not be forgotten or denied or rewritten. It was a firewall against revisionism.

And here was one more thing she shared with Hazel. Maybe even more remarkably, while not exactly thankful for the photograph, Hazel recognized the good it had brought *her*. Yes, it had been a terrible burden. Yes, it would define her long after she was gone. ("To them it's a picture," she said once. "To me, it's *me*.")

She didn't like the word "unlucky," and "cursed" wasn't quite right either, but was there ever another image that so doggedly refused to die? At the same time, it had propelled her out of Central, away from people who would have only compounded her shame. It gave her firsthand experience with racism, and helped her—at least she thought so—surmount it. It had made her a better person, and, incidentally, helped her to find a loving husband. Maybe she had been chosen, like Jonah going to Nineveh, to convey a message. She still looked at the picture with horror: it was that awful. It continued to make her weep. But she also knew that she was a kind person who had done everything she could to atone, and she had lived a good life besides.

Eight years after starting my story, I finally wrote some of it down. An article on Elizabeth and Hazel—the genesis of this book—appeared on the website of *Vanity Fair* in September 2007, just as everyone was gathering for the fiftieth anniversary in Little Rock. It broke the impasse between Hazel and me, and we began to speak—tentatively at first and, later, more comfortably. Courteous and amused, yet probably disapproving, Antoine made himself scarce whenever I came around (that is, when I saw him at all; Hazel seemed to fit me in when he was out).

As for Hazel's children, I never did meet, or speak with, any of them. Hazel was determined to protect them. But from what? The pain of reliving their mother's shame? The embarrassment of revealing their disapproval of what she had done then, or was doing now, or the fact that they didn't much care about either? The repercussions they might suffer in their businesses were their mother revealed as a "nigger lover"? Or of being unable to hide their hostility toward some untrustworthy northern reporter, out to stir up old troubles for his own gain? I could never be sure. That the children of both Elizabeth and Hazel were almost equally uninterested in their stories and unavailable to talk about them to me was striking, and discouraging.

Elizabeth's statements about her in the article were, she told me, like a voice from the dead: they hadn't spoken in six years, hadn't seen each other for seven. After reading it, Hazel couldn't sleep for three nights, even with pills. She was excited and hurt and, mostly, confused. Which Elizabeth in it should she believe? The one who had called her a liar, seeking reconciliation on the cheap, or the one who had acknowledged all her help, and even that she missed her? She was tempted to call Elizabeth—she knew another birthday was approaching—but decided, instead, to write. She put down a few sentences, only suddenly to stop. "I'm not very good at expressing my thoughts and feelings, and besides, it would fill many pages," she explained. "I do want you to know I care about you still and if you want to talk I'm here. Call me." She then added one more thing, something I'd neglected to mention in my article. She recounted that, the day after Erin was killed, she and Antoine had come by to see her, and that they had left a note for her. Instead of mailing the letter, though, Hazel stuck it in a drawer. After all, what good would it do? If she didn't send it, then at least, like so many other letters she had sent off, it couldn't go unanswered.

Reviewing Hazel's comments with Elizabeth, however, I did mention that condolence call. Elizabeth said nothing, and I moved on. Elizabeth, though, did not. A few weeks later, she told me how surprised, and pleased, she had been to learn what Hazel had done.

At some point, she said, maybe she would write Hazel to say so. But she never did.

I would have loved it if, during the long gestation of this book, Elizabeth and Hazel had again reunited. How nice it would have been if, simply by being part of this joint enterprise, they had put aside their suspicion and hurt and started afresh. It would have been good for them and also, of course, for me: what author would not want a happy ending to his tale, particularly one so filled with sadness? Never, though, did I consider asking them to do it. I did not want to stage-manage anything, nor to have them view me as yet another manipulator, using them for his own ends. As best I could, I honored the boundaries they had established: going between their homes, or speaking with them on the phone, I only rarely mentioned one to the other. Planting a rose bush in Elizabeth's front yard, I did not mention that I used Hazel's shovel. Should the two women ever see each other again, I figured, it should be on their own terms, and in their own good time.

But as the book neared completion, a photographer friend who had offered to take individual portraits of the two asked—inevitably—if he could also photograph them together. I changed the subject. He persisted. I resisted. He pressed—it was really a matter of recording history, he said—and eventually I agreed at least to ask. Perhaps, I rationalized, I'd be doing them a favor, supplying the nudge they both needed, and maybe even wanted. I knew the need for delicacy. I would call them well in advance, before we got to Little Rock, so that they would feel no undue pressure. I would stress that they owed me no favors.[1] It would be done quietly, I would assure them, with no fanfare; no one would know anything until this book appeared. We could choreograph everything—comings and goings, who was present when and for how long—in whatever way they wished. They would still fashion their own ending, happy or otherwise.

Because I thought Elizabeth both more unpredictable and more likely to take offense, I called Hazel first. Just as I had done when I first met the two, and notwithstanding everything I had ostensibly learned since, I misread things completely. Hazel answered unhesitatingly: she wasn't interested. Her tone I recognized—I'd heard it early on, when she refused to meet with me—and I knew there was nothing more to discuss: even asking her to mull things over was pointless. She was perfectly gracious; we simply moved on to other topics: what she should wear, how to do it all while Antoine was out of the house. My call to Elizabeth, then, was easy: I need only tell her what had happened and, just for the record, ask her how she felt. She seemed a bit surprised by Hazel's attitude. She then said, equally unhesitatingly, that she would have sat with her, even though they'd have little to say. Perhaps, she speculated, Hazel had still not forgiven her for her comments about her father. To Elizabeth, the issue seemed less personal, more abstract. Reuniting with Hazel now was simply one more claim that the picture—indeed, that history itself, which she appreciated and respected—had placed on her.

I reproached myself: had I asked Elizabeth first, might Hazel have reacted differently? Might she relent now once she was told? Perhaps there was still some hope. The question hovered over us that chilly Sunday morning in March when we drove out to her house. Knowing Hazel's punctuality, we arrived precisely at noon, just as the cookies she had baked for us were coming out of the oven. She had dressed casually but was impeccably made up, as if for a special occasion. Her silver hair shimmered; I don't think I'd ever seen her wearing lipstick before. First in her backyard, near the budding tulip tree, then in her living room, she endured three hours of picture-taking, as different as different could be from her fleeting encounter with Will Counts fifty-four years earlier. When the photographer urged her to look serious—befitting the gravity of her story—she did her best to comply, though that was really not her way: she is more lighthearted than that. Only once it was over, and I took my leave, did the photographer ask Hazel to reconsider. She would not. Perhaps she could sleep on it, he said. In our mind, at least, the matter was still not closed. We reached Elizabeth late afternoon. The sun was perilously low, but cast a warm glow as she sat down on the brick wall in front of her house, the house that had witnessed so many chapters of her story. Behind her, the first flowers of spring, yellow and purple pansies, blossomed brilliantly. As the photographer worked, Elizabeth held her head high.

We did not call Hazel, and never heard from her. At this point, only Photoshop could bring them together. Just as Elizabeth and Hazel represented racial reality in 1957, it could be argued, they still do in 2011: yes, the worst excesses are past, the chasm somewhat narrower. But new barriers had replaced the old: while black suspicions remain, now whites feel, in addition to their residual prejudices, maligned, belittled, aggrieved. If two people of such obvious intelligence, goodwill, and empathy, who even liked each other for that brief moment in time, can't bridge the racial gap, then who can? But consider their catastrophic start, and how far they had come. And still could, even as each nears seventy. Perhaps somewhere down that road, when no one else is looking, they will find a way to meet again. Elizabeth is ready. And, to be precise about it, Hazel never did say "no." She only said "not now."

Notes

CHAPTER TWO

1. The phrase was coined by Relman Morin of the Associated Press and soon became commonplace.

CHAPTER THREE

1. For some previously undisclosed details in this account, I'm grateful to Jennifer Singleton Miller, who devoted her 2011 master's thesis to the lynching of John Carter.

2. Little Rock's senior black lawyer, Robert Booker, described to Harold Isaacs of MIT the electoral appeal Faubus made to his community. "You can't go with the other side: they're out-and-out segregationist," he'd say. "But you know me. You know what I am. You know I'm for you. I might wink at them now and again out of need, but you know I'll do my best for you every time."

3. The WPA investigators found the racial chasm enormous. Most parks were segregated, as were the hospital wards and movie theaters (though two of them offered blacks "gallery accommodations"). The black public library had 9,709 books, the white 276,995. As of 1945, Little Rock's black library could not subscribe to black weeklies like the *Chicago Defender* and the *Pittsburgh Courier*. These papers were the main sources of news, and among the principal voices for racial justice, in black America, and the white city fathers apparently didn't want to subsidize anything so subversive. (The papers nonetheless reached Little Rock and towns like it via sleeping car porters who tossed them off their trains at certain designated locations.)

4. It was a case establishing the principle of equal pay for equal work for black teachers that first brought Thurgood Marshall to town.

5. When white school officials asked another of the Little Rock Nine, Jefferson Thomas, whether he'd talked to "Mrs. [Daisy] Bates" about enrolling in Central, Thomas failed at first to realize that they were referring to the head of the local NAACP; he'd never before heard a white man call a black woman "Mrs."

6. "It appeared that there is a certain social mixing at the whorehouse level," Isaacs wrote. "I did not investigate."

7. Booker recalled that once, while he was buying something at the cigar stand in the café by the courthouse, some white lawyers sitting at a nearby table invited him over for a soda. He didn't know what to do: blacks could enter the place, but normally could not sit down. Again he was asked to join the group. As everyone watched him, he went over and took a seat; he drank his Coke, uncomfortable from first sip to last.

CHAPTER FOUR

1. After the first day, these black employees received special identification cards allowing them to go in.

2. Like other particulars in Bates's book, *The Long Shadow of Little Rock*, some of this doesn't compute. At least one other student, Terrence Roberts, showed up for school on his own that day. Another, Melba Patillo, has said she did, though it's unclear whether she was present at all. And a third, Minnijean Brown, denied receiving any such call from Bates. According to Bates's biographer, Grif Stockley, numerous passages in her memoir are either incomplete, unverifiable, misleading, or incorrect, partly because her publisher sought a heroic self-portrait—something to which Bates herself was clearly not opposed.

CHAPTER SIX

1. So deeply etched were the racial lines that blacks never pressed to come on, and the program never thought to invite them. Without any court orders to integrate, and no soldiers patrolling its dance floor, *Steve's Show* represented Little Rock far more faithfully than did Central: it remained restricted long after Central's barriers came down.

CHAPTER SEVEN

1. The seven included Jane Hill (who quickly dropped out of the group) but not Terrence Roberts (who, like Elizabeth, had come to school by himself that day) or Melba Patillo.

2. It marked the first and last time that Dhonau, beginning his thirty-year run at the paper, ever stepped into one of his stories.

3. Still, he joked about it, telling reporters he'd come to add "color to the situation."

4. Schakne was sufficiently honest, and respectful of history, to admit later that he'd been overly aggressive. Aggressiveness had not been his only sin that day; when his cameraman had missed some protestors chanting anti-integration slogans, he asked them to do it again. Faubus quickly learned of this manipulation, which neatly corroborated his claim that the out-of-town press was stirring up trouble.

CHAPTER EIGHT

1. And Hazel never saw Lorch at all. But afterward, Lorch expressed sympathy for her and the other whites in Counts's photograph, invoking the famous language from Franklin Roosevelt's second inaugural address. "The people who made up that mob, many of them 'ill-fed, ill-clad, ill-housed,' need to look back at the picture," she wrote. "Their children too have walls to break down, not as direct victims of race prejudice, but as victims of poverty and ignorance."

2. Lee Lorch's contract with Philander Smith was not renewed; effectively blacklisted from every college in the United States, he and his family moved to Canada, where he was to live and teach for the next fifty years. Grace Lorch's experiences in Little Rock and the exile that followed thrust her into a depression from which she never really recovered. She died in 1974.

CHAPTER NINE

1. Taken with a Rolleicord, it was square rather than horizontal, showing more of Elizabeth's skirt. Her face was sharper and clearer than in Counts's picture, and ever more inscrutable. Hazel was again at mid-epithet, but at a slightly different point: her mouth is more wide open, her teeth less clenched.

2. As Hazel remembered it, Sammie Dean's father had been behind them, and had called to his daughter at the precise instant Counts took his picture. Parker did not recall why she turned around. Sammie Dean's father *was* concerned at her conspicuousness; if in fact he shouted at her at that moment, he protected her far better than he could ever have intended.

3. The remainder of the article has not been preserved.

4. Interviewed by the writer Linda Monk many years later, Pauline Bryan remained irked that Hazel had been singled out for criticism. She was taken aback when Monk described to her what Elizabeth had suffered through that day. "I didn't know it was like that, I really didn't," she said. "Oh, how frightful!"

CHAPTER TEN

1. The man to whom the girls made their remarks was the same fellow who had comforted Elizabeth on the bench: Benjamin Fine of the *New York Times*. For that, and for being a northerner and a Jew representing a liberal newspaper, he quickly became a whipping boy for the segregationists, who accused him of stirring the pot to spice up his reportage. He heard from the home office, too. Convinced that he'd made himself part of his own story—and belatedly realizing that events in Little Rock warranted a first-rank reporter rather than a somewhat tweedy education editor—the *Times* dispatched the famed war correspondent Homer Bigart to replace him. Fine, who evidently had lost favor at the paper for other reasons, left the *Times* shortly thereafter.

2. After four days of harassment, Dorothy Counts gave up, and soon moved with her family to Philadelphia.

CHAPTER TWELVE

1. Only with a last-minute $790 donation from Philadelphia could the *Worker* afford to send Gardner, a veteran left-wing reporter and rabble-rouser, to Little Rock. From its glory days two decades earlier, the Communist paper had dwindled down to only a few pages. Still, Gardner managed to reach people (including Elizabeth's grandparents and parents) that better-heeled reporters either missed or ignored.

2. "Go home, niggah! Go back north where you belong!" a woman shouted at Nall during one protest. "But I'm from Nashville," Nall replied.

CHAPTER THIRTEEN

1. "I remember the face of only one of those children," Julius Lester—a sophomore at Fisk when the picture appeared, later a professor and author—was to write. "I wanted to be there beside her. It was hard for me to live with myself if I couldn't at least suffer with her. . . . I knew that they would have to pay for making her cry. . . . Someday. Somewhere. They would pay." To David Shipler, a twelve-year-old from an all-white New Jersey town, the picture was "like a punch in the stomach"—his first, life-altering, encounter with racial hatred. It helped inspire a journalistic career in which he often wrote on racial issues. Martin Luther King had said that only when white Americans became sufficiently aroused, and engaged, could the civil rights movement succeed; experiences like Shipler's illustrated how compassion for Elizabeth (and embarrassment over Hazel) catalyzed that process.

CHAPTER FOURTEEN

1. When I located him in the summer of 2007, Lubenow had never told his story publicly before. A shorter, G-rated version of this account first appeared as "The Day Louis Armstrong Made Noise" in the *New York Times* on September 23, 2007, marking the fiftieth anniversary of the events in Little Rock.

2. Set to defend his middleweight title against Carmen Basilio later that month, Robinson interrupted his training to echo Armstrong. "I never interfere in politics, no kind of way," he told *Time*. "But I'd give that Faubus my whole purse and taken him on right after Basilio." Then he took a swing at the president. "I think Mr. Eisenhower's somewhat faulty, too," he said. "There he is playing golf and his country['s] damn near in a revolution."

3. As for Lubenow, he got paid $3.50 ($1.75 an hour times two) for the story. But his editor was miffed (he'd gotten into politics, after all), and when the paper barred him from talking about Armstrong on a local radio show sponsored by the Farmers Union (which the *Herald* considered communistic), Lubenow walked out. After two tours of duty in Vietnam, he eventually went into public relations in Texas.

CHAPTER FIFTEEN

1. That the turmoil around Central did not worsen European opinion, one USIA report concluded, "may be owing to the fact that America's standing in the area of race relations was already in a very depressed state."

2. Still, for Faubus it was never anything personal. Many years after he was out of office Elizabeth shared a stage with him, speaking before he did. He was very cordial to her, grumbling amiably that she was a tough act to follow.

3. It was for these pictures, and not for the one of Elizabeth and Hazel, that he was nominated for a Pulitzer Prize.

4. She was carted off to the police station in a paddy wagon, but that was as rough as it ever got for her. Instead, she settled into the status of a minor celebrity: in the ensuing months, she gave numerous interviews, was photographed kissing Faubus, and went to *Steve's Show* with a bodyguard. *Life* did a piece on her (and *Ebony*, surely facetiously, offered her a chance to pose nude). Always, she was good for an outlandish quote—that the NAACP was paying the Little Rock Nine, for example, or that Ernest Green, the only senior in the group, had asked her out on a date. Sammie Dean's stunts were all public, which was later a source of pride for her. "I was not one of those students who put gum in their chairs or their hair or laughed at them when they got hurt or pushed down the stairs," she said. When she faced expulsion, Governor Earl Long of Louisiana offered to let her attend school in Baton Rouge, with free room and board in the governor's mansion.

5. One of Central's librarians later described her encounter that day with a black maid in the building. "She was that queer green-gray color that a negro turns when he is frightened," she wrote. "Afterwards I realized that she was desperately afraid of what might happen to her if the crowd outside broke into the school."

6. In an oral history, Jefferson Thomas recounted that the police actually allowed a representative of the mob into the building, then negotiated with him. If the police handed them one of the Nine to lynch, the man said, it would calm everyone down. "That makes sense," the officer replied. "Now, how do I determine which one I turn over to you?" Thomas missed the rest of the conversation.

7. Real, but effectively still segregated, at least for present purposes: its blacks were confined to barracks, and never posted around Central.

CHAPTER SIXTEEN

1. "Gosh, everybody was so friendly. We didn't think it would be nearly this nice," she told another reporter. "A lot of kids knew my name and introduced themselves. We got along real fine." To a third, she said: "I had a good time. The only incidents were very, very minor." Melba's 1994 memoir, *Warriors Don't Cry*, tells a dramatically different story, contradicting not only her own contemporaneous statements but the recollections of the other black students. Only to Melba, and only decades later, were things nightmarish from the outset; to the others, the process was more gradual, and subtle, and complex.

CHAPTER SEVENTEEN

1. Once, after he'd had lunch with Jefferson Thomas in the cafeteria, a group shoved Reinhardt to the floor. Another time he was punched in the face. "I guess you're proud of your nigger-loving son," an anonymous caller told his parents over the phone. The delicacy of the situation was nicely captured in a written exchange between another of the Nine, Gloria Ray, and a white student. "Becky, if you saw me in the halls one morning and I spoke to you, would you speak to me?" Ray asked her. It would be best if she didn't, Becky replied: it would endanger her friendships and family. "But I do notice you in the hall," she said. "I hope you understand."

2. So much of a pillar, in fact, that when segregationists closed down the Little Rock schools for the 1958–59 school year and some classes were taught (briefly) on television, her history course was broadcast, by popular demand, for the entire school year.

CHAPTER EIGHTEEN

1. The *Democrat* duly noted all such absences, "apparently hopeful," the historian Elizabeth Jacoway has written, "that the nine youngsters would lose heart and return to Horace Mann High School."

2. Jefferson Thomas told Ted Poston that as the segregationist students shouted "Two! Four! Six! Eight! We ain't going to integrate!" the black students muttered, "Eight! Six! Four! Two! Ten to one, we bet you do!"

CHAPTER NINETEEN

1. Little Rock's Jewish community was not unusual. "By and large, the Southern Jew does not like segregation, but he is unwilling to expose himself to public calumny and economic reprisals by identifying himself with the integrationist cause," Albert Vorspan of the Union of American Hebrew Congregations wrote in November 1957.

CHAPTER TWENTY

1. "Melba Patillo and her mother are probably the only one of these families who seemed to be unduly conscious of their celebrity role in this situation," he wrote, noting Mrs. Patillo's proposal that the black schoolchildren sell stories of their experiences to the newspapers. Clark stressed, however, that this was but a preliminary conclusion; he did not speak to Melba for long.

CHAPTER TWENTY-ONE

1. In all likelihood, the agent probably came from the Federal Bureau of Investigation.

2. In his memoirs, Terrence Roberts recalls that Martin Luther King also came to Little Rock to instruct the Nine in nonviolence. Elizabeth had no such recollections, though she remembered meeting King at Ernest Green's graduation a few months later. He struck her as a country preacher, not at all the sophisticated, citified figure he later became.

3. In a much-discussed article in *Dissent* in 1959, Arendt criticized the federal courts, the NAACP, and the parents of the Nine for placing burdens on them too great for them to bear. She focused on Elizabeth, whom she never mentioned by name. "The girl, obviously, was asked to be a hero—that is, something neither her absent father nor the equally absent representatives of the NAACP felt called upon to be," she wrote. "Have we now come to the point where it is the children who are being asked to change or improve the world? And do we intend to have our political battles fought out in the school yards?" Arendt's article was much criticized on other grounds—particularly for arguing that bans on interracial marriage were more objectionable than segregated schools. That criticism only stiffened her spine. Were she a black mother in the South, she subsequently wrote, "under no circumstances would I expose my

child to conditions which made it appear as though it wanted to push its way into a group where it was not wanted. . . . I would feel that the Supreme Court ruling, unwillingly but unavoidably, has put my child into a more humiliating position than it had been in before." The novelist Ralph Ellison countered that history and tradition had conditioned southern blacks—parents and children alike—for such sacrifice. "The child is expected to face the terror and contain his fear and anger *precisely* because he is a Negro American," he wrote. "It is a harsh requirement, but if he fails this basic test, his life will be even harsher." Arendt ultimately conceded the point.

4. The awards that the *Gazette* won, along with one to Relman Morin of the Associated Press, effectively kept Will Counts from winning a Pulitzer. The Pulitzer jury recommended him, but the board, apparently unwilling to bestow too many awards for a single story, overruled it.

5. To Miss Middlebrook, hostility to blacks was nothing new. While editing the *Tiger* a few years earlier, Jerry Dhonau had written a column urging that the school's new field house be named for Riley Johns, the longtime caretaker of Central's football field, who was black. Claiming that it would upset the principal and the school board, Miss Middlebrook spiked the column, prompting Dhonau to resign. Five years later Dhonau, by then with the *Gazette,* was among those reporters who'd positioned themselves protectively around Elizabeth as she waited for the bus.

CHAPTER TWENTY-TWO

1. Mildred Bond Roxborough, the NAACP's field secretary at large during that time, doesn't disagree. "It seems cold, but someone winds up being a martyr no matter what," she later said. With the new battles and battlefields the NAACP faced, there was little time to tend to Central's wounded. Or, as Roxborough put it, "Little Rock became of less consequence after they got those doors open."

2. On the SIU campus in Carbondale, students at a fraternity house shouted racial epithets at them. En route, Elizabeth and the film's editor, Robert Pierce, who was white, were initially refused service in a café in Xenia, Ohio.

3. Though blacks appear conspicuously in the film, Central had but twenty of them when the short was made; they still could not participate in sports, debates, or anything involving public competition.

CHAPTER TWENTY-FIVE

1. Haley's brother had been among the first black law graduates of the state university at Fayetteville.

2. For Cassells, who was to be nominated for a Pulitzer Prize and win many awards, it became his most anthologized poem; once he got to read it aloud on the White House lawn.

CHAPTER TWENTY-SIX

1. See Chapter 13, note 1.

2. Like so many others connected to the Little Rock saga, Sammie Dean deemed herself a victim. Like Elizabeth, she felt that she had been enlisted to fight for others, and that it had ruined everything; had she been less linked to the segregationists, she believed, she'd have been Miss Little Rock of 1959 instead of only first runner-up.

CHAPTER TWENTY-SEVEN

1. The unreliability of Beals's book is apparent from the outset, when she describes the horror of encountering "my friend Elizabeth" besieged by the mob; in fact, Elizabeth and Melba had yet to meet. If Beals is to be believed, moreover, her ordeal that morning made Elizabeth's look mild: she writes that she and her mother were assaulted, then chased by five men (or an indeterminate number of men and women: her account is inconsistent), one with a rope, another with a large branch, and a third with a brick, with which he smashed the windshield of their car. Though two blacks standing close enough to the action to have witnessed Elizabeth's walk—even two blacks merely standing around, let alone being attacked—would have been highly conspicuous that day, no eyewitnesses, including the many newsmen and others giving statements to the FBI, reported seeing Beals and her mother at all. More significantly, Beals's 1994 account bears no resemblance to what she told the FBI the day after it happened. In her statement of September 5, 1957, she said she'd never been to Central at all, including on the day of Elizabeth's walk, because "she was afraid of being physically harmed in the event any incident occurred." She also told the FBI that she "did not receive any threats, either direct or implied, against her going to Central High School." There were no references to ropes, branches, or bricks.

Beals, a journalist herself, declined to explain this discrepancy; of the Nine, only she refused to be interviewed for this book. (Others who have written on the Little Rock schools crisis report the same thing.) Her unwillingness to discuss, or defend, what she has written only fortified my belief that *Warriors Don't Cry* is untrustworthy. For that reason, I have not relied upon it in any way.

Like the others, Beals deserves great respect for what she suffered at Central, and perhaps even some literary license. But she's not entitled to a free pass from scholars and journalists, especially since her book is read (and credited) by many schoolchildren and, indeed, sold at the Central High School visitor center. One hopes that, despite their ties to one another, those members of the Nine who shared their reservations about the book privately with me do so publicly at some point as well; after all, this is ultimately *their* history. Anyone taking liberties with this story, black or white, should be rebuked.

2. Jacoway had grown up in town, graduating from Hall High School, before earning a doctorate in history at the University of North Carolina. As a member of a prominent local family, she had known several of the key players in the drama; Virgil Blossom—"Uncle Virgil" to her—was married to her mother's first cousin.

3. After taking the picture, Jenkins had moved to Austin, Texas, where he worked for a time at the local newspaper. Later, he opened his own commercial photography lab. Though he had won a Polk Award for the photo, he never took another famous one and did not even keep a copy of this one around. He died in 1992.

CHAPTER TWENTY-EIGHT

1. The long rivalry between the two newspapers ended in 1991, when the *Gazette* closed and was folded into the *Democrat*.

CHAPTER THIRTY

1. Clinton was still thinking about Elizabeth and Hazel a week later. Talking to the writer Taylor Branch, he remarked that their "painful accord marked a second phase of progress, when nameless antagonists became human to each other and everyone else."

CHAPTER THIRTY-ONE

1. It wasn't the only letter of hers that went unanswered. Hazel had also written to Vivian Counts to thank her and her husband for what they had just done. "I felt so nourished by your understanding and acceptance," she'd said. "Words cannot express how much the opportunity for a second picture (a second chance) means to me. THANK YOU. I only wish the 1997 picture had the impact of the 1957 one." She asked them to please let her know of any places in which the new picture appeared. Here, too, she got no reply.

2. It was not Elizabeth's only concern. Hazel had warned her that although the man who ran the iris garden was very friendly, his wife was not. Perhaps, Elizabeth replied, she should not go there. Hazel was taken aback, and enlightened: It had never occurred to her that Elizabeth might not be welcome, or might feel unwelcome, somewhere because of her color.

CHAPTER THIRTY-FOUR

1. After reading the book and inscription, Hazel had written Melba a long letter, describing how shocked, and moved, she had been to learn what the Nine had experienced inside Central. "I cried a number of times reading your story. I must not be warrior material," she wrote. "Thank you for embracing me and making me your 'spiritual partner.' 'The God in me sees and honors the God in you.' We are all one." Here, too, she never got a reply.

2. At least three photographers, it turns out, trained their cameras on the knot of students, Elizabeth among them, standing outside Central that day. The picture Brodie fastened upon was taken by an unidentified Associated Press photographer. Also recording the scene were Bern Keating of Black Star and the Magnum photographer Burt Glinn. While in the AP photo Elizabeth is speaking to another student, Priscilla Thompson, in others she stands apart. In still more, she is across from a student, but it's unclear whether they're conversing. The pictures were also manipulable; *Paris Match* cropped one of Glinn's to make Elizabeth look *more* isolated than she actually was. Thus, on the matter of how Elizabeth was received on her first day at Central, the only conclusion to be drawn from these photographs is that they offer no conclusion at all.

3. Elizabeth said, for instance, that the letters written afterward by students attending their joint appearances generally criticized Hazel, when in fact most were highly complimentary. She also believed that a snapshot taken by a Cen-

tral student named Craig Rains on the first day of school showing a Guardsman walking alongside her as the mob was on her heels had to have been fabricated.

4. Even had she been able to, Elizabeth would have refused to donate to a fund for Bates, who lived out her life in poverty, believing that simply not disclosing the truth about her—that she had used the black students, many of whom disliked her—constituted enough of a contribution. Asked once how it felt to drive down Daisy L. Gatson Bates Drive—the former 14th Street, from which Elizabeth began her walk—she let out a simple harrumph.

CHAPTER THIRTY-FIVE

1. Simply as a matter of racial solidarity, I had assumed that Hazel would receive me more openly than Elizabeth. In fact, it was the other way around, and it was to Elizabeth I initially gravitated. Hazel, I later learned, felt slighted. Things only worsened when, as she remembered it, I told Elizabeth that "we"— that is, Jews and blacks—were "special." I don't recall saying it and can't imagine I did. But recollections vary and, I came to know, Hazel wasn't one to make things up. As part of her self-education on racial matters, Hazel had learned of the historic ties between blacks and Jews, and my remark convinced her that in any dispute between the two, I would side with Elizabeth. (Such a fear puzzled Elizabeth; Jews were like any other white people to her.) Eight years passed before Hazel spoke with me again.

2. Ten months earlier Ross, a doctor who would have succeeded Ralph Brodie as student body president had Little Rock's high schools not shut down, wrote that he and other white students "went out of our way to befriend and help those nine black students." Like the officers in Vietnam many went on to become, he claimed, Central's whites had never been properly thanked for their heroism during that period. Elizabeth remembered Ross, though not that they had ever been friends.

3. One former Central student who did sympathize with Hazel was David Sontag, who had been suspended for pouring soup on Minnijean. "I've always said, 'Thank God I wasn't there. Thank God it wasn't me doing that,'" he said. One of the principal segregationist students, in 1998 Sontag apologized on *Oprah* for his misbehavior. He died in 2010.

CHAPTER FORTY

1. I told Lorch, then in his nineties, that Elizabeth considered his late wife a provocateur. Surely Elizabeth had not felt that way at the time, he theorized; such bitterness was the result of a hard-lived life. Touched by his reaction, Elizabeth conceded that perhaps she had judged Grace Lorch too harshly.

CHAPTER FORTY-TWO

1. Brodie subsequently collected and cowrote a collection of recollections from Central's "good" students, aptly titled *Central in Our Lives*. For Brodie, setting the record straight (as he sees it) has not been cheap: the book project and other activities have, by his estimate, cost him more than $100,000.

2. In her own way, Burleson tried to make amends years before going on television: when her daughter was born in 1960, she named her Elizabeth. At some point in the 1970s, she, too, tried calling Elizabeth Eckford to apologize, but had never reached her. She died in 2009.

3. And it was true: Jefferson Thomas died, at age sixty-eight, in September 2010.

CHAPTER FORTY-FOUR

1. Early on in this project, years before Elizabeth raised the subject very gingerly herself, I had resolved that once my reporting was substantially done I would compensate her for her cooperation. Once it was, I did. Hazel preempted this issue entirely, informing me at one point that she did not expect, nor did she want, any payment. Neither Elizabeth nor Hazel ever asked to see this book before publication, though as a courtesy, I showed the final manuscript to each of them. Each suggested a few corrections; neither asked that anything substantive be changed.

Acknowledgments

Imagining a book, then pitching it, can be as daunting as writing the book itself. Sometimes, though, things fall magically into place. That was what happened when I wandered into the Mobil station–turned–museum across the street from Little Rock Central High School in the spring of 1999 and first saw the poster on the wall of Elizabeth Eckford and Hazel Massery—standing alongside each other, smiling. Could such a thing really have come to pass? And how? Therein lay a tale. And, as it turned out, a book.

It took me a dozen years to do it, and I encountered many helpful people along the way. They include Annie Abrams, Charlene Jackson Allen, Ethel Ambrose, Alice Lorch Bartels, Martha Boveia, Gene Bowman, Max Brantley, the Hon. Wiley Branton, Jr., Ralph Brodie, Phyllis Brown, Linda Caillouet, Cyrus Cassels, Cathy Collins, Dr. Helen Cooks, Bill Corker, Vivian Counts, Eric Engberg, Annette Gilbert, Anna Eckford Goynes, Grace Guggenheim, Peggy Harris, Steele Hays, the Hon. Marion Humphrey, George Iggers, Bill Jersey, Heather Jurgensen, Michael Krenn, Michael Leahy, Linda Lee, Judith Leonard, Johanna Lewis, Mike Maddell, Antoine Massery, Josh McHughes, Laura Miller, Angela Park, Ken Reinhardt, Curtis Ricks, Nancy Rousseau, Mildred Roxborough, Skip Rutherford, Charles Sawrie, Jack Schnedler, David

Shipler, David Smith, Professor Valerie Steele, Jeff Steinberg, Steve Stevens, the Rev. Hezekiah Stewart, the late Mary Ann Burleson Thompson, Morris Thompson, Spirit Trickey, Robin Ward, Linda Wells, Lynn Whittaker, Emogene Wilson, and Nina Zagat.

I was assisted selflessly by people at several research institutions: Anne Prichard, formerly the librarian in special collections at the University of Arkansas at Fayetteville; Rhonda Stewart at the Butler Center for Arkansas Studies; Linda Pine of the University of Arkansas at Little Rock; Jane Hooker and Linda McDowell of the Arkansas History Commission; the ever-helpful Charles Niles at the Howard Gotlieb Center at Boston University; Michael Cogswell and Ricky Riccardi of the Louis Armstrong House Museum; Anna St. Onge of the Clara Thomas Archives at York University; and the kind workers in the microfilm rooms of the Schomburg Branch of the New York Public Library and the Mother Ship on 42nd Street and Fifth Avenue. As always, I am indebted to Jeff Roth, the vigilant protector of the precious *New York Times* morgue. I also want to thank Skip Isaacs, who miraculously managed to find—sitting in a box at the back of a closet in his home— the notes of his late, remarkable father's 1957 trip to Little Rock and Augusta, Arkansas.

Despite their entirely understandable interview fatigue, eight of the Little Rock Nine agreed to speak with me, and I am grateful to them all: in addition to Elizabeth Eckford herself, Ernest Green, Gloria Ray Karlmark, Carlotta Walls LaNier, Terrence Roberts, the late Jefferson Thomas, Thelma Mothershed Weir, and, particularly, Minnijean Brown Trickey. As I have told Minnijean, my biggest mistake in this entire enterprise was failing to write a separate book simultaneously on her, for she is equally deserving of one; I look forward to reading her forthcoming memoir. Most of the other players in this drama are gone, but I was fortunate to catch up with Lee Lorch, for whom the epochal events in Little Rock were but one more stop in a remarkable journey, and Larry Lubenow, the man who prompted Louis Armstrong to weigh in on the schools crisis. I'm thankful to those reporters who covered the story and shared with me their memories: Jerry Dhonau, Gene Foreman, Farnsworth Fowle, the late Walter Lister, Ray Moseley, Moses Newson, Roy Reed, and Claude Sitton. Luckily, I got to know, and to listen to, Will Counts a bit before his death in 2001. He was a lovely man. I hope I have done him justice here.

But for *Vanity Fair,* on whose website a shorter version of this story first appeared, *Elizabeth and Hazel* would never have happened. I'm grateful to Graydon Carter, Doug Stumpf, and Mary Flynn for making that possible. Jonathan Brent of Yale University Press backed this book from the beginning; when he moved on to new challenges, it was my great fortune that Ileene Smith inherited it, and me. Her careful editing, intelligence, and encouragement buoyed me. Together with Sarah Miller, John Palmer, Dan Heaton, Mary Valencia, and Maureen Noonan, they have made this book as beautiful as I had always imagined it would be. Also at the Press, Jay Cosgrove, Heather D'Auria, and Brenda King have done everything they could to ensure that this book finds its audience.

Brian Chilson, Phyllis Colazzo, Brad Cook, Bay Fitzhugh, Laura Harris, Jeff McAdory, and Paul Robert Walker helped with the pictures. Michael Henry Adams, David Bray, Elizabeth Cohen, the late Neal Hartman, Elizabeth Jacoway, Phil and Ruthe Kaplan, Joel Klein, Andrew Margolick, Gert Margolick, Jonathan Margolick,

Joseph Margolick, Linda Monk, Grif Stockley, and Tim Zagat all read the book in draft, offering suggestions, spotting mistakes. The chefs at Sims Barbecue fed me during my many trips to Little Rock.

Rhonda Chahine has been a constant source of love, support, and good judgment throughout my work. I want, too, to thank the remarkable Lawrence Schiller, who took the contemporary portraits of Elizabeth and Hazel (and then, with his son Howard Schiller, designed an elegant cover around them). Beyond his uncanny storytelling instincts, Larry is a treasured and loyal friend; his encouragement lifted my spirits and improved this book. Most important, I want to thank Elizabeth Eckford and Hazel Bryan Massery. This story is painful for them both, and neither was eager to revisit it. I'm more grateful than I can express that each of them—in her own way, at her own pace—took me into her confidence, then endured endless hours of interviews, invariably followed by requests for still more. Neither sought special treatment; each asked only that her story be honestly told. I've done my best to comply. A dear and tenderhearted friend once faulted an earlier project of mine for having had no heroes. In this book, I was blessed with two.

David Margolick
New York, March 2011

Index

Page numbers in *italics* refer to illustrations.